A Practical Guide to Critical Religion

SERIES: *CRITIQUING RELIGION: DISCOURSE, CULTURE, POWER*

Series editor: Craig Martin

Critiquing Religion: Discourse, Culture, Power publishes works that historicize both religions and modern discourses on 'religion' that treat it as a unique object of study. Using diverse methodologies and social theories, volumes in this series view religions and discourses on religion as commonplace rhetorics, authenticity narratives, or legitimating myths which function in the creation, maintenance and contestation of social formations. Works in the series are on the cutting edge of critical scholarship, regarding 'religion' as just another cultural tool used to gerrymander social space and distribute power relations in the modern world. *Critiquing Religion: Discourse, Culture, Power* provides a unique home for reflexive, critical work in the field of religious studies.

Christian Tourist Attractions, Mythmaking and Identity Formation
Edited by Erin Roberts and Jennifer Eyl

Fieldnotes in the Critical Study of Religion
Edited by Vaia Touna and Richard Newton

French Populism and Discourses on Secularism
Per-Erik Nilsson

Reframing the Masters of Suspicion: Marx, Nietzsche, and Freud
Andrew Dole

Religion, Nationalism and Foreign Policy
Filiz Coban Oran

Representing Religion in Film
Edited by Tenzan Eaghll and Rebekka King

Rethinking Christian Martyrdom: The Blood is the Seed?
Matt Recla

Stereotyping Religion II
Edited by Craig Martin and Brad Stoddard

Spirituality, Corporate Culture, and American Business: The Neoliberal Ethic and the Spirit of Global Capital
James Dennis LoRusso

Stereotyping Religion: Critiquing Clichés
Edited by Brad Stoddard and Craig Martin

A Practical Guide
to Critical Religion

Edited by

ALEXANDER HENLEY

BLOOMSBURY ACADEMIC
LONDON · NEW YORK · OXFORD · NEW DELHI · SYDNEY

BLOOMSBURY ACADEMIC

Bloomsbury Publishing Plc, 50 Bedford Square, London, WC1B 3DP, UK
Bloomsbury Publishing Inc, 1359 Broadway, New York, NY 10018, USA
Bloomsbury Publishing Ireland, 29 Earlsfort Terrace, Dublin 2, D02 AY28, Ireland

BLOOMSBURY, BLOOMSBURY ACADEMIC and the Diana logo are trademarks
of Bloomsbury Publishing Plc

First published in Great Britain 2026

Copyright © Alexander Henley and contributors, 2026

Alexander Henley has asserted his right under the Copyright, Designs and Patents Act,
1988, to be identified as Editor of this work.

For legal purposes the Acknowledgements on p. xvii constitute an extension of this
copyright page.

Series design by Dani Leigh
Cover image © Yi Lu/EyeEm/gettyimages.co.uk

All rights reserved. No part of this publication may be: i) reproduced or transmitted in
any form, electronic or mechanical, including photocopying, recording or by means of
any information storage or retrieval system without prior permission in writing from the
publishers; or ii) used or reproduced in any way for the training, development or operation
of artificial intelligence (AI) technologies, including generative AI technologies. The rights
holders expressly reserve this publication from the text and data mining exception as per
Article 4(3) of the Digital Single Market Directive (EU) 2019/790.

Bloomsbury Publishing Plc does not have any control over, or responsibility for, any third-
party websites referred to or in this book. All internet addresses given in this book were
correct at the time of going to press. The author and publisher regret any inconvenience
caused if addresses have changed or sites have ceased to exist, but can accept no
responsibility for any such changes.

A catalogue record for this book is available from the British Library.

ISBN: HB: 978-1-3502-5646-0
PB: 978-1-3502-5647-7
ePDF: 978-1-3502-5648-4
eBook: 978-1-3502-5649-1

Series: Critiquing Religion: Discourse, Culture, Power

Typeset by Deanta Global Publishing Services, Chennai, India
Printed and bound in Great Britain

For product safety related questions contact productsafety@bloomsbury.com.

To find out more about our authors and books visit www.bloomsbury.com and
sign up for our newsletters.

For Tim Fitzgerald, who coined the term 'critical religion' and who has helped many of us see the world otherwise.

'The invention of generic religion and its binary opposite, the non-religious secular, is fundamental in generating the illusion that today's dominant system of exploitation and inequality is sane, rational, normal, natural and the only possible game in town.'

'It is these pairs of opposites, which operate as binary signalling, that keep us enthralled and unable to have any new ideas.'

(Quotations from Fitzgerald's chapter in this volume.)

Contents

Preface: 'Critical religion' and the purpose of this volume ix
Contributors xiv
Acknowledgements xvii

PART I Introducing critical religion: A toolkit of critiques, methods and trajectories 1

1   What is wrong with the category 'religion' and what can we do about it? *Alexander Henley* 3

2   What is critical religion? Past, present and future of critical scholarship *Alexander Henley* 21

PART II Perspectives on being critical about 'religion' and the 'secular' 45

3   The reluctant genealogist: Why it matters where our terms come from *Aaron W. Hughes* 47

4   Classification matters: Why you should care about scholarship on the category religion *Russell T. McCutcheon* 61

5   *The Ideology of Religious Studies* then and now: The author's view *Timothy Fitzgerald* 77

PART III Applying critical approaches in the field 99

6 The projection of 'religion' upon Japan by the United States since the 1850s *Mitsutoshi Horii* 101

7 Religionization of minorities and culturalization of Christianity: How to study boundary cases? *Teemu Taira* 121

8 Researching 'religion' in Indigenous cultures *Suzanne Owen* 141

9 Managing 'faith' in a modern state: 'Time for Reflection' in the Scottish Parliament *Steven J. Sutcliffe* 157

10 Thinking outside of the 'religion and politics' duality: The Jewish-Israeli case *Yaacov Yadgar* 179

11 The category of religion in the technology of governance: An argument for understanding religions as vestigial states *Naomi Goldenberg* 195

12 The implications of critical religion for (gendered) Religious Education *Alison Jasper and John I'Anson* 209

Notes 229
Index 239

Preface

'Critical religion' and the purpose of this volume

In case you haven't heard, the study of religion is in the throes of a revolution – one that is significant for anyone talking about 'religion'. A steadily growing body of scholarship now challenges the basic assumption that religion is a thing in the world that we can (or ought to) identify, describe or analyse within and across cultures, past and present. This movement, sometimes called 'critical religion', has opened the way for radical re-interpretations and fresh approaches to the things we have habitually called 'religions' or 'religious', as well as a constellation of conceptual fields imagined as 'non-religious' or 'secular' – such as politics, economics, culture and society. Its practitioners build on several decades of reflexive scholarship that has provincialized the study of religion within a particular post-Enlightenment Euro-American knowledge regime, one that makes 'religion' and 'the religious' comprehensible only in a binary relationship with the secular and that reifies a set of discrete 'world religions' as meaningful objects of study. If you are unsure what that means, or what it means to you, please read on: this book is for you.

While critical religion has been gaining traction over the past twenty years or more, it has also met with reluctance, puzzlement and sometimes even vehement opposition. A sizeable part of this latter reaction stems from a concern that critical theory gets in the way of the important work of studying the beliefs, practices or worldviews of others. Many students and scholars are understandably wary of excessive introspection or deconstruction; they may see it as impractical, or worry about its debilitating effect on knowledge production, or simply feel at sea in theoretical jargon. I hope this book will help by clarifying what critical religion is all about and by showing its practical relevance and usefulness for empirical research and teaching on a wide range of contemporary subjects in various disciplines.

PREFACE

This *Practical Guide to Critical Religion* is designed firstly to make critical theory on 'religion' accessible to students, teachers and researchers who may be unfamiliar with or sceptical of it. The book serves secondly as a *Practical Guide* to the state-of-the-art in critical methods, presenting snapshots of the work of scholars who are pushing the boundaries of their fields. Don't worry if theory is not really your thing: this is not so much a theory textbook as a guidebook for theory-informed practice. Nor is this book intended to prescribe a singular interpretation or method of doing critical religion; instead, its authors model a range of approaches and tools they have used to achieve new insights and create new knowledge. We use the term 'critical religion' in this book as shorthand for a critical orientation to 'religion' and related categories (see Chapters 1 and 2), while representing a diversity of voices – including those who tend to use other terms for what they do (e.g. Chapters 3 and 4).

Part I introduces critical religion. Chapter 1 explains what is wrong with the category 'religion' and what we can do about it. This opening chapter sets the stage by exploring the problems and limitations of treating religion as a fixed or self-evident kind of thing in the world. Then it offers a roadmap for productive scholarship that avoids these pitfalls in conventional thinking about religion. Chapter 2 turns to the critical scholars behind these ideas. Beginning with what they mean by 'critical religion', this chapter traces the development of critical theory and methods, introducing a series of transformative thinkers in religious studies and setting them in the context of a broader critical and post-colonial turn. Considering the present state and future directions of critical religion as an evolving, interdisciplinary orientation to scholarship, this chapter also addresses counter-arguments and highlights ongoing debates. Whether you are new to critical religion or curious about why these debates matter, Part I provides an accessible entry point and a foundation for the discussions and case studies that follow.

Part II presents first-hand perspectives from three of the most influential theorists in religious studies as they reflect on the practical importance of being critical about 'religion' and the 'secular'. They challenge us to reflect on our positionality as scholars and to be more conscious of the hidden work done by the words we tend to take for granted. The stakes are high, as these chapters show through different kinds of examples. Aaron Hughes (Chapter 3) uses a dialogue between a theorist/genealogist and a textual historian to emphasize that neither can do meaningful scholarship without the other; we are all theorists, whether we see ourselves as such or not. Russell McCutcheon (Chapter 4) uses everyday examples from American life to illustrate how labels of 'religious' or 'non-religious' are deployed differently from one context to another; we need to stop taking them as neutral descriptors and pay attention to their uses and effects as tools of social classification. Timothy Fitzgerald (Chapter 5) uses examples of cultural mistranslation from his work in India and Japan, and the difficulty of representing those cultures faithfully to his religious studies students in the UK, to explain his motivations for writing his now-classic critique in *The Ideology of Religious Studies* (2000). Fitzgerald goes further than Hughes or McCutcheon, who primarily advocate for a shift in the way we do religious studies; for him, critical religion is aligned with a wider-ranging project of 'extended critique' aimed at a bigger target, unpicking the numerous ways our language reinforces dominant systems of inequality. Helpfully for readers who, like me, are trying to figure out how to navigate the challenges raised by critical religion, Fitzgerald shares his raw, honest reflections on a career spent grappling with its ethical and practical implications.

Part III offers seven case studies from scholars applying critical approaches in various fields. Each one highlights ways in which critical religion has enriched their empirical research and their analysis of the particular contexts and issues they study. Cases have been selected to represent scholarship on diverse contexts from Japan to the Middle East to Europe and North America; colonial history as well as contemporary anthropology, sociology, political science, gender studies and education policy; international, national and local dynamics; elite and state actors as well as minority and Indigenous actors. Chapters touch on different ways the category 'religion' is constructed, deployed, managed, negotiated or contested – from above and from below – in relation to other categories including 'politics', 'culture', 'society', 'heritage', 'nation', 'ethnicity', 'spirituality', 'superstition' and 'faith', as well as through intersections with gender. They suggest how we might analyse such data from various perspectives to understand causes – motivations, strategies or systemic drivers – as well as effects and who stands to benefit from such acts of categorization. These case studies offer a rich sample of potential applications, intended to provide food for thought as readers consider how to engage critical religion in their own work.

Teaching applications are also discussed in Part III, first by Teemu Taira (Chapter 7) through his experiment with a class research project and then in a systematic treatment by Alison Jasper and John l'Anson (Chapter 12). In that closing chapter, Jasper and l'Anson analyse problems with 'religious education' in UK schools in order to propose a more critical, ethical and experimental framework that can be applied at all levels of education; they offer ideas on how this critical religion framework could engage issues of violence, gender, normativity and thinking otherwise in teaching and learning.

The motivation for this *Practical Guide* arose out of an interdisciplinary seminar series on *Critical and Decolonial Approaches to 'Religion'*, which I hosted with Lauren Morry at the University of Oxford in 2020. Most of the contributors to this volume were speakers at that seminar, invited to address three core questions in relation to their own fields:

1. What's wrong with the category 'religion'?
2. What should we do about it?
3. And how can critical approaches create new knowledge?

We wanted to see how others in different fields and disciplines are responding seriously to the problems with 'religion' as a category of analysis and to learn more about the variety of cutting-edge research and pedagogy grounded in critical religion. Lauren and I did not really consider ourselves theorists, so we were particularly keen to discuss these questions with others who are also not primarily theorists.

Meanwhile, the experience of organizing such a seminar was almost as instructive. On one hand, the advertised theme proved extremely popular with students at all levels on various humanities and social science programmes who had had little or no exposure to critical methodologies in their courses on religion – except perhaps as a token nod towards problems in defining that concept or translating it outside Western Christian contexts. Some students had encountered critical or decolonial approaches in other forms – for example critical race theory, feminist critique of gender categories, post-colonial studies, or calls to decolonize education – and were eager to learn how these might apply to religion. Many of them asked us to recommend an introduction to critical religion, but we had trouble finding readings broad enough and readable enough for complete newcomers, let alone an up-to-date entry point into a literature that has grown exponentially. Others struggled to figure out how to relate seemingly complex critical theory to their own fields of study, so were looking for inspiration. On the other hand, we were surprised at the extent of scepticism we encountered among faculty colleagues and some students, especially those most invested in the work of studying religions. With visiting speakers from other institutions, we found ourselves comparing experiences we had all had of colleagues dismissing critical religion off-hand as 'self-referential theory of theory', 'a distraction', 'a niche interest', 'faddish', 'pointless deconstruction', 'counter-productive', 'dangerous' or just 'silly'. It seemed clear that gut-reaction negative perceptions remain the biggest obstacle to wider understanding of the issues raised by more than thirty years of critical scholarship. Hence our goal in this book is to address those concerns and preconceptions directly by showing what critical religion can *do*.

Genealogical studies – revealing where our terms come from – have been foundational to critical religion, but we have found that many social scientists regard genealogy as a subject for historians. After all, the language of 'religion' appears to be widely shared between researchers and the people they study today. Along similar lines, other sceptics concede that the colonial history of 'religion' may be important for studying formerly colonized societies, but not for studying European and North American societies where the religion-secular binary originated and is the dominant paradigm. In response to such preconceptions about the limited relevance of critical religion, this book pays special attention to explaining why genealogy matters to all of us and showing how critical religion proves equally useful – and important – for understanding modern and contemporary societies on every continent, including Europe and North America.

Critique is challenging and intentionally so – but not in the debilitating ways that some fear. Theorists like Timothy Fitzgerald, Russell McCutcheon and Aaron Hughes have set out to rock the boat, to shake the methodological foundations of the study of religion and other disciplines in which religion is treated as a distinct phenomenon in society, culture or politics. They critique, deconstruct, historicize and provincialize the common-sense language we habitually use to describe the world, organize academic departments and courses, and identify ourselves as students and scholars. They expose the troubling colonial genealogies and ideological effects of the basic conceptual categories we were trained in or raised with. Yet all of this book's authors have rocked the boat – or had their boats rocked – and lived to tell the tale. Critical religion has enabled them to set new and exciting courses for their research and teaching. Running with this analogy, our aim for this book is to reassure others that they need not drown if they, too, allow themselves to have their boats rocked. To borrow an alternative analogy from Fitzgerald, coming to see the world without the category 'religion' is like discovering one day that you have been wearing tinted glasses your whole life. This change of lenses likely involves a profoundly disorientating shift of perspective, but also the invigorating potential of renewed sight. You gain new vistas and a capacity to see vivid colours you never noticed before. By giving our readers glimpses of the world as we see it through critical lenses, we hope to provide you with both guidance and encouragement to discard your own 'religion'-tinted glasses. In different ways, each chapter emphasizes that critique is productive; deconstruction is constructive; provincializing terms helps us achieve a more global vision; and historical genealogies shed light on contemporary realities.

Contributors

Timothy Fitzgerald was Reader in Religion at the University of Stirling from 2001 to 2015, having previously worked in Japan for thirteen years; he now lectures at the University of Kent. He coined the term 'critical religion', founded the Critical Religion Association with colleagues at Stirling and is an associate of the Center for Critical Research on Religion. He is the author of *The Ideology of Religious Studies* (2000), *Discourse of Civility and Barbarity: A Critical History of Religion and Related Categories* (2007) and *Religion and Politics in International Relations: The Modern Myth* (2011).

Naomi Goldenberg is Professor of Religious Studies in the Department of Classics and Religious Studies at the University of Ottawa, Canada. Books she has authored include *Resurrecting the Body: Feminism, Religion and Psychoanalysis* (1993) and *Changing of the Gods: Feminism and the End of Traditional Religions* (1979). Vestigial state theory, the subject of her chapter in this volume, is the focus of *The End of Religion: Feminist Reappraisals of the State* (2021), a collection of essays co-edited with Kathleen McPhillips.

Alexander Henley is a programme leader and lecturer at the Institute of Ismaili Studies, directing its Graduate Programme in Islamic Studies and Humanities in partnership with SOAS University of London. He is also an associate member of Oxford's Faculty of Theology and Religion, where he was previously a lecturer and Marie Curie Research Fellow. He teaches the study of religion, Islam and politics in the modern Middle East. His research interests revolve around 'religion' as a category of practice and governance in Middle Eastern states, especially how contemporary 'religious leaderships' are shaped by connected processes of religionization, institutionalization and sectarianization.

Mitsutoshi Horii is a professor at Shumei University, Japan, in the Faculty of Global Management and principal of Chaucer College, UK. His research interests focus on categories of human sciences that authorize and normalize modern ways of doing, knowing and being. He co-edits with Tisa Wenger the journal *Method and Theory in the Study of Religion*. His most recent books are *The Category of 'Religion' in Contemporary Japan: Shūkyō and*

Temple Buddhism (2018) and *'Religion' and 'Secular' Categories in Sociology: Decolonizing the Modern Myth* (2021).

Aaron W. Hughes is Dean's Professor of the Humanities and the Philip S. Bernstein Professor of Religion at the University of Rochester, NY. Hughes specializes in three fields: Islamic Studies, Jewish Studies and Theory and Method in the Study of Religion. He has written numerous books in all three and is co-editor of the book series 'Advances in the Study of Islam' at Edinburgh University Press and of the *Journal of Religious Minorities Under Muslim Rule*.

John l'Anson is Senior Lecturer in Education in the Faculty of Social Sciences at the University of Stirling. His writings address a range of educational thematics that include work on equity and inclusion, children's rights, cultural and religious difference and pharmacy education. These writings tend to be interdisciplinary and intercultural in scope.

Alison Jasper moved from school teaching into higher education in 2001 and was Senior Lecturer in Religion and Gender at the University of Stirling until 2019. She has published on topics in feminist theory, feminism and critical religion, biblical interpretation and theology. Collaborations with John l'Anson have resulted most recently in the publication of *A Poetics of Education: Edupoetics and Pathways Towards New Educational Collectivities* (2025).

Russell T. McCutcheon is University Research Professor at the University of Alabama, where he had also been the long-time chair of the Department of Religious Studies. His work, which is widely published, is mostly focused on the history of the field and the conditions and implications of scholarship while also producing and editing an array of materials to help others reinvent how they practice and teach the study of religion.

Suzanne Owen is an associate professor at Leeds Trinity University, lecturing on the study of religion and researching British Druidry and indigeneity in Newfoundland. She has also published on the state of religious studies in the UK and on Paganism more generally. Her first book was *The Appropriation of Native American Spirituality* (2008) and she has a second one forthcoming on British Druidry.

Steven J. Sutcliffe is Visiting Fellow in Religious Studies at the Open University and was previously Senior Lecturer in the Study of Religion at the University of Edinburgh. His research interests include the effects of category formation on social life and cultural production. His publications include *Children of the New Age: A History of Spiritual Practices* (2003) and, as co-editor with

Carole Cusack, *The Problem of Invented Religions* (2016). He is completing a monograph on the Life Reform movement as a precursor to New Age spirituality.

Teemu Taira is Senior Lecturer in the Study of Religion at the University of Helsinki. His work focuses on public discourses on religion; methodology; religion in media; and atheism and nonreligion. He is the author of *Taking 'Religion' Seriously: Essays on the Discursive Study of Religion* (2022), editor of *Atheism in Five Minutes* (2022) and co-author of *Media Portrayals of Religion and the Secular Sacred* (2013). More information can be found at teemutaira.wordpress.com.

Yaacov Yadgar is the Stanley Lewis Professor of Israel Studies at the University of Oxford. He is the author of *To Be a Jewish State: Zionism as the New Judaism* (2024), *Israel's Jewish Identity Crisis: State and Politics in the Middle East* (2020) and *Sovereign Jews: Israel, Zionism, and Judaism* (2017).

Acknowledgements

This volume arose out of a series of productive seminar discussions at the University of Oxford; several participants suggested we turn those discussions into a book. Thanks are owed to all who contributed so enthusiastically to our seminars and to this publication. As convenor/editor, I am particularly grateful to the senior colleagues involved for their commitment to nurturing students and would-be academics – I hope this book will also benefit many more. It is worth acknowledging that in the time since those seminars, many among us have struggled with the impacts of the Covid pandemic in combination with the increasing precarity of academic careers and financial pressures plaguing the humanities.

Dr Lauren Morry co-convened our seminar series on *Critical and Decolonial Approaches to 'Religion'* in January–March 2020. Lauren and I had planned to co-edit this book and include a chapter on her research; life took her in a different direction, but she shares credit for its inception.

Our seminar series was kindly hosted by Mansfield College, with funds from the European Commission as part of a Marie-Skłodowska-Curie Fellowship, which also kept me in hot dinners for two years. That grant enabled us to bring wonderful speakers from afar to spend time hashing out ideas together with our interdisciplinary medley of academics and graduate students.

For their work on the production of this volume, I thank the team at Bloomsbury who have been wonderfully patient. Craig Martin, as series editor, was enthusiastically supportive of this book project and I am delighted to see it included in an excellent series of titles on *Critiquing Religion: Discourse, Culture, Power* – several of which I already keep on my easy-reach shelf for teaching. An anonymous reviewer gave particularly constructive feedback, giving me the encouraging nudge I needed to improve and expand the trickiest bits of my introductory chapters. Finally, I gratefully acknowledge the permissions granted to reproduce copyright material in Chapters 4, 5 and 11. The costs of reproducing that material were kindly covered by the Institute of Ismaili Studies.

A last word of personal thanks must go to my colleagues and mentors at Oxford's Faculty of Theology and Religion. Among them I am most deeply indebted to Justin Jones, Anna Sapir-Abulafia, Jenn Strawbridge and Joel Rasmussen for their generosity and faith in me. And for entertaining my interest in critical religion against their better judgement.

PART I

Introducing critical religion

A toolkit of critiques, methods and trajectories

1

What is wrong with the category 'religion' and what can we do about it?

Alexander Henley

Asking what we mean by 'religion' is a rite of passage for induction into the study of religion (or religious studies), but it is a singularly unsatisfying one. Any initiate will have rehearsed the tired old debates over a definition of religion and likely emerged none the wiser. Typically, the teacher recites a litany of definitions; students respond by acknowledging the flaws of each, finally confessing that no definition is adequate to encompass this profoundly elusive phenomenon of religion. Some may go on to pick a favourite formula to use for the sake of consistency, caveated with a ritual nod to the problem. Others revert to the dictum 'we know it when we see it'. Either way, we are back where we started. We have no common way of knowing our religious apples from our non-religious oranges.

This book does not debate definitions of religion. Nor do its authors ignore the problem. Instead, we want to move the conversation in a more productive direction by getting at the root of the definitional problem: there is something wrong with the term 'religion' itself. The first section of this chapter – *What's wrong with the category 'religion'?* – introduces the most common critiques of 'religion' as an analytical category. The second section – *Where do we go from here?* – discusses their significance and our options moving forward. This section offers something of a roadmap for what comes after critique or through it: how we can create new knowledge by applying critical approaches to 'religion' out in the world. The following chapter – *What is critical religion? Past, present and future of critical scholarship* – turns to the pioneering scholars behind these ideas, painting a broad-strokes picture of this critical turn in scholarly thinking around religion. Collectively, I hope these two chapters may serve as a handy inventory of a critical religionist's toolkit of critiques, lenses, concepts, terms, methods, issues and resources.

What is wrong with the category 'religion'?

You may think you know more or less what is meant by the word 'religion', along with its plural 'religions' and adjectival form 'religious'. No doubt you could name several religions and all sorts of religious beliefs, practices or institutions that seem to fall easily into a box labelled 'religion'. How much do we need to worry about the odd-shaped things that do not quite fit, or those things that might also fit into other boxes? Some say that it is better to get on with studying the things that do fit rather than bickering endlessly over borderline cases or the exact shape of the box. But the real trouble is in what we do with the box: What are we doing when we categorize something as 'religion'? Is the category actually useful? Does it help us analyse our subject by drawing meaningful connections and does it help us spot false comparisons? I begin by presenting the argument that 'religion' is simply not useful as a descriptive, let alone analytical, category. That is only the beginning of the critique posed by a recent generation of scholars; these critical religionists go on to argue that using the category 'religion' may be misleading or even dangerous. I will outline a series of interconnected critiques, which target in turn the essentialist, discursive, ideological and theological underpinnings of the category 'religion'. (In this section I draw significantly on Timothy Fitzgerald's classic book, *The Ideology of Religious Studies* (2000), which still offers one of the most strident, wide-ranging and accessible critiques of the category 'religion'.)[1]

To start with, **the term 'religion' is inherently vague**. '"Religion" and "religions" are used in such a vast variety of contexts and include so many different things that they have no clear meaning' (Fitzgerald 2000: 6). When someone refers to the role of religion in society, for instance, they may be talking about any or all of a baffling array of beliefs, doctrines, texts, experiences, rituals, practices, actors or institutions. In certain contexts we may see all these intuitively as components of a familiar 'religion', given coherence within an institutionalized tradition that is jurisdictionally circumscribed – most notably in the European Christian context of a distinction between church and state. But when trying to determine a common denominator for 'religion', scholars define it in relation to belief in the supernatural or other-worldly. Their aim is to extend a Judeo-Christian notion of God beyond monotheism to include not only polytheism but also other belief systems that are supposedly similar. Options for a definition include belief in the divine, transcendent, numinous, mystical, sacred, or in superhuman agents, an ultimate concern, or soteriological commitment. While trying to pin down some underlying referent for religious belief, these definitions really only fudge the matter further. Timothy Fitzgerald explains this problem of definition neatly:

> It cannot be assumed at the outset that what is loosely referred to as belief in the supernatural in one context (for example, propitiation of angry ghosts in Japan) shares any significant *a priori* semantic properties with what is loosely described as belief in the supernatural in another context (for example, possession by the goddess Mariai in central India). (2000: 6)

Whatever definition we may have in mind, using the label 'religious' mystifies rather than clarifies our understanding of what we are looking at and it leads us to assume a commonality with other supposedly 'religious' phenomena that is likely to 'confuse and impoverish analysis, conceal fruitful connections that might otherwise be made . . . and generally maximize our chances of misunderstanding' (2000: 6).

As well as being vague in meaning, **'religion' has no fixed boundaries**. All of the characteristics we associate with religion are equally present in things we do not normally categorize as such. Supernatural beliefs, rituals and sacred things are found everywhere. Attempts to define religion have therefore 'given rise to intractable problems of marginality', as Fitzgerald neatly puts it (2000: 5): 'For example, are ghosts, witches, emperors, and ancestors gods? How about film stars? What is the difference between a superhuman being and a superior person?' Obvious examples of supposedly non-religious things that could equally be called religions include football (as a cult with fanatics, idols, sacred vestments, hymns, shrines, etc.) and nationalism (as a system of belief in something greater than ourselves, with scriptures written by founding fathers; hallowed places of pilgrimage; ritual pledges of allegiance to a sacred symbol that must be honoured and protected from desecration; and of course armies of willing martyrs). With such a vast range of possibilities encompassed by any definition of 'religion', we are left with no way to decide which to include or exclude.

An analogy that comes to mind is the children's shape-sorter toy with various holes into which to sort shaped blocks. You may have seen the 2021 viral video showing someone dropping all the differently shaped blocks into a single square hole because it turns out everything fits into the square.[2] In one version of the video, an observer becomes increasingly frustrated and distressed as successive blocks are miscategorized. 'Religion' is the square hole into which all things fit, making it a useless tool for sorting data into categories for analysis. In the famous words of Jonathan Z. Smith, '**there is no data for religion**' (1982: xi). So why do many of us find that such a strange and unsettling thought? It disturbs our common-sense way of seeing and describing the world and calls into question the way we have habitually interacted with it. Like the distressed observer in the video, we may never have thought twice about the self-evident logic – even the necessity – of putting certain blocks into square holes and other ones into round holes. That is what we were taught to do and what we might have taught our own children to do.

How much does this categorization issue actually matter? Part of the problem is that our 'common sense' is not shared by everyone, so applying the concept of religion to other cultures is to make **a category mistake in cross-cultural analysis** (Fitzgerald 1997, developed further in 2000). It turns out that the English word 'religion' – along with European cognates – does not translate straightforwardly into non-European languages. In order to capture that Europhone notion of religion as the domain of beliefs and practices pertaining to the supernatural, most people in the world have had to invent new words or re-purpose old ones. Nineteenth-century Chinese scholars, for example, translated it by combining a pictogram of an ancestral altar with a character meaning 'teaching' to create a compound word *zong-jiao*. The same novel combination of characters was then adopted into Japanese as *shu-kyo*. Now-familiar words for 'religion' in languages all across Asia are similarly recent adaptations: for example, Hindi's *dharma*, from a Sanskrit word meaning 'duty'; Bengali's *niyama*, likewise expanded from 'rules' or 'duties'; Khasi's *ka niam*, borrowed earlier from Bengali to refer to a variety of traditional 'customs'; Arabic's *din*, from a Qur'anic term for 'law' or a 'debt' to authority, which was rarely used in plural or adjectival forms (*adyan, dini*) before modern discussions of 'world religions' and a separable sphere of 'religious' life. We now have a well-established and ever-growing body of scholarship that has traced these inventions of 'religion' in each language to the era of European powers' global exploration and colonization. Europeans were also behind the categorization and naming of belief systems we now know as 'world religions': 'Hinduism', 'Buddhism', 'Shintoism', 'Confucianism', 'Taoism' and 'Judaism' were all coined in the eighteenth or nineteenth centuries (see e.g. Masuzawa 2005). 'Islam' appears to be the only exception as a term dating back to the Qur'an, where it referred to an act of 'submission'; its adoption as the name of a religious system and community, however, is a surprisingly recent development, only gaining widespread recognition among Muslims and non-Muslims alike in the twentieth century (W. C. Smith 1981: 41–77).

The vast majority of people in the world had no indigenous words for 'religion' or 'religions' because they did not make such distinctions between one belief versus another, one customary practice versus another, one institution or authority versus another and so on, as religious as opposed to non-religious. For example, it may not make sense to distinguish between religious versus secular duties if the same code of conduct governs one's duties to one's parents, ancestors, elders, teachers, emperor and god. Over recent centuries there has been a gradual globalization of Euro-American terminology – and with it the ways of thinking and organizing societies that its word-concepts represent – but it is crucial to realize that these have been adopted, adapted, subverted or rejected in varied ways and to different extents that can only be understood contextually. So when we apply the conceptual vocabulary of religion across cultures, or across history, we do so 'in the face of a mass of contradictory evidence' (Fitzgerald 2000: 6).

Rather than a thing we can observe in the world, or a universal dimension of human experience, **'religion' is a modern reified concept**. Wilfred Cantwell Smith famously identified 'reification' as a process of 'mentally making religion into a thing, gradually coming to conceive it as an objective systematic entity' (1962: 50), a process that can be traced historically to the peculiar circumstances of Western modernity. As such, religion does not exist apart from human discourse. In talking about religion, we are imagining a trans-cultural and trans-historical essence that is somehow manifested in the world. The danger in this religion-talk is that we read into people's actions and motivations something that may not be there. Rather than helping us to understand how people think and act in particular contexts, it implicitly assumes essential 'religious' characteristics or even attributes agency to 'religion' as an invisible force of nature like gravity.

Talking about specific 'religions' is no better. It still implies an essential equivalence between those belief systems we choose to call religions – like species of a common genus – and groups them together as a fundamentally different kind of thing from other belief systems presumed to be non-religious or secular. So, for example, to talk about 'Islam' as 'a religion' is to obscure or outright deny certain Muslims' belief in the incomparability of God's revelation in the Qur'an, or in the universal applicability of shari'a as a holistic way of life or social order. It also takes for granted the existence of 'Islam' as a timelessly bounded and cohesive belief system that defines what it means to be Muslim. It therefore obscures the varied and even conflicting ways in which people have defined themselves as Muslims and others as non-Muslims. Further, it reduces what it means to be Muslim to a certain conception of belief, that is, cognitive assent to a 'belief system', an internally coherent set of pre-determined doctrines, by a self-conscious and consistent individual (see e.g. McCloud 2017). So when we describe Muslims as adherents of a religion called Islam, we devalue or misunderstand many people's experience of *islam* as a practice of submission (its literal meaning in Arabic), which may be less a ritual expression of doctrinal belief than a means to cultivate faith or an ongoing struggle to understand and commit to God's will as part of a collective project. In other words, the language of generic 'religion' and singular or plural 'religions' conjures into our imagination an objective systematic entity that is simply not there to be found. It misdescribes individuals and groups, stereotyping them and skewing our own understanding. Like other stereotypes, it has been reinforced by continual repetition until it feels so self-evident that we may find it difficult not to see it in people and in patterns of behaviour or historical trends.

Far from a neutral descriptor, **'religion' is an implicitly normative category**. In order to grasp this point, it is important first to remember that 'religion' is never a stand-alone concept but rather a category distinction. When we call one thing 'religious', we are setting it apart from other things that are 'non-religious' or 'secular'. These categories operate as two sides of a binary pair: one always implies the existence of the other. Talal Asad highlighted this binary relationship as an extension of Wilfred Cantwell Smith's observation that religion only exists as a reified concept in the modern imagination: '"religion" is a modern concept not [only] because it is reified but because it has been linked to its Siamese twin "secularism"' (Asad 2001: 221). These twin categories were born together in sixteenth- and seventeenth-century Europe as the conceptual underpinnings of an ideology that aimed to displace the all-encompassing authority of Christian Truth. By classifying certain truth claims and moral authorities as subjectively 'religious', it became possible to assert a separate 'secular' conceptual space of objectivity and moral neutrality as the exclusive basis for 'scientific' knowledge, the 'politics' of nation-states and liberal democracies, the 'economics' of capitalist markets, and so on. Fitzgerald explains the significance of the category 'secular' as:

> the arena of the 'really real' . . . an appearance of undeniable factuality that hides (from westerners, but not from so many members of third world societies) the value-laden assumptions upon which so much of the western view of the world rests. This is not to deny the importance of scientific values, or the advocacy of human rights, or even the value of capitalist productivity. What I wish to point out is that the secular is itself a sphere of transcendental values, but the invention of religion as the locus of the transcendent serves to disguise this and strengthen the illusion that the secular is simply the real world seen aright in its self-evident factuality. (2000: 14–15)

When we describe something as 'religious', therefore, we are placing it on one side of a binary that is normatively loaded – predominantly in favour of the secular.[3] Our use of these seemingly innocuous words has effects we may not intend or even be aware of: applying and/or reinforcing a hierarchy of values in which some people or projects are empowered while others are disempowered.

To understand what this means in practice, we need only look back at colonial history – a history in which the so-called scientific study of religion was deeply implicated. Most students in religious studies or anthropology are aware that their academic disciplines were born in European and North American universities at the height of colonialism, whose global information-gathering made it possible to study the religions and cultures of the world systematically. What may be less immediately obvious is that their role in colonial knowledge production went far beyond simply collating and circulating information about local peoples that could be used to exploit them. Scholarly classification of religions equipped colonial officials with a covert ideological weapon: by classifying large swathes of a colonized people's culture as being part of their local 'religion', they could exclude virtually any indigenous forms of expression or organization from the new secular institutions they built. This meant that they could invite locals to participate freely in liberal democratic politics and capitalist commerce while setting terms of engagement that invisibly hobbled any real competition. These secular public spaces were presented as level playing fields where all people – regardless of their 'private' religious commitments – could engage in a purportedly universalistic rational negotiation of interests. In effect, however, the language of secular universalism served as a cover under which to privilege a particular Western system of beliefs and values. Meanwhile, supposedly positive protections on 'freedom of religion' as a private matter of individual conscience had the effect of compartmentalizing and marginalizing indigenous values, symbols, institutions and leadership structures – all the cultural resources that might be used to mobilize a meaningful resistance or to articulate alternative ways of knowing or being in the world.

Even in contemporary contexts where religious-secular categories may seem fully embedded as a shared frame of reference, we still see their boundaries being continually negotiated in ways that matter to the people involved. It matters, for instance, whether Islam is counted as a religion or a political ideology, whether a headscarf is treated as a religious symbol, or whether ISIS militancy is genuinely Islamic. Yet these are not the kind of questions that can be resolved empirically; instead, their answers are invocations of normative discourses that have the potential to sway public attitudes or change legal statuses. Outcomes similarly depend entirely on discursive contexts. Take three instances of a community space for Muslims in New York: in one instance, claiming 'religious' status helped gain building permissions and tax breaks; in a second instance, announcing the opening of an 'Islamic Center and Mosque' near the site of New York's 9/11 attack prompted a national uproar over the idea of a 'Ground Zero Mosque'; in a third instance, rebranding the same site as a 'cultural center for Muslims with a prayer space' allowed it to open without further controversy. Rather than reflecting a fixed social reality, we see classifications of religion or non-religion as discursive tools that are used strategically to achieve something in a given context. So whenever we come across a claim that something is either religious or non-religious – be it secular, political, cultural, social or whatever stands for the other side of the binary – we need to recognize that claim as a discursive strategy rather than a factual description that can be proven or disproven.

A final problem to mention here, as part of the problem of covert normativity in the terms we take to be neutrally descriptive, is that **the category 'religion' is implicitly theological**. Hidden in the language of religion and religions is what Fitzgerald calls 'a disguised form of liberal ecumenical theology' (2000: 6). That is to say, it rests on an unverifiable assumption about the commonality of human experience underlying the various phenomena we call religious: 'a natural and/or a supernatural reality in the nature of things that all human individuals have a capacity for, regardless of their cultural context' (5). As I noted earlier, grouping all so-called religions together as equivalent forms of metaphysical belief, or ritual responses to the supernatural, is to paint over the very different – and frequently incompatible – ways in which people conceive of their own experiences or actions and articulate their own worldviews. When Fitzgerald calls this assumed commonality a form of 'ecumenical theology', he is referencing a Christian theological movement for unity among churches, which has argued for a re-interpretation of their differences not as rival truth claims but as equally valid paths to salvation or complementary ways of worshipping the same God. The notion of universal religion implicitly extends that idealized vision of unity to all 'religions'. At this point some readers may be wondering what is so bad about emphasizing unity among the world's religions. The trouble is not necessarily with the ideal itself, but with a misleading representation of what one thinks *ought* to be the case as though it simply *is* the case.[4] I would say this comes down to a matter of intellectual honesty as well as accuracy. Whether or not you intend to express any such normative commitment when you talk about 'religions', you are nevertheless using language that aligns with some people's theological truth claims over others. Deciding what should or should not count as legitimate 'religion' is ultimately a theological judgement: the same kind of judgement Christians make on excommunication or Muslims make on *takfir*, deciding who belongs in one's community of believers and who does not. You cannot avoid the negative implications of such judgements by taking an expansive approach because that is precisely the liberal ecumenical project that whitewashes over real differences and, in Russell McCutcheon's words, 'can also be described in political terms as . . . [an] instance of the liberal effort to domesticate and homogenize diversity' (McCutcheon 1997: 125). Meanwhile, our habitual decision to call some other metaphysical beliefs 'secular' – such as faith in the natural necessity of nation-states or capitalist markets – may protect those from scrutiny as similarly transcendental values.

Where do we go from here?

Defining our key terms and concepts should help us identify what kind of thing we are looking at and why. It should help us make sense of our data – that is, classify and organize the mess of stuff we see in the world – allowing us to draw meaningful connections, comparisons or generalizations. It should help us talk about our findings in ways that others can understand and engage with. It should also help us spot conclusions that do not make sense, so that we avoid comparing apples and oranges. Attempts to define 'religion' have yielded no such benefits nor resulted in any meaningful consensus, despite a century and a half of scholarly efforts in its name. You might counter by pointing out that every academic discipline has similar debates over the terms that define its field of study, but there is something more pernicious about this one. Naomi Goldenberg explains the difference nicely:

> The category 'religion' is unique in the pantheon of reified Western concepts that must be deconstructed. Unlike other speculative and generalized abstractions that resist precise delimitation, 'religion' is treated as if it were a defined, agreed-upon, ahistoric and non-contingent object in laws and constitutions. The 'it' that is hypostasized as 'religion' is given special protections, exemptions, privileges and institutions. 'It' is spoken of as a mysterious agentic force that is sometimes dormant, but always returns. 'It' is both blamed for violence and discord by detractors and extolled for promoting peace and harmony by advocates. In short, reification of 'religion' seriously distorts clear thinking about issues that are essential to communal life. (Goldenberg 2020b: 314)

Or as Russell McCutcheon puts it: '*the category of religion is up to something*, making it not just a neutral descriptor of obvious spiritual and thus apolitical, otherworldly states and dispositions' (Chapter 4; emphasis added). If you are not yet convinced, I urge you to read McCutcheon's chapter for a more extended statement of the problem, which he illustrates with everyday examples of what words do: how naming things as 'religious' or 'non-religious' has practical, legal or social consequences that are anything but neutral. When we use such labels uncritically – as though they describe some objectively identifiable kind of phenomenon – we fall into a series of traps: (1) we risk distorting our own analysis of important issues; (2) we miss what these labels are doing as folk categories, or discursive practices of social classification, in the contexts we study; and (3) we unwittingly feed into wider discourses that do things beyond our control. So where do we go from here? Over the rest of this section, I will take each of these three traps as a starting point to suggest ways to escape them and move forward.

Escaping trap 1: Analytical distortion

If the first trap is analytical distortion, we can often escape it by being more specific about what we mean. The words 'religion', 'religions' and 'religious' are so ingrained in our everyday vocabulary that it is easy to forget how vague and slippery they are. We may know intuitively what they refer to in certain contexts, where they are commonly used and understood as what scholars might call 'folk categories' or 'categories of practice', but that does not mean they work as categories of analysis. Because their meanings and boundaries shift depending on context and usage, it is helpful to think of these terms as 'floating signifiers' that are continuously constructed and negotiated, or even as 'empty signifiers' that acquire meaning only in opposition to other categories (see Taira 2022: 20–1). Fitzgerald calls them 'empty abstractions that appear concrete, and that unconsciously operate and organize our knowledge', or 'empty signs operating in an automatic signalling system' which therefore 'operate us more than we operate them' (Chapter 5). So, rather than try to pin down a working definition of religion for one's own analytical purposes, it may be safer and more productive to leave it empty and look instead for more specific terms.

Once we think of 'religion' as an empty abstraction, it becomes easier to ask what we really mean. Within the panoply of possible things that might be described as religious, what are the specific practices, social formations, dynamics, factors or motivations we can pick out for analysis? Take, for instance, the endlessly unresolved debates over the so-called problem of religious violence. Rather than assume we know or can discover what distinguishes 'religious' violence from 'secular political' violence, we can treat the term as an empty placeholder for something else. What are the specific forms or causes of violence at issue in this debate? Perhaps what we really mean is violence that is motivated by belief or ideology; devoted to absolute ideals, principles or truth claims; framed by an overarching mythology, worldview, cosmology, eschatology or good/evil dichotomy; directed at symbolic targets or pursuit of sacrifice or redemption; fought over indivisibly sacred goods or identities; performed through ritual acts; organized or mobilized by non-state actors, institutions or networks. Any of these factors may be picked out as a focus for more fruitful analysis that allows for comparison across contexts, without needing to group them under a catch-all category so elusive as 'religion'. Freeing ourselves to look for the same factors in any context, without confining our analysis to the arbitrary boundaries of the 'religious', we quickly realize that every one of them can also be found in so-called secular or political violence. Besides calling into question a religious-secular dichotomy that 'seriously distorts clear thinking about issues that are essential to communal life' (Goldenberg as quoted above) – in this case by leading us to perpetuate 'the myth of religious violence' (Cavanaugh 2009) – what we gain by breaking down 'religion' into specific components is, first, a granular clarity of focus and, second, a rich potential to analyse cross-cutting categories of human practice or belief over a wider field. So, next time you find yourself describing something as 'religious', it is worth pausing to consider whether you could be more specific. Or when you see a statement about 'religion', ask yourself – or, at the risk of making yourself unpopular, ask your colleague or student: What does this really mean, if it means anything at all?

Escaping trap 2: Missing the categories at work

The second trap in talking about religion is that we miss what the category is doing right under our noses, in the very contexts we are trying to understand and analyse. There is often a great deal of insight to be gained by paying critical attention to how people use words like 'religion' and 'religious'. Being 'critical' in this sense means, to begin with, not taking it for granted that such labels refer to some inherent characteristic in the things being described. Instead, we can put the words in quotation marks – literally and figuratively – as folk categories that deserve to be objects of study in their own right. We can then ask some probing (critical) questions about their contextual meanings and significance: How does labelling something as 'religious' – or as 'a religion' – distinguish it from other categories of things? Why is this distinction being made? What does it achieve? What purposes does it serve, and for whom? Who benefits from it, and how? Each of these questions follows from the last, and they become progressively more 'critical' in the sense that they delve deeper under the skin of the descriptive language to reveal underlying social dynamics and power relations. First, they help us interpret meanings in the context of a conceptual vocabulary used by the people we are studying to organize their knowledge of the world around them. Further, they help us see how this organizing system of knowledge – what critical theorists call a 'discourse' – functions to organize and shape people's social reality. By this point, what we are doing is more than linguistic analysis; we are analysing the way people use words like 'religion' as *discursive practices* of social classification: 'walling things off from one another, so as to promote or demote them in relation to other things in society, all depending on the social interests of the speaker' (McCutcheon in Chapter 4).

There are all sorts of ways to study 'religion' discourse. We can look at individual 'speech acts' – a term coined by J. L. Austin in *How to Do Things with Words* (1962) – by examining what particular words are doing rhetorically in a given conversation, oration or text, analysing them situationally as strategic deployments of a wider discourse. Zooming out a little, we can look at how language is used on different sides of a debate (e.g. Teemu Taira's case studies of legal claims to 'religion' status and their contestation, in Chapter 7; or Suzanne Owen's discussion of various terms used by or about Indigenous people to represent their identity, in Chapter 8). Zooming out further, we can look at how categories are employed at the level of institutions or states, drawing attention to large-scale effects of discourse on social organization and governance (e.g. Steven Sutcliffe's ethnographic study of how the Scottish Parliament represents 'faith' in state ritual, in Chapter 9; or Yaacov Yadgar's historical and institutional analysis of the Israeli state's formulations of Jewish 'religious' and 'national' identities, in Chapter 10; or Mitsutoshi Horii's use of longue-durée history and sociology to trace changing US projections of an alien concept of 'religion' onto Japan and their effects on diplomatic negotiations and Japanese statecraft, in Chapter 6). If we look for changes in how categories are used over time, we start to see how discourses are constructed and re-constructed, how they emerge and gain dominance, and how they reshape social relations, practices and institutions. It can be productive to compare cases across contexts, or across moments in history, in order to spot patterns or specificities (e.g. Naomi Goldenberg draws together observations from various continents and historical periods into her 'vestigial state theory' that religion is a classification used by governments to disarm and contain the remnants of former governmental structures in a diminished but still privileged status, in Chapter 11; Teemu Taira highlights two opposite trends of 'religionization' and 'culturalization' in contemporary European negotiations of religious-secular boundaries, explaining them as parallel discursive strategies that serve the different interests of minority and majority groups, in Chapter 7). To get a more granular sense of how one might carry out such a study, I recommend reading Teemu Taira's step-by-step walkthrough of his research process in Chapter 7. (For further reading on discourse analysis methods and theory, see Taira 2022; Johnston and von Stuckrad 2021; Martin 2021; Wijsen and von Stuckrad 2016; Lincoln 2014.)

The study of discourse is not limited to language. Speech acts are one kind of discursive practice, but if we are interested in what religious-secular categories *do*, then the emphasis should be on *acts* and *practices* of social classification – whether performed verbally or non-verbally. For example, Sutcliffe's study of state discourse (Chapter 8) uses ethnographic observations to examine how social categories are represented – and thereby constructed – through a parliamentary ritual called 'Time for Reflection'. As well as looking at the textual content of weekly 'Reflections' and the parliament's framing language of 'non-denominational faith', he takes their performance itself as data: ritualized styles of speech, bodily actions and deportment; material elements such as the architecture and spatial organization; and roles of performers and audience members. Another option for discursive study of 'religion' is to explore how categories are institutionalized or operationalized on a larger scale. For example, Horii's analysis of Japanese statecraft (Chapter 6) reveals religious-secular categories enacted through the separation of powers and arrangement of hierarchical relationships, as well as through the government's differential treatment of social institutions according to their shifting designations as 'religion', 'non-religion' or 'superstition'.

Whatever the focus of your studies – in whatever discipline and regional/historical context – paying critical attention to key terms and categories is always important and valuable. You don't have to do all the critical work yourself: there is now a well-established literature on the genealogies – that is, the historical origins and discursive formations – of common terms like 'religion', 'religions', 'secular', 'politics', 'culture', 'race', 'gender' and so on. We can draw on those genealogies to reflect on the terms we use to describe, organize and analyse our data. Firstly, understanding where our words come from helps us assess what they may be doing as building blocks in the scholarly narratives we construct. Secondly, by tracing the local/provincial origins of words as we currently understand them, genealogy shows us that the conceptual categories they represent are neither universal nor naturally occurring. In other words, genealogy *provincializes* our received categories so that we can *problematize* how they apply to the contexts we study. If you are worried that all this business of genealogy and critical reflection may distract you from the work you really want to do – immersing yourself in great texts, histories, life-worlds or social dynamics – please do read Aaron Hughes' discussion of 'why it matters where our terms come from', in Chapter 3. That chapter is addressed to you, 'the reluctant genealogist'.

Genealogies of terms and concepts should not be seen as a niche interest but as a resource for other researchers. For historians, a major benefit of knowing the modern genealogies of now-familiar concepts is to defamiliarize the conceptual worlds of the past. Classicist Brent Nongbri illustrated this in his book *Before Religion* with a myriad of ancient Latin, Greek and Arabic texts 'that appear to self-evidently proclaim a religious/secular divide to modern people ("Render unto Caesar...")', but which in fact 'seem to have been understood quite differently by ancient readers' (2013: 5). Genealogy therefore guides us to look out for those anachronisms we would not otherwise be aware of committing. Once we spot our mistranslation of categories, we may get closer to reading historical texts on their authors' terms instead of our own. More ambitiously, this defamiliarization 'would allow what we have been calling "ancient religions" (that is, the contents of all those books called *Mesopotamian Religion, Religions of Rome, Ancient Greek Religion*, etc.) to be disaggregated and rearranged in ways that correspond better to ancient peoples' own organizational schemes' (Nongbri 2013: 159). If we turn to more recent history, Horii's study of nineteenth- and twentieth-century Japan (Chapter 6) also shows the importance of genealogy. His narrative begins not in Japan but in early modern Europe with the invention of 'religion', following its discursive spread to America and from there to the shores of Japan, allowing Horii to set the global scene in which to think critically about 'religion' in nineteenth-century Japan. For those of us who study contemporary society, genealogy can be thought of as the 'history of the present' (Foucault 1977: 31; for a light introduction to Foucault's influential ideas about discourse and genealogy, see Gutting 2019). Genealogy traces the origins of present discourses, structures, or institutions as a means to question whether they are really as natural or necessary as they seem. So, for example, feminist scholars may find in genealogy an opportunity to dispel 'the mystified aura of ancient specialness in which religions are cloaked' (Goldenberg 2020a: 19), allowing them to question how this special status has protected spaces of masculine hegemony from critical discussion internally and from legal accountability externally (see Chapter 11; also the collected 'feminist reappraisals' in McPhillips and Goldenberg 2020).

Escaping trap 3: The discursive web

The third trap to consider is that, in using certain terms, we unwittingly feed into wider discourses that do things beyond our control. Here we get into ongoing debates about the scale on which one should respond to the problems with the category 'religion'. Should we stop using the word altogether? Some scholars have focused on distancing themselves from particularly problematic uses – those they identify as most analytically troublesome in whatever they are studying – while keeping the words 'religion', 'religious' or equivalents in their descriptive vocabulary. Nongbri notes this as common in historians' writings: 'They can (correctly) recognize that religion was not a concept in ancient cultures, but they can continue speaking as if it were' (2013: 151). It may seem intuitive to write in language familiar to one's readers, but that comes at the risk of undermining the point of historicizing the concept in the first place. So we must beware of how our vocabulary might result in 'the reinscription of religion as something eternally present in all cultures' (151). This is not only a trap for historians. McCutcheon similarly notes the danger of thinking that we can reject the abstraction of religion as a generic universal concept only to 'raise a mission accomplished banner and then get on with the business of studying religions – in the plural, on the ground, on the move' (2010: 254). Pluralizing religion or emphasizing local particularity may help dispel the myth of monolithic 'world religions' with fixed boundaries, but it does not avoid the implication that the things being described are instances of a universal phenomenon distinct from non-religion. The same trap appears if we try instead to use the adjective 'religious', or other words like 'religiosity' or 'faith' or 'spirituality', which seem to describe an authentic attitude or quality: all end up naturalizing the theological idea of a unique inner dimension to human life that is somehow distinguishable from cultural expression or political orientation. On the other hand, Taira suggests the possibility of using the vocabulary of religion 'heuristically in specific research designs in order to solve some problems', so long as it is done 'reflectively and self-consciously' (Chapter 7). Ultimately, though, it may be simpler and safer to avoid these generic terms. Dropping such common words might initially feel counter-intuitive, but, like Taira, I find that I have little need to talk about 'religion' once I get into the habit of using more specific terms.

Clearly 'religion' is not the only word to be wary of. Substituting different words for broadly the same underlying idea (e.g. 'faith') does not resolve the problem, not least because they perform the same discursive function of constructing their binary other: a secular sphere of factual knowledge and objective reason. Because these are not stand-alone categories but 'empty signs operating in an automatic signalling system', Fitzgerald warns us that we cannot control what the words do in the broader framework of modern discourse (Chapter 5). This applies to abstract concepts on both sides of the religious-secular binary, so he argues that we should also jettison the terminology of the secular. That would mean we stop trying to identify things – or aspects of things – as 'political', 'cultural', 'scientific', 'economic' and so on, because these are equally empty categories that are premised on their opposition to religion. 'It seems we are trapped by language', he says, and 'need to dissolve these reified binaries if a new paradigm is to have a chance to get articulated in public discourse' (Fitzgerald 2007: 38). Meanwhile, some scholars worry that such an extended, perhaps never-ending, critique of categories becomes impractical. Goldenberg, for example, argues that an expansive conception of 'politics' as power relations can be a useful tool: 'Positioning "religion" *as politics* . . . demystifies the term and implies that historical, contingent human motives and goals are always operative'

(2020b: 315; emphasis added). She sees this as a strategic inversion of the dominant paradigm, a strategy that echoes and extends the feminist maxim that 'the personal is political' (see Goldenberg 2020a). Notably, what scholars like Fitzgerald and Goldenberg have in common is an *ethical* commitment to challenging discourses responsible for 'generating the illusion that today's dominant system of exploitation and inequality is sane, rational, normal, natural and the only possible game in town' (Fitzgerald in Chapter 5). On one side of the debate, Goldenberg proposes to overturn the discourse from within: 'To dismantle the master's house, what else could you possibly use except what you have at hand – that is, the master's toolbox?' (2020b: 314). On the other side, Fitzgerald argues that those tools are too fundamentally compromised: we must lay down the tools 'that keep us enthralled and unable to have any new ideas' (Chapter 5). An example of a scholar who has taken up this radical call is Horii (2021), who sees it as integral to the task of decolonizing the social sciences. Unravelling the web of modern categories allows us to understand and engage with others on a more equal footing:

> When we abandon the religious-secular distinction and stop wearing it as a conceptual lens, the lifeworld of moderns appears to be full of strangeness. . . . In this mindset, I believe, self-identified 'secular' moderns can find lots of things in common with those who used to be regarded as non-modern 'religious' others. This should be the foundation upon which any meaningful dialogue takes place between multiplicities of lifeways to facilitate their co-existence based on mutual respect. (Horii 2021: 250–1)

In this chapter I have sought to explain why so many scholars have come to regard the term 'religion' with suspicion, and how that suspicion can be a healthy thing. In sum, the category 'religion' is not a self-evident or neutral descriptor, but a historically contingent, normatively loaded and often problematic tool that shapes and sometimes distorts our understanding of the world. Recognizing the traps and limitations inherent in this category is not simply a semantic exercise; it is a vital and vitalizing step towards more precise, honest and equitable scholarship. By interrogating the terms we use and the assumptions they carry, we open up new possibilities for analysis and dialogue, both within and beyond the academy. The question, then, is not only what is wrong with the category 'religion', but how we might think and work differently in its wake. In the next chapter I go on to introduce the scholars asking these questions, map the intellectual trajectories behind them, and highlight ongoing debates.

References

Asad, Talal (2001), 'Reading a Modern Classic: W. C. Smith's "The Meaning and End of Religion"', *History of Religions*, 40 (3): 205–22.
Austin, J. L. (1962), *How to Do Things with Words*, Cambridge, MA: Harvard University Press.
Cavanaugh, William T. (2009), *The Myth of Religious Violence: Secular Ideology and the Roots of Modern Conflict*, Oxford: Oxford University Press.
Fitzgerald, Timothy (1997), 'A Critique of "Religion" as a Cross-Cultural Category', *Method and Theory in the Study of Religion*, 9 (2): 91–110.
Fitzgerald, Timothy (2000), *The Ideology of Religious Studies*, Oxford: Oxford University Press.
Fitzgerald, Timothy (2007), *Discourse on Civility and Barbarity: A Critical History of Religion and Related Categories*, Oxford: Oxford University Press.
Foucault, Michel (1977), *Discipline and Punish: The Birth of the Prison*, trans. Alan Sheridan, New York: Vintage.
Goldenberg, Naomi (2020a), 'The Religious Is Political', in Kathleen McPhillips and Naomi Goldenberg (eds), *The End of Religion: Feminist Reappraisals of the State*, 7–25, London: Routledge.
Goldenberg, Naomi (2020b), 'Timothy Fitzgerald and the Revival of Religious Studies', *Implicit Religion*, 22 (3–4): 309–18.
Gutting, Gary (2019), *Foucault: A Very Short Introduction*, 2nd edn, Oxford: Oxford University Press.
Horii, Mitsutoshi (2021), *'Religion' and 'Secular' Categories in Sociology: Decolonizing the Modern Myth*, Cham: Palgrave Macmillan.
Johnston, Jay and Kocku von Stuckrad, eds (2021), *Discourse Research and Religion: Disciplinary Use and Interdisciplinary Dialogues*, Berlin: De Gruyter.
Lincoln, Bruce (2014), *Discourse and the Construction of Society: Comparative Studies of Myth, Ritual, and Classification*, 2nd edn, Oxford: Oxford University Press.
Martin, Craig (2021), *Discourse and Ideology: A Critique of the Study of Culture*, London: Bloomsbury.
Masuzawa, Tomoko (2005), *The Invention of World Religions: Or, How European Universalism Was Preserved in the Language of Pluralism*, Chicago, IL: University of Chicago Press.
McCloud, Sean (2017), 'Religions are Belief Systems', in Brad Stoddard and Craig Martin (eds), *Stereotyping Religion: Critiquing Cliches*, 11–21, London: Bloomsbury Academic.
McCutcheon, Russell T. (1997), *Manufacturing Religion: The Discourse of Sui Generis Religion and the Politics of Nostalgia*, Oxford: Oxford University Press.
McCutcheon, Russell T. (2010), 'Religion Before "Religion"?', in Panayotis Pachis and Donald Wiebe (eds), *Chasing Down Religion: In the Sights of History and the Cognitive Sciences*, 251–66, Thessaloniki: Barbounakis.
McPhillips, Kathleen and Naomi Goldenberg, eds (2020), *The End of Religion: Feminist Reappraisals of the State*, London: Routledge.
Nongbri, Brent (2013), *Before Religion: A History of a Modern Concept*, New Haven, CT: Yale University Press.

Smith, Jonathan Z. (1982), *Imagining Religion: From Babylon to Jonestown*, Chicago, IL: University of Chicago Press.
Smith, Wilfred Cantwell (1962), *The Meaning and End of Religion*, New York: Macmillan.
Smith, Wilfred Cantwell (1981), *On Understanding Islam: Selected Studies*, Berlin: De Gruyter.
Taira, Teemu (2022), *Taking 'Religion' Seriously: Essays on the Discursive Study of Religion*, Leiden: Brill.
Wijsen, Frans and Kocku von Stuckrad, eds (2016), *Making Religion: Theory and Practice in the Discursive Study of Religion*, Leiden: Brill.

2

What is critical religion? Past, present and future of critical scholarship

Alexander Henley

What is 'critical religion'?

'Critical religion' is a shorthand for the critical study of 'religion' and related categories. That is, for the kinds of critique and critical approaches outlined in the previous chapter. In this chapter, I offer a survey of scholarship associated with these perspectives. This survey can hopefully provide an entry point into a diverse and rapidly growing literature, indicating resources for further exploration. I start by discussing the term 'critical religion' itself, along with alternatives proposed by scholars thinking along similar lines, which reflect their positioning in relation to the field of religious studies and to other disciplines. I go on to point out some significant trajectories in this literature, tracing its chief inspirations and major developments, then finally highlighting several counter-arguments that have generated ongoing debates.

The term 'critical religion' was coined in the 2000s by Timothy Fitzgerald with his colleagues in the Religion subject group at the University of Stirling: Alison Jasper, Andrew Hass and Michael Marten. They wanted a new label to indicate that they were trying to do something different in their teaching and research, departing from then-conventional understandings of 'religious studies' – that is, as a unique field or phenomenological discipline whose subject is a universal phenomenon that can be studied through (but not reduced to) its historical and cultural manifestations. This departure reflected Fitzgerald's critique in *The Ideology of Religious Studies* (2000), which targeted both the conceptual basis for religious studies and the role of university departments in naturalizing a religious-secular dichotomy:

> The industry known as religious studies is a kind of generating plant for a value-laden view of the world that claims to identify religions and faiths as an aspect of all societies and that, by doing so, makes possible another separate 'non-religious' conceptual space, a fundamental area of presumed factual objectivity. (Fitzgerald 2000: 9)

Adopting the banner of 'critical religion' has therefore been a counter-branding exercise for scholars to position and present themselves differently, albeit while trying to keep jobs at secular universities that continue to advertise Religion as a subject for study. The term echoes 'critical race' theory, which gained currency in the 1990s and reflected a similar move away from studying racial characteristics or inter-race relations towards studying 'race' as a system of socially-constructed categories. 'Critical religion' is also intended to be inherently inter-disciplinary: a collective project that incorporates many disciplines and aims to inform scholarship in all of them, while ultimately collapsing the categories that separate them. (For more on what its advocates mean by 'critical religion', see the Critical Religion Association website; the preface and introduction to Barbato, Montgomery and Nadadur Kannan 2020; and Fitzgerald's reflections in Chapter 5.)

The Stirling group established the Critical Religion Association[1] as a forum to promote broader collaboration across disciplinary and other boundaries. That platform also helped popularize the term 'critical religion', now commonly used in UK and European academia and gradually gaining recognition among interested professionals globally. Scholars with all sorts of job titles have adopted it as a conveniently pithy label for what they do or how they do it. Some might call themselves critical religionists because they engage directly in the study of religious-secular categories, applying methods like genealogy or discourse analysis; others can identify critical religion simply as an influence on their thinking, perhaps informing what they *don't* do or say more than the kinds of work they actually do – in much the same way as my basic knowledge of critical race theory may hopefully help me spot and avoid racializing language even though I do not explicitly work on 'race'.

I use the term 'critical religion' here – and in the title of this book – at the risk of giving you the misleading impression that it describes a homogenous school of like-minded scholars all marching in the same direction. Others use different labels for their critical orientation to 'religion', which can reflect widely varying methods, agendas and conclusions. In this volume, for instance, Russell McCutcheon (Chapter 4) refers to 'the critical study of religion' in contrast to what he elsewhere calls 'pre-critical' approaches, which ignore or minimize the theoretical gains of recent decades (2021: 11–60). Aaron Hughes (Chapter 3) deliberately talks in more general terms about 'theory and method', saying: 'I tend not to call what I do anything as I work on the naïve assumption that a critical posture is a hallmark of all scholarship and thus should function as the default position for everyone in our field.' Both McCutcheon and Hughes have dedicated a great deal of their careers to advocating for a fundamental shift in religious studies (e.g. McCutcheon 1997, 2021; Hughes and McCutcheon 2021) and in Hughes' case also the associated fields of Islamic and Jewish studies (e.g. Hughes 2013, 2014, 2015). Because their aim is to reshape religious studies from within, they find the label 'critical religion' superfluous or perhaps even counter-productive: they want to bring the discipline with them rather than distance themselves from it. These scholars share with Fitzgerald a driving concern to change the way people think about 'religion', but they diverge in how they do it, why they do it and the direction they see it going.

Fitzgerald (Chapter 5) casts the central difference as a choice between either 'limited critique' of the category religion within existing disciplinary frameworks or 'extended critique' of a web of modern categories and of the academic disciplines that reproduce them (see also Fitzgerald 2007a, 2011). He makes an intellectual and ethical/ideological case for extended critique as the only way to liberate our thinking enough to generate new ways of imagining and being in our world. Meanwhile, he acknowledges that it presents professional academics with a dilemma: 'choosing between expanding employment opportunities and the survival of religious studies departments on the one hand and following the logic of critique on the other' (Chapter 5).

So why use the term 'critical religion' here? First, it is pithier than *the critical study of 'religion' and related categories*. Second, it echoes the familiar logic of 'critical race' theory with its similar focus on categories. Third, it need not be tied to a particular discipline in the same way as 'the critical study of religion' or 'theory and method in religious studies'. Fourth, and most importantly, it is a handy way to distinguish this kind of critical scholarship from various other uses of the word 'critical' in the study of religion. Other uses range from 'critical thinking' in general to all sorts of more specific attempts to cast one's analytical approach as questioning conventional knowledge in some way. For instance, the Center for Critical Research on Religion promotes a '*critical* approach' it defines as one which 'examines religious phenomena according to both their positive and negative impacts';[2] while critical in the sense of offering multifaceted analyses to challenge received wisdom, this is clearly *not* an approach that is much concerned with questioning how certain phenomena are classified as 'religious' or not (see McCutcheon 2018: 96–120 for a discussion of this and other varieties of critical scholarship).

'Critical religion' is a label we can use to distinguish a kind of critical scholarship concerned with the categories themselves, the kind that tends to put 'religion' in quotation marks. But – as with any of our key terms – we need to be aware of its limitations and how we or others use it. In this chapter, I apply the label in this way to a loose constellation of scholars who do not necessarily use it for themselves. They might not thank me for lumping them together, since they disagree as often as they agree. Recently there has been a heated debate over whether they can be said to constitute a 'methodological school' (as claimed by Watts and Mosurinjohn 2022), to which many objected that their methods differ widely (see Horii 2024). Among those somewhat reluctantly associated with critical religion, Craig Martin suggested that 'what the scholars named share is perhaps their *conclusions* – [i.e. that] the concept of "religion" is deeply problematic – more than their methods' (2022: n.p.; emphasis added). Timothy Fitzgerald, whose name is most associated with critical religion, called it 'a broad alliance on the need for critique', whose members 'share some significant *critical tendencies*' but 'have our own starting points and trajectories' (2024: 240). As those trajectories diverge, he now worries that the idea of critical religion may 'become over-extended and lose any clear shape' (245) and that his 'own use of the term might become confused with theirs and might get lost in the widening stream' (246). None of us are reducible to one label, so I would urge you to explore and engage with each scholar's arguments on their own terms. You could start with the perspectives captured in the chapters of this book. You can also go see their debates play out in the wild: a few journals have gained a reputation for hosting theoretical and methodological discussions around critical religion, especially *Method and Theory in the Study of Religion*,[3] *Critical Research on Religion*,[4] and *Implicit Religion*.[5] For now, I hope my colleagues will forgive me if I generalize somewhat about their critical tendencies or conclusions, for the sake of painting you a picture of the extraordinary shift in thinking to which they have contributed. I still see in 'critical religion' a valuable banner under which to identify – and thereby promote – a change of *orientation* toward scholarship.[6]

Where does critical religion lead us?

Many scholars working in religious studies departments have worried that critical religion puts their profession at risk of an existential crisis, undermining the very ground upon which they stand. While Fitzgerald (Chapter 5) urges us to move to new, more fertile ground, there are others who see in critical religion quite the opposite: the revival of religious studies with a new raison d'etre (Goldenberg 2020: 314). Religious studies professionals are arguably best equipped to examine constructions of religion and secularity with a critical eye; indeed, as Teemu Taira points out, 'if we do not do the critical work, no one will, because people in other fields have shown very little interest in historicizing and deconstructing "religion"' (Chapter 7). Going a step further, perhaps critical religion is not the source of a crisis for religious studies departments but actually the solution to their pre-existing problem of marginality. After all, religious studies has been a victim – at least in certain respects – of religion's second-class status in the secular university's hierarchy of knowledge. McCutcheon, in his classic analysis of the state of religious studies, noted that its traditional claim to study a sui generis (i.e. unique, one of a kind) subject has an unfortunate side-effect: it 'isolates and excludes the study of religion' from meaningful engagement in wider knowledge production (1997: xi, also 192–213). From this perspective, critical religion may spell the end of sui generis religion but not the end of religious studies departments. It offers a release from the silo of esoteric scholarship, placing critical religious studies squarely within the social sciences where it can speak on issues of common concern.

The stuff of 'religion' is not essentially different from what other disciplines study, but students trained in religious studies are better prepared to recognize dynamics that others have historically missed. Once we re-mystify the so-called secular world (Horii 2021: 250–1), we can apply many of the conceptual tools of religious studies to a limitless field. Wherever we look, we will find ritual, symbolism, mythology, eschatology, soteriology, prophecy, charismatic leaders, canonical texts, orthodoxies and orthopraxies, ecstatic or numinous experiences, sacred/profane dichotomies and so on. On the other hand, the traditional data of religious studies can be brought into productive conversation with other data and disciplines if we redescribe it as ordinary. This means treating each thing we study as an example not of religion but 'of some even wider, common, and even seemingly mundane human process that we also see elsewhere in history or in contemporary culture' (McCutcheon 2024c: 20). When we widen our comparative lens, we get to apply what scholars in other disciplines have learnt about those human processes to our own case study and vice versa. McCutcheon, having been a long-time religious studies department head, emphasizes the potential to make the discipline more widely relevant and therefore valuable:

> Such work would, therefore, explicitly be aimed at producing conclusions with application well beyond any one . . . tradition, scripture, region, or group, not to mention honing skills applicable to the study of a variety of other items well outside our field, both of which are significant steps beyond

the current model that assumes that each site where scholars of religion invest their energy is unique and self-evidently important. (McCutcheon 2024c: 20)

Equipped with the toolbox of their trade and critically attuned to religious-secular categories at work, graduates of religious studies programmes therefore have a great deal to offer wherever they go next.[7]

In short, critical religion has opened doors rather than closed them. It does not close the door to studying any of the things that have been treated under the rubric of 'religion', nor does it need to discard the resources of the religious studies literature. Instead, it provides new resources – genealogical, theoretical and methodological – to inform a critical re-reading of received scholarly literature (e.g. King 2017; Newton and Touna 2023), as well as of human history and the modern world we inhabit. Critical theory encourages and helps us to pay closer attention to the terms we use to describe and analyse our subject matter (see Hughes in Chapter 3), to the ways others use words and conceptual categories as subtle tools of social classification (see McCutcheon in Chapter 4), and to the ethical and ideological impact of our knowledge production (see Fitzgerald in Chapter 5). Much of this work has been pioneered by scholars in religious studies departments, originating partly in self-reflection on their own disciplinary heritage, while also being an inherently interdisciplinary project.

Critical religion builds on developments across the humanities and social sciences, and it speaks to issues that concern all academic disciplines as well as professions and constituencies beyond academia. If you count yourself in the latter groups, I recommend reading Chapter 4 on *Why you should care about scholarship on the category religion*. McCutcheon wrote that chapter 'with an intended audience in mind who might have better things to do than to stay up to date with the latest news from the academic study of religion'. For teachers of religious studies in schools or universities, critical religionists have proposed ways to move from a descriptive, essentializing mode towards more generative, experimental and ethically sensitive modes to engage students in thinking outside fixed boxes (see Jasper and l'Anson in Chapter 12; also e.g. Cotter and Robertson 2016; Ellis 2022; l'Anson and Jasper 2017). Insights from critical religion have been brought to bear on numerous other fields, including – to name just a few examples – politics and international relations (e.g. Fitzgerald 2011; Martin 2010; McCutcheon 2025; Stack, Goldenberg and Fitzgerald 2015; Yadgar 2020); sociology (e.g. Horii 2021; Martin 2014; Moberg 2022); gender studies (e.g. McPhillips and Goldenberg 2020); critical race studies (e.g. Nye 2019; Vial 2016); media studies (Sheedy 2022b); and the natural sciences (e.g. Harrison 2015; Schaefer 2022).

Where does critical religion come from?

The ideas presented in this book emerge out of religious studies scholars' engagement with critical theory – by which I mean an array of ideas associated with the 'critical turn' in the humanities and social sciences since the 1960s. Critical theory is distinguished from traditional empirical theory, which attempts to describe and understand the world from a neutral, objective standpoint. Theory is critical, by contrast, when it aims to critique and challenge established ways of understanding the world that it sees as bound up with social inequality or oppression.

The term 'critical theory' was coined by the Frankfurt School in the 1930s, but it was arguably the French philosophers of structuralism and post-structuralism who did most to galvanize a global critical turn in the 1960s onwards; their ideas are heavily referenced in critical religion. Michel Foucault (1926–84) developed the genealogical method – first proposed by Friedrich Nietzsche (1844–1900) – using it to explore the interdependence of knowledge and power by tracing discourses that have come to define what we consider normal. Louis Althusser (1918–90) developed Karl Marx's (1818–83) infamous claim that religion is 'the opiate of the masses' into a more generalized theory of ideology as a means of social control – 'ideology' here being a set of beliefs or values produced by an 'ideological state apparatus' to shape people into obedient subjects. Jacques Derrida (1930–2004) developed a method of challenging taken-for-granted concepts through linguistic 'deconstruction' of their meaning, showing how they depend on shifting binary oppositions between words.

Various forms of critical theory have called into question Western modernity's grand narratives, moral universalisms and scientific certainties. Post-colonial theory has had a particularly overt influence on critical religion. Edward Said, in his landmark book *Orientalism* (1978), critiqued Western representations of 'the Orient' as figments of the West's own imagination, showing how they serve dual purposes: on one hand serving colonial ideology by classifying 'Oriental' peoples as inferior, irrational and dangerous; on the other hand serving as an 'Other' against which to define 'Western civilization' as rational, moral and generally superior. Said's arguments paved the way for 'religion' and 'world religions' to be seen as classificatory tools of Orientalist discourse (e.g. Asad 1993, 2003; Chidester 1996, 2014; Dubuisson 2003, 2019; Fitzgerald 2000, 2007a, b; King 1999; Masuzawa 2005). Seen in this light as part of Orientalist discourse, the category 'religion' does various things: it projects Protestant Christian assumptions onto the world under a universalist guise; it serves colonial ideology by classifying peoples into a hierarchy of world religions, which can be associated with varying levels of irrationality and danger to themselves or others; and it serves as the 'Other' against which to define Western secular modernity as rational, moral and generally superior. Since the 1990s, global academia has seen a gradual shift from post-colonial critique towards decolonial theory, which aims to escape the ongoing coloniality of modern knowledge by thinking through indigenous epistemologies. Reflecting that wider shift of emphasis, some scholars inspired by critical religion are now looking for ways to decolonize knowledge production in religious studies and beyond by thinking *with* rather than only *about* the traditions they study (e.g. Ahmed 2016; Horii 2021; Tayob 2018, 2025; Thatamanil 2020).

A third broad area of critical theory to mention here is the deconstruction of gender and race categories since the 1980s and 1990s. Naomi Goldenberg suggests that feminist theorists like Judith Butler deserve much of the credit for laying the groundwork for critical religion:

> Several decades of questioning long-held notions about the essential nature of male/ female and masculine/feminine binaries have made it possible to imagine the queering of other dominant and reified principles of institutions and ideology. If gender and sex are not 'really real,' but rather appear so due to the way authority is asserted through chains of citation and performance, questions arise about what else might be similarly contingent. Religion and secularity eventually come to mind as focal concepts that support conventional power arrangements and thus are worthy of critical attention. (Goldenberg 2015: 310)

Critical gender theorists have helped us see gender as a social construction rather than an inherent dimension of human nature, shifting the focus of study from essences to processes of 'gendering' or 'genderization'. Similarly, critical race theory has shifted our focus from race as an essential human characteristic to 'racialization' as a process of collective imagination and social formation. The same logic is applied to all sorts of categories: 'nations' are no longer regarded as primordial identity groups but as 'imagined communities' invented by modern nation-building projects (Anderson 1983; Gellner 1983); 'rituals' are approached not as a unique kind of action but as products of 'ritualization' (Bell 1992). Across the social sciences, critical theory has driven a shift from *essence* to *process*, providing a framework for us to think about 'religion' and 'religions' not as naturally occurring things with their own essential nature but as products of 'religion-making' or 'religionization' (see Taira in Chapter 7; Dressler 2019; Dressler and Mandair 2011).[8] Critical theories of race and gender have also emphasized the importance of intersectionality – that is, how various layers of social classification intersect and overlap – which provides a backdrop against which to think about 'religion' as part of an interlocking system of modern categories rather than a stand-alone concept (see Fitzgerald on overlapping binaries in Chapter 5; Owen on intersections of 'religion' and 'indigeneity' in Chapter 8).

Religious studies scholars have brought these wider developments into conversation with the intellectual heritage of their own discipline. There is a longstanding tradition of self-reflection and debate – as old as the academic study of religion itself – on the definition of religion, as well as on the methods and positionalities of those who study it. We can trace the beginnings of a critical turn within that tradition to Wilfred Cantwell Smith's influential book *The Meaning and End of Religion* (1962). Addressing the question 'What is religion, or a religion?' (1962: 7), W. C. Smith proposed we take a critical approach to the term for two reasons: first, because 'the way we use words . . . is a significant factor in determining how we think'; second, because 'to understand other people and other ages, it is requisite that we do not presume uncritically that their meanings for words are the same as ours' (20). Ultimately he argued for an end to the terminology of 'religion' because it is a peculiarly modern Western reification, abstracted from the raw personal experience of faith. Although his work is foundational to the genealogical study of 'religion', W. C. Smith ended up replacing one problematic universal category with another: faith. The problem with his substitution of 'faith' is that, as Fitzgerald puts it, 'He assumes that all people in all cultures are responding in faith to the same notion of transcendence that he himself does' (2000: 46).

Twenty years later, Jonathan Z. Smith extended the argument into an epistemological and methodological critique of the way scholars project their own categories onto the world. His book *Imagining Religion* opens with the provocative and oft-quoted claim that 'there is no data for religion' (Smith 1982: xi). He explains: 'Religion is solely the creation of the scholar's study. It is created for the scholar's analytic purposes by his imaginative acts of comparison and generalization. Religion has no existence apart from the academy.' What he concluded from this is that we must own up to the artificiality of our concepts, becoming 'relentlessly self-conscious' about how we define and use them as second-order categories of analysis. Our goal should not be to find the most *accurate* definition of 'religion' (or 'faith', etc.), but to choose a *useful* definition by which to organize and redescribe our data to answer a given analytical question. Not only did J. Z. Smith doubt the existence of a unifying phenomenon out there awaiting our definition, he also encouraged us to critique the discourse of universal religion by interrogating its ideological motivations. 'As the anthropologist has begun to abandon a nationalist view of culture . . . so we in religious studies must set about an analogous dismantling of the old theological and imperialistic impulses toward totalization, unification, and integration' (Smith 1982: 18; see also his short summary of the issues in Smith 1998).

In the 1990s we see the beginnings of critical religion as we know it today, attributed usually to the work of three scholars: Talal Asad (1993, 2003), Russell McCutcheon (1997) and Timothy Fitzgerald (1997, 2000, 2007a). In distinct but overlapping ways, these three built on the Smiths' critiques of the term 'religion' while raising the stakes by widening the focus of their critique. Instead of aiming only to deconstruct that word and the concept it represents, they would emphasize its key role in larger discourses and power structures. What makes 'religion' key is its binary relationship with the secular: twin creations of the modern imagination that have been deeply entangled with ideological projects from the nation-state to colonialism and capitalism. This troubling discursive context makes the discipline of religious studies itself a target of critique, such that the scholar can no longer claim to be a detached observer innocently playing with categories – as some have (mis-)interpreted J. Z. Smith's picture of the scholar conjuring up 'imaginative acts of comparison'.

There is now a rich literature on the genealogies of religious-secular categories, tracing their emergence out of the Protestant Reformation, the European 'Enlightenment', colonial encounters and the rise of modern nation-states. This includes numerous studies on local 'inventions of religion(s)' in different contexts around the globe.[9] Scholarship in the global South has played a formative role in critical religion, prompting religious studies scholars – and anthropologists and so on – to reflect on the Eurocentrism of the academic discipline they inherited. For example, the problem of translating the term 'religion' across cultures was what prompted W. C. Smith's early genealogical adventures; for Asad it was his work in the anthropology of Islam in the Middle East; for Fitzgerald it was time spent researching and teaching in India and Japan. By taking seriously other people's terminologies and conceptual categories, critical scholars have been able both to deconstruct their universalized Euro-American categories and to reconstruct their understanding of local contexts. Some have sought to map the globalization of a Western conceptual system, exposing the machinations by which colonial powers exported it and nation-states imposed it, while also revealing its effects in the restructuring of local societies. On the flip side of the same coin, some have looked to rediscover how people saw their worlds before 'religion', or to identify instances where the globalized discourse has not (yet) erased local alternatives. Such studies have also raised important questions: What nuances might be left out in all this talk of 'global' versus 'local' or 'Western' versus 'non-Western' discourses? Was the discourse of religion simply a Western invention and export, or has it perhaps been produced through global interactions (as per Chidester 2014)? What roles or agency do local actors have in this, and what interests are at stake for them (see Josephson 2012)? These questions and more are discussed through a variety of case studies in the following ten chapters of this volume, which reflect growth areas in current scholarship with an emphasis on contemporary issues and on complicating our understanding of 'Western' contexts.

Counter-arguments and debates around critical religion

As the critical turn has gathered momentum in the study of religion, it has inevitably provoked counter-arguments and generated searching debates. While this chapter has traced the emergence of critical religion as a response to the limitations and pitfalls of conventional categories, this newer kind of scholarship is, of course, far from immune to critique itself. Questions have been raised about the coherence of critical religion as a methodological project; the risks of reproducing normativity in new guises; and the consequences of relentless critique for our ability to make meaningful claims about the world. Some have even asked whether critical religion is simply hostile to religion and theology. In what remains of this chapter, I touch on each of these debates and address some of the most pressing concerns.

When considering such debates, it is important to remember that they rarely have only two sides, nor are those sides fixed. Indeed, ongoing self-reflection and robust debate are part and parcel of critical scholarship as a process rather than an end point. Critical religion, therefore, is not a finished project and presumably never will be. (Which is why I prefer to speak of it in dynamic terms as a critical orientation, turn or movement.) In Fitzgerald's words, 'We all have to take risks, we all get things wrong, and none of us are standing still' (2024: 263). This book is an invitation to join us in making better paths forward.

Can critical religion play by its own rules?

This question was posed by Galen Watts and Sharday Mosurinjohn in the title of a provocative and much-discussed article (2022). The authors situate themselves as sympathetic to the broad goals of critical scholars like Fitzgerald, McCutcheon and Martin, but see them as going too far: 'in our view, they have appropriately encouraged increased self-reflexivity, emboldening us to become aware of the contingencies of the concepts we employ . . . Yet, taken to its logical ends, CR is fraught with contradictions and double-standards' (2022: 332). I should note that some of the 'contradictions' identified in this article were not actually logical flaws but simply points of disagreement between different scholars, which highlights the need to avoid treating critical religion as if it were a unified 'methodological school'.[10] For now I want to focus on addressing a few key concerns raised, but I would also recommend delving into the flurry of responses to that 2022 article (see overview in Horii 2024) – there you will see a diverse range of perspectives on critical religion and ongoing negotiation of the challenges in doing critically reflexive scholarship.

So why do Watts and Mosurinjohn think critical religion cannot play by its own rules? Their first argument is that critical religionists are guilty of 'inconsistent historicization' (2022: 319–22). That is to say, critical religionists bang on about the need to historicize our concepts – that is, contextualizing 'religion' as a product of modern Western history rather than a natural or universal phenomenon – but do not do it consistently with all the other concepts we use. 'The problem . . . is that in the process of historicizing *religion*, McCutcheon and his fellow CR scholars have simultaneously reified and naturalized a whole panoply of concepts (and indeed social worlds) that are themselves neither universal nor neutral' (320). Critical religion (CR) scholars inevitably end up using other concepts like '*Western, European, Christian, colonialism, culture, modernity*' as if those were stable and uncontroversial, which they are not (320). Observing this inconsistency leads Watts and Mosurinjohn to ask: 'can CR scholars justify abandoning the category *religion* without contradiction?' (326). They call out critical religion for its 'arbitrary abandonment' of one category over all the others one could problematize (326–31). Ultimately, Watts and Mosurinjohn conclude that the logic of critical religion sets 'an impossibly high bar – meaning the rigorous and consistent application of CR principles can only lead to either one of two undesirable outcomes: hypocrisy or silence' (331). Either we fall into hypocrisy through 'inconsistent historicization' and 'arbitrary abandonment' of the category religion, or we zealously purge our entire conceptual vocabulary until we cannot say anything at all and simply fall silent – are those really the choices that critical religion presents us with?

Responses in defence of critical religion have converged around a central theme: that 'historicization is aspirational, not a metric that can be perfectly achieved' (Sheedy 2022a: n.p.). Matt Sheedy succinctly expresses this consensus that 'scholars should aim to historicize and contextualize their concepts as much as possible. Failure to do so in each and every instance does not undermine this argument. It merely points to how difficult it is to achieve this level of conceptual depth and critical reflexivity'. This aspiration is both individual and collective, so we move forward as a community of critical scholars partly by pointing out where each other's work has been relatively more or less successful in achieving it. Given how heated these exchanges can get, Sheedy also acknowledges that 'there is a legitimate debate to be had about *how* we criticize our colleagues' work, whether it is charitable enough, and whether attempts at productive provocations may have turned, in some cases, into counter-productive rivalries'. Perhaps the real problem here is with the critical *tone* used by some scholars, rather than their critical analysis. In other words, people on all sides need to stop accusing each other of hypocrisy and accept that – as Horii helpfully advises – 'There are no bad intentions in all these different positions' (2024: 235).

'Religion' is not the only problematic concept around, and I don't think anyone is arguing that it is. In fact, all the biggest names associated with critical religion have also attempted to historicize and deconstruct other key terms that tend to shape our thinking. To name a few examples, Aaron Hughes and Russell McCutcheon together published a set of two books that critically examine the wider vocabulary of religious studies (2022a, b); Timothy Fitzgerald has long been concerned with the concept of 'politics' (2007a, 2011); and Craig Martin has also written extensively on the language of liberal and capitalist discourses (2010, 2014, 2021, 2023). On the other hand, Martin points out that 'no one can historicize their entire vocabulary at once, and criticizing a scholar for historicizing x, y, and z but not a, b, and c would be like criticizing a sociologist for not focusing on psychology, or criticizing a climate change scientist for not focusing on the latest string theory' (2022: n.p.). So we might expect someone specializing in religious studies to be most attentive to the category 'religion', while for any given study one may need to decide strategically which other terms of analysis are most significant to historicize.

Underlying this debate is a lingering question: Where should we draw the line between useful concepts and less useful or simply bad ones? We all draw a line somewhere, since there are many concepts that scholars have already dropped from their analytical vocabulary – for example, primitive, savage, negro, oriental, crazy, uncivilized, cult, heresy, ether, phlogiston and so on. In that light, our move to abandon the category 'religion' is not arbitrary (contrary to Watts and Mosurinjohn 2022); it is just another analytical tool we have found not to benefit our understanding of the world. Given the serious concerns raised by so many critical scholars over several decades (see Chapter 1 for a catalogue of those concerns), it seems appropriate now to turn the question around on sceptics like Watts and Mosurinjohn: how do they justify *keeping* 'religion' in their analytical toolbox? 'What does it pick out from the world, and how does it pick it out in a way that is more useful than other vocabularies?' (Martin 2022: n.p.).

Among those of us who do *not* think 'religion' is a concept worth saving, the question of where to draw the line remains much debated. Do we stop at 'religion', or use it as a starting point to identify other similarly problematic concepts? 'Religion', after all, is not a stand-alone concept. It is problematic partly because of the way it functions as one side of binary pairings with 'secular' categories such as 'politics', 'culture', 'science' and so on (see Chapter 1). That is why critical religion has been glossed as the critical study of 'religion' *and related categories*. 'The "related" part is crucial', says Fitzgerald (2024: 242). He argues that critique of one category cannot be divorced from the others because they operate together 'in an automatic signalling system' (Chapter 5). For instance, if I describe a certain Muslim organization as political, I have automatically signalled that it is not religious, or perhaps not properly religious. So if I want to avoid imposing one category, I need to avoid the other too; only then might I stand a chance of analysing how the organization is framed in its own context, where these categories may turn out to be strategically significant, perhaps even highly contested, or simply irrelevant. Fitzgerald is also dissatisfied with the way some critical scholars try to use one category to subvert another, as in the title of William Arnal and Russell McCutcheon's book *The Sacred is the Profane: The Political Nature of 'Religion'* (2013). If everything is political, or if everything is religious, then nothing is. Fitzgerald dismisses these expansive uses of categories as 'vacuous expressions' (2024: 242); they do not help us think outside the discursive box. Worse, every use of these words reinforces our intuitive sense that they do have some inherent meaning after all. Whereas Watts and Mosurinjohn see Fitzgerald's dismantling of our common-sense vocabulary as leading only to silence, he sees it as the only way to say something more meaningful: 'We need to find a new language that frees us from the burden of abstractions that construct the 'modern', like 'religion' or 'politics' or 'economics' . . . and that grounds us more in community and collective consciousness' (Chapter 5).

In a survey of these debates, Mitsutoshi Horii concludes that 'They reflect different moral grounds on which each scholar stands' (2024: 235). Rather than reducing the differences to black-and-white judgements of logical inconsistency, let alone hypocrisy, we can more helpfully understand the variety of approaches through scholars' moral stances, motivations and strategies. At one end of the critical spectrum, Fitzgerald is most pessimistic about the state of the world we live in, so believes we must find better ways of being human by radically liberating our thinking. Along the spectrum, we find scholars like McCutcheon, Martin and Goldenberg pursuing relatively smaller victories they believe likely to make a more immediate difference. Towards the other end, Watts and Mosurinjohn do not think things are all that bad – not bad enough to risk rocking the boat – so prefer to tweak its rudder towards a better course.

Who is being normative now?

A key premise of critical religion is that the category 'religion' is implicitly normative. The word sounds innocently descriptive, but on closer inspection is rarely, if ever, neutral. Critical religionists therefore warn against using it as an analytical category because they believe 'scholars are obligated to retire words, ideas, or concepts that carry unduly burdensome normative baggage' (Martin 2015: 299). One of the counter-arguments raised by Watts and Mosurinjohn is that critical religion cannot play by its own rule of academic neutrality, so is itself 'crypto-normative' (2022: 322–6). By 'crypto-normative', they mean 'seemingly offering a "critique from nowhere" (Hjelm 2020: 1016), while furtively embedding a cadre of normative assumptions into their interpretations of social life as well as their taxonomies' (Watts and Mosurinjohn 2022: 325).

In fact, critical religion is not meant to be neutral or objective. Responses to the charge of crypto-normativity all protest that this is a misunderstanding of critical scholars' intentions. They do want to distance themselves from 'concepts that carry *unduly burdensome* normative baggage' (Martin 2015: 299; emphasis added), but they also agree that normative baggage and scholarly distance are always relative. Some concepts are better or worse than others, though how we judge them will depend on where we stand. I think 'religion' is a particularly problematic concept for two main reasons: first, because it has been used to support numerous forms of inequality and domination, including colonialism, capitalism, patriarchy and elitist orthodoxy; second, because people tend not to notice that it is normative. When I point out this second problem, I do not mean to say we must be objective instead of normative. On the contrary, by pointing out the first problem, I have already taken a normative position against inequality and domination. I also realize that words like 'colonialism', 'patriarchy' or 'elitist' are not neutral; they are really only used with a negative moral judgement. But I am less concerned about historicizing and deconstructing *these* loaded terms because I think they usefully label things I consider bad.

Addressing inequalities is what motivates many scholars to this kind of critical study, albeit with significant variations that 'reflect different moral grounds on which each scholar stands' (Horii 2024: 235). Martin, for example, spells out his normative standpoint on the opening page of *A Critical Introduction to the Study of Religion*:

> because I sympathize with those who are victims of oppression, I have chosen to focus this text on . . . social domination – something which is often ignored in other introductions, or, if addressed, considered briefly or marginally. As an instructor, my primary teaching goals are, first, to demonstrate to students that societies are never set up in ways that serve everyone's interests equally, and, second, to give students the skills to identify who benefits and who does not, and how disproportionate social structures are legitimated and maintained. (Martin 2023: ix)

Whether or not we state it so explicitly, it seems critical scholars can all agree with Watts and Mosurinjohn that normativity is part of good scholarship: 'any social theory that actually tells us something of interest (goes beyond minimalist interpretation) cannot avoid making normative judgments, for in interpreting social action (organizing, explaining, judging) one must avail oneself of a normative framework, which distinguishes consequential from inconsequential, relevant from irrelevant, good from bad' (2022: 325). Perhaps the real question to come out of this debate is how well we actually articulate our normative frameworks or standpoints in practice. Sheedy rightly suggests there is a need to develop better 'training in matters of positionality and standpoint epistemology' across all fields of study (2022a: n.p.).

Can there still be degrees of neutrality in scholarship? While critical religionists would reject the notion of a perfectly objective academic standpoint – which smacks of the universalizing supremacism of 'secular' knowledge claims – there are nevertheless those who see their critical approach as *more* neutral than alternative approaches. That is the thrust, for example, of McCutcheon's call for religious studies scholars to be *Critics Not Caretakers* (2024a):

> our role as scholars . . . is not to be caretakers for or representatives of the groups that we happen to study but to be critics – prepared to *historicize* the ordinary sources or practical effects of the claims, actions, productions, and institutions that . . . are often represented *as if* they were somehow free of discernable causes, untethered from context, innocent of interests or agendas, and just obviously full of deep meaning. (McCutcheon 2024a: xi)

Like a culture critic – say, of theatre, literature, food or film – the critical scholar's role is not to serve the interests of any particular group or tradition, but to step back a certain distance in order to see them in context. We all know that no critic is neutral, and indeed the most insightful critics are reflective and honest about their own predispositions, but we can still benefit from their analysis to the extent that it contextualizes and balances insider claims. One of those insider claims is what counts as 'religion', or 'Christianity', 'Islam' and so on. So, Sheedy explains, 'what most, if not all scholars of this stripe are arguing . . . is that when we uphold insiders' terms as analytic categories, we end up reifying what, for example, certain liberal Protestant Christians, Sunni Muslims, or Reform Jews interpret as "true" religion' (2022a: n.p.). By distancing ourselves from these categories altogether, we avoid falling into the trap of reproducing one insider's classification over another's. Hence critical religion can produce analysis that is neutral with respect to those insider claims, and that provides valuable insight regardless of whether you share the analyst's specific normative motivations.

Is anything real after critique?

People sometimes worry that critical religion takes us away from the 'real' stuff of religion that we want to study. Watts and Mosurinjohn, for instance, argue that 'much would be lost were we to limit the critical study of religion to CR' (2022: 319). They present this as a stark choice which 'comes down to whether we, as critical scholars of religion, should focus our energies on mapping the discursive battles over the uses of *religion*, or instead study the cultural structures, collective practices, and social performances that the term *religion* is used to refer to (Goldstein 2020: 84; Schilbrack 2020: 89)' (Watts and Mosurinjohn 2022: 331). But this choice is, in fact, a bogus one – a false dilemma – because the two options are not mutually exclusive.

Critical religion does not magically make disappear the whole swathe of structures and practices that have been labelled 'religion'. Nor is anyone suggesting we turn our backs on them. Quite the contrary, critical religion allows us to see better and more. We see *better* by removing the 'religion'-tinted glasses that have distorted our analysis of the data, flattened local nuances and superimposed ill-fitting categorical divisions (as explained in the first half of Chapter 1). We see *more* by adding the layer of discourse as data for our analysis, which includes not only looking at battles over the uses of words but also discursive practices of social classification (as explained in the second half of Chapter 1). Discourse analysis is a key method for studying 'religion' and related categories, but it is by no means the only method available for critically oriented scholarship.

There is an associated debate about whether critical religion is anti-realist in a philosophical sense. Kevin Schilbrack (2014, 2017, 2020, 2024) has argued for a 'critical realist' alternative, which he says can take critiques of the category religion seriously while also reclaiming it for scholarly use. Craig Martin (2021), on the other hand, has defended an anti-realist position as the basis for critique. Jason Josephson-Storm (2021), another major contributor to critical religion, has proposed a theoretical framework he calls 'metarealism', within which he uses a 'process social ontology' to understand the world in terms of processes rather than essences. While there are interesting ideas being advanced through this debate, for our immediate practical purposes I would agree with Taira's conclusion that critical religion 'is not essentially connected with either a realist or anti-realist standpoint' (Chapter 7).

Is critical religion anti-religion (or anti-theology)?

Finally, I think it is worth addressing those who fear that critical religion may somehow be anti-religious, or that its practitioners may simply be 'religion's despisers' (as per Strenski 1998). This apprehension is partly just an unfortunate side-effect of the word 'critical', which sometimes leaves us having to explain that we are not in the business of *criticizing* religion. Leslie Smith put this nicely in a discussion of McCutcheon's classic book *Critics Not Caretakers* (2024a; first published 2001):

> It strikes me that one way that *Critics Not Caretakers* has been fundamentally misread is in the idea that a critic is someone who opposes or even seeks to subvert something (in this case, religion). Rather, I read the term 'critic' here in the way that we understand the titles 'movie critic' or 'culture critic' – these are not people who are attempting to undermine movies or culture (in these particular examples), but who are attempting to uncover the dynamics – large and small – that make these things what they are. (Smith et al. 2024: 139)

A movie critic is rarely, I dare say, someone who hates movies. Coming back to the question at hand – *Is critical religion anti-religion?* – a critical scholar would go a step further to question the terms of the question itself. We cannot be anti-religion if we don't think religion exists out there as a thing for us to love or to hate universally. The whole point is to move the conversation onto more nuanced ground and avoid making such sweeping generalizations.

Critical religion may occasionally appear anti-theological when we critique the category religion as implicitly theological. But that is not the intention, as Fitzgerald spells out: 'I must stress that this argument is not antitheological. It is an argument against theology masquerading as something else' (2000: 20). It is an argument directed specifically against conventional approaches to the study of religion, which have long been framed as methodologically agnostic – and therefore non-theological – but which turn out to reproduce 'a disguised form of liberal ecumenical theology' (6). McCutcheon, in *Critics Not Caretakers* (2024a), argues for a clearer separation between the discipline of *theology*, whose scholars are caretakers of a particular theological tradition and make absolute truth claims from within their tradition, and the discipline of *religious studies*, whose scholars should act as public critics, analysing all traditions (including the categories they use to self-designate) without advocating for or adjudicating between their truth claims. While an individual may move between these roles, intellectual honesty and rigour demand that the two forms of scholarship not be conflated.

A better question might be: What is the relationship between critical religion and theology? McCutcheon's views on this are clear but one-sided, since he is only really interested in the future of religious studies, not of theology. For someone coming at the question from the other side, there remains plenty of scope to explore the implications of critical religion for theological thinking. Alternatively, Fitzgerald's extended critique of secular social sciences could potentially open the way for a more fundamental revaluing and reintegration of theological forms of knowledge. Critical religion challenges the modern 'distinction between the subjective faith bias of religion and the objective knowledge production of secular reason' (Fitzgerald in Chapter 5). In modern universities, this distinction enforces a hierarchy of knowledge in which theology has been relegated to a second- or third-class status. Theologians of all stripes, along with many other humanities scholars, share legitimate concerns about the wholesale devaluing of local traditions of knowledge and ethics: 'After all, if "religious" thinking does not constitute real knowledge that we can or ought to make judgments about, then presumably the place left for *'aqīda* [Islamic theology] is that of a life accessory, a commodity to be bought and sold on the basis of aesthetics or utility' (Henley 2020: 386). The secular hierarchy of knowledge limits how we engage with all those numerous ways in which people have made sense of our world, reducing many of them to private lifestyle preferences, cultural entertainments, optional add-ons to the 'real' needs and certainties of secular society. Hence I share Horii's hope 'that the deconstruction of the religious-secular distinction frees sociologists and social scientists from this confinement, and helps them to renew their interests in other intellectual traditions developed in other parts of the world and in different times in human history' (2021: 252).

One way or another, I would go further than merely defending critical religion as methodologically agnostic; I tend to see the end of 'religion' as generally beneficial for those people and lifeways sometimes called 'religious'. Critical religion liberates our thinking – about ourselves and others – from profound inequalities on which the language of 'religion' and 'religions' has been built. To begin with, the 'world religions' paradigm has privileged the identities of tiny elites of literate male intellectuals, projecting their identity onto vast swathes of people as the archetype of 'Christianity' or 'Islam' or 'Hinduism'. Moving away from that paradigm of normative 'religions' levels the playing field, making diversity and change more visible, more comprehensible and ultimately more viable (see e.g. Ahmed 2016; Henley 2022). In general, the concept of 'religion' has given a privileged place to doctrinal belief systems and textual traditions. The projection of 'religion' onto the world as a universal dimension of human experience has even, through a remarkable sleight of hand, privileged a certain brand of universalist theology, which Fitzgerald (2000) calls 'liberal ecumenical theology' and McCutcheon (1997) calls a 'theology of religious pluralism'. Each of these features of the discourse suits some people but not others, some purposes but not others. Whatever our own ideals or motivations, there is surely a benefit – when we set aside the broad brushes of our reified categories – in understanding the multiplicity of human lifeways, with all their messy contradictions and conflicting truth claims, as they are now and have been through history.

References

Ahmed, Shahab (2016), *What Is Islam? The Importance of Being Islamic*, Princeton, NJ: Princeton University Press.

Anderson, Benedict (1983), *Imagined Communities: Reflections on the Origin and Spread of Nationalism*, London: Verso.

Arnal, William and Russell T. McCutcheon (2013), *The Sacred Is the Profane: The Political Nature of 'Religion'*, Oxford: Oxford University Press.

Asad, Talal (1993), *Genealogies of Religion: Discipline and Reasons of Power in Christianity and Islam*, Baltimore, MD: Johns Hopkins University Press.

Asad, Talal (2003), *Formations of the Secular: Christianity, Islam, Modernity*, Stanford, CA: Stanford University Press.

Barbato, Malanie, Cameron Montgomery and Rajalakshmi Nadadur Kannan, eds (2020), *Critical Religion Reader*, Pembroke, Ontario: Studio Dreamshare Press.

Bell, Catherine (1992), *Ritual Theory, Ritual Practice*, Oxford: Oxford University Press.

Bloch, Esther, Marianne Keppens and Rajaram Hegde, eds (2010), *Rethinking Religion in India: The Colonial Construction of Hinduism*, London: Routledge.

Center for Critical Research on Religion website, https://criticaltheoryofreligion.org/ (accessed 15 July 2025).

Chidester, David (1996), *Savage Systems: Colonialism and Comparative Religion in Southern Africa*, Charlottesville, VA: University Press of Virginia.

Chidester, David (2014), *Empire of Religion: Imperialism and Comparative Religion*, Chicago, IL: University of Chicago Press.

Cotter, Christopher R. and David G. Robertson, eds (2016), *After World Religions: Deconstructing Religious Studies*, Oxford: Routledge.

Critical Religion Association website, https://criticalreligion.org/ (accessed 1 February 2025).

Dressler, Markus (2019), 'Modes of Religionization: A Constructivist Approach to Secularity', Working Paper 7, HCAS 'Multiple Secularities – Beyond the West, Beyond Modernities', Leipzig: Leipzig University.

Dressler, Markus and Arvind-Pal S. Mandair, eds (2011), *Secularism and Religion-Making*, Oxford: Oxford University Press.

Dubuisson, Daniel (2003), *The Western Construction of Religion: Myths, Knowledge, and Ideology*, trans. William Sayers, Baltimore, MD: Johns Hopkins University Press.

Dubuisson, Daniel (2019), *The Invention of Religions*, trans. Martha Cunningham, Sheffield: Equinox.

Ellis, Justine (2022), *The Politics of Religious Literacy: Education and Emotion in a Secular Age*, Leiden: Brill.
Fitzgerald, Timothy (1997), 'A Critique of "Religion" as a Cross-Cultural Category', *Method and Theory in the Study of Religion*, 9 (2): 91–110.
Fitzgerald, Timothy (2000), *The Ideology of Religious Studies*, Oxford: Oxford University Press.
Fitzgerald, Timothy (2007a), *Discourse on Civility and Barbarity: A Critical History of Religion and Related Categories*, Oxford: Oxford University Press.
Fitzgerald, Timothy, ed. (2007b), *Religion and the Secular: Historical and Colonial Formations*, London: Equinox.
Fitzgerald, Timothy (2011), *Religion and Politics in International Relations: The Modern Myth*, London: Continuum.
Fitzgerald, Timothy (2024), '"What Is Critical Religion?" A Response to Galen Watts and Sharday Mosurinjohn, "Can Critical Religion Play by Its Own Rules?"', *Method and Theory in the Study of Religion*, 36 (3–4): 238–66.
Gellner, Ernest (1983), *Nations and Nationalism*, Ithaca, NY: Cornell University Press.
Goldenberg, Naomi (2015), 'Afterword', in Trevor Stack, Naomi Goldenberg and Timothy Fitzgerald (eds), *Religion as a Category of Governance and Sovereignty*, 309–12, Leiden: Brill.
Goldenberg, Naomi (2020), 'Timothy Fitzgerald and the Revival of Religious Studies', *Implicit Religion*, 22 (3–4): 309–18.
Goldstein, Warren (2020), 'What Makes Critical Religion Critical? A Response to Russell McCutcheon', *Critical Research on Religion*, 8 (1): 73–86.
Harrison, Peter (2015), *The Territories of Science and Religion*, Chicago, IL: University of Chicago Press.
Henley, Alexander (2020), 'Islam as a Challenge to the Ideology of Religious Studies: Failures of Religious Studies in the Middle East', *Implicit Religion*, 22 (3–4): 373–90.
Henley, Alexander (2022), 'Normalization Through Religious Representation: A Lebanese Druze Response to the "Muslim Question"', *Implicit Religion*, 23 (4): 363–87.
Henley, Alexander (2023), 'Why Is It So Difficult to Get Critical Religion into the Mainstream? Reflections on Horii's *"Religion" and "Secular" Categories in Sociology*', *Critical Research on Religion*, 11 (1): 116–19.
Hjelm, Titus (2020), 'Mapping the Discursive Study of Religion', *Journal of the American Academy of Religion*, 88 (4): 1002–25.
Horii, Mitsutoshi (2018), *The Category of 'Religion' in Contemporary Japan: Shukyo and Temple Buddhism*, Cham: Palgrave Macmillan.
Horii, Mitsutoshi (2021), *'Religion' and 'Secular' Categories in Sociology: Decolonizing the Modern Myth*, Cham: Palgrave Macmillan.
Horii, Mitsutoshi (2024), 'Editorial: Introduction to Special Issue on Critique', *Method and Theory in the Study of Religion*, 36 (3–4): 219–37.
Hughes, Aaron W. (2013), *The Study of Judaism: Authenticity, Identity, Scholarship*, Albany, NY: State University of New York Press.
Hughes, Aaron W. (2014), *Theorizing Islam: Disciplinary Deconstruction and Reconstruction*, New York: Routledge.
Hughes, Aaron W. (2015), *Islam and the Tyranny of Authenticity: An Inquiry into Disciplinary Apologetics and Self-Deception*, Sheffield: Equinox.

Hughes, Aaron W. and Russell T. McCutcheon, eds (2021), *What Is Religion? Debating the Academic Study of Religion*, Oxford: Oxford University Press.

Hughes, Aaron W. and Russell T. McCutcheon (2022a), *Religion in 50 Words: A Critical Vocabulary*, New York: Routledge.

Hughes, Aaron W. and Russell T. McCutcheon (2022b), *Religion in 50 More Words: A Redescriptive Vocabulary*, New York: Routledge.

I'Anson, John and Alison Jasper (2017), *Schooling Indifference: Re-Imagining RE in Multi-Cultural and Gendered Spaces*, London: Routledge.

Josephson, Jason Ananda (2012), *The Invention of Religion in Japan*, Chicago, IL: University of Chicago Press.

Josephson-Storm, Jason Ananda (2021), *Metamodernism: The Future of Theory*, Chicago, IL: University of Chicago Press.

King, Richard (1999), *Orientalism and Religion: Post-Colonial Theory, India and 'The Mystic East'*, London: Routledge.

King, Richard, ed. (2017), *Religion, Theory, Critique: Classic and Contemporary Approaches and Methodologies*, New York: Columbia University Press.

Mahmood, Saba (2016), *Religious Difference in a Secular Age: A Minority Report*, Princeton, NJ: Princeton University Press.

Mandair, Arvind-Pal Singh (2009), *Religion and the Specter of the West: Sikhism, India, Postcoloniality, and the Politics of Translation*, New York: Columbia University Press.

Martin, Craig (2010), *Masking Hegemony: A Genealogy of Liberalism, Religion, and the Private Sphere*, Sheffield: Equinox.

Martin, Craig (2014), *Capitalizing Religion: Ideology and the Opiate of the Bourgeoisie*, New York: Bloomsbury.

Martin, Craig (2015), 'Theses on the Critique of "Religion"', *Critical Research on Religion*, 3 (3): 297–302.

Martin, Craig (2021), *Discourse and Ideology: A Critique of the Study of Culture*, London: Bloomsbury.

Martin, Craig (2022), 'Norms and Concepts: A Response to Watts and Mosurinjohn', *Craig Martin Religion* blog, 19 July. Available online: https://craigmartinreligion.wordpress.com/2022/07/19/norms-and-concepts-a-response-to-watts-and-mosurinjohn/ (accessed 20 July 2022).

Martin, Craig (2023), *A Critical Introduction to the Study of Religion*, 3rd edn, New York: Routledge.

Masuzawa, Tomoko (2005), *The Invention of World Religions: Or, How European Universalism Was Preserved in the Language of Pluralism*, Chicago, IL: University of Chicago Press.

McCutcheon, Russell T. (1997), *Manufacturing Religion: The Discourse of Sui Generis Religion and the Politics of Nostalgia*, Oxford: Oxford University Press.

McCutcheon, Russell T. (2018), *Fabricating Religion: Fanfare for the Common e.g.*, Berlin: De Gruyter.

McCutcheon, Russell T. (2021), *On Making a Shift in the Study of Religion and Other Essays*, Berlin: De Gruyter.

McCutcheon, Russell T. (2024a), *Critics Not Caretakers: Redescribing the Public Study of Religion*, 2nd edn, New York: Routledge.

McCutcheon, Russell T., ed. (2024b), *Religious Studies Beyond the Discipline: On the Future of a Humanities Ph.D.*, Sheffield: Equinox.

McCutcheon, Russell T. (2024c), 'Religious Studies: Wither and Why?', *Religious Studies Review*, 50 (1): 17–24.
McCutcheon, Russell T., ed. (2024d), *Teaching in the Study of Religion and Beyond: A Practical Guide for Undergraduate Classes*, New York: Bloomsbury.
McCutcheon, Russell T. (2025), *Religion and the Domestication of Dissent: Or, How to Live in a Less Than Perfect Nation*, 2nd edn, London: Routledge.
McPhillips, Kathleen and Naomi Goldenberg, eds (2020), *The End of Religion: Feminist Reappraisals of the State*, London: Routledge.
Moberg, Marcus (2022), *Religion, Discourse, and Society: Towards a Discursive Sociology of Religion*, Oxford: Routledge.
Newton, Richard and Vaia Touna, eds (2023), *Fieldnotes in the Critical Study of Religion: Revisiting Classical Theorists*, London: Bloomsbury.
Nye, Malory (2019), 'Race and Religion: Postcolonial Formations of Power and Whiteness', *Method and Theory in the Study of Religion*, 31 (3): 210–37.
REL Toolbox website, https://reltoolbox.ua.edu/ (accessed 15 July 2025).
Religious Studies Project website, https://www.religiousstudiesproject.com/ (accessed 1 February 2025).
Said, Edward W. (1978), *Orientalism*, New York: Pantheon Books.
Schaefer, Donovan O. (2022), *Wild Experiment: Feeling Science and Secularism After Darwin*, Durham, NC: Duke University Press.
Schilbrack, Kevin (2014), *Philosophy and the Study of Religions: A Manifesto*, Oxford: Blackwell.
Schilbrack, Kevin (2017), 'A Realist Social Ontology of Religion', *Religion*, 47 (2): 161–78.
Schilbrack, Kevin (2020), 'A Metaphysics for the Study of Religion: A Critical Reading of Russell McCutcheon', *Critical Research on Religion*, 8 (1): 87–100.
Schilbrack, Kevin (2024), 'The Realist Discursive Study of Religion', *Method and Theory in the Study of Religion*, 36 (3–4): 419–39.
Sheedy, Matt (2022a), 'Critical Religion and the Critical Study of Religion: A Response to Galen Watts and Sharday Mosurinjohn', 2 parts, *Culture on the Edge: A Peer Reviewed Blog*, 22 and 24 August. Available at https://edge.ua.edu/chapter-3/critical-religion-and-the-critical-study-of-religion-a-response-to-galen-watts-and-sharday-mosuringjohn/ (accessed 23 August 2022).
Sheedy, Matt (2022b), *Owning the Secular: Religious Symbols, Culture Wars, Western Fragility*, London: Routledge.
Smith, Jonathan Z. (1982), *Imagining Religion: From Babylon to Jonestown*, Chicago, IL: University of Chicago Press.
Smith, Jonathan Z. (1998), 'Religion, Religions, Religious', in Mark C. Taylor (ed.), *Critical Terms for Religious Studies*, 269–84, Chicago, IL: Chicago University Press.
Smith, Leslie, Mitsutoshi Horii, Suzanne Owen and Titus Hjelm (2024), 'The Conversation: *Critics Not Caretakers* ... The Public Study of Religion 20+ Years In', *Bulletin for the Study of Religion*, 52 (4): 129–48.
Smith, Wilfred Cantwell (1962), *The Meaning and End of Religion*, New York: Macmillan.
Stack, Trevor, Naomi Goldenberg and Timothy Fitzgerald, eds (2015), *Religion as a Category of Governance and Sovereignty*, Leiden: Brill.
Strenski, Ivan (1998), 'On "Religion" and Its Despisers', in Thomas A. Idinopulos and Brian C. Wilson (eds), *What is Religion?*, 113–32, Leiden: Brill.

Tayob, Abdulkader (2009), *Religion in Modern Islamic Discourse*, London: Hurst.
Tayob, Abdulkader (2018), 'Decolonizing the Study of Religions: Muslim Intellectuals and the Enlightenment Project of Religious Studies', *Journal for the Study of Religion*, 31 (2): 7–35.
Tayob, Abdulkader (2025), 'Muslim Publics between Discourses of Religion and Islam', in Frank Peter, Paula Schrode and Ricarda Stegmann (eds), *Conceptualizing Islam: Current Approaches*, 108–20, Oxford: Routledge.
Thatamanil, John J. (2020), *Circling the Elephant: A Comparative Theology of Religious Diversity*, New York: Fordham University Press.
Vial, Theodore (2016), *Modern Religion, Modern Race*, Oxford: Oxford University Press.
Watts, Galen and Sharday Mosurinjohn (2022), 'Can Critical Religion Play by Its Own Rules? Why There Must be More Ways to Be "Critical" in the Study of Religion', *Journal of the American Academy of Religion*, 90 (2): 317–34.
Yadgar, Yaacov (2020), *Israel's Jewish Identity Crisis: State and Politics in the Middle East*, Cambridge: Cambridge University Press.

PART II

Perspectives on being critical about 'religion' and the 'secular'

3

The reluctant genealogist
Why it matters where our terms come from

Aaron W. Hughes

One of the goals of this volume is to make 'critical religion' less jargony and foreign-sounding, with the noble aim of making it more accessible. Though I have never employed the term critical religion before, I use it interchangeably with terms more familiar to me such as 'theory' or 'theory and method'. In fact, the more I think about it, I tend not to call what I do anything as I work on the naïve assumption that a critical posture is a hallmark of all scholarship and thus should function as the default position for everyone in our field. This, rather surprisingly, comes as a shock to many. Much scholarship on religion, on the contrary, often involves taking a set of untheorized terms and categories, our own, that we then assume to be both universal and an objective model for *accurately* transcribing the world around us. Our goal as scholars of religion, again so it is assumed, is then to *describe* this world to the best of our abilities. Often lost in such descriptions is the fact that it is we who impose order on it and not vice versa. Since none of these assumptions or activities are new, later scholarship does after all stand on the shoulders of earlier work, we ought to be mindful of the importance of understanding the history of the field. Where it came from, in other words, helps us to understand where it might be going.

Rather than conceive of 'theory' as excessive or deconstructive, let alone dangerous, I prefer to imagine such a critical posture as denoting a sensitivity and a certain self-reflexivity when it comes to the terms, categories and narratives that we have inherited, and which we often continue to employ without sufficient attention to their genealogies. Such a self-reflexivity, I submit, should ideally mean that we constantly reflect upon the questions we ask, how they have been asked (and answered) in the past, and the uses to which such answers have been put. Scholarship – but especially scholarship on religion – we would do well to remember has never been a value-neutral nor an objective affair. Since religion in general (and specific religions in particular) is ostensibly what many hold dear, it is perhaps not surprising that we – as scholars, as practitioners, or as scholar-practitioners – have a difficult time approaching it critically. Indeed, the field of religious studies is littered with the corpses of bad comparisons, faulty interpretive strategies, and hopelessly vague terms and categories. Critical religion is necessary because it forces us to consider a host of meta questions that simmer under the surface of scholarship that should be, but rarely are, given sufficient attention.

What follows makes the case that we avoid theory at our own peril. To 'do theory', however, need not set off alarm bells, nor does such engagement necessarily lead one down the slippery epistemological slope towards atheism or, even worse, nihilism. Far from it, an attunement to theoretical matters reveals a certain comfort level with one's data, so much so that one is willing to inquire into its contemporaneous production and its subsequent reception in secondary literature. Here it might be worth noting that just as people carry around a lifetime of emotional baggage with them, so too do the terms and categories of scholarly analysis. If therapy helps us reflect upon and deal with our individual baggage, theory is what permits something similar on a disciplinary level.

After a brief autobiographical discussion, I wish to turn my attention to the importance of genealogy. By genealogy I mean nothing more (nor less) than the tracing of lines of descent from there (our past) to the here and now. Since the world we encounter does not neatly self-taxonomize, rather we taxonomize it, we need to be aware of the history of the terms that we use and be cognizant of whence they came, including how their meanings have (or have not) changed over time. Terms like 'experience', 'shamanism', 'secular', even 'religion' all come from somewhere and none are value neutral, though we often use them as if they were. It is important that we be aware that our terms, categories, and the scholarly narratives they construct – our entire conceptual toolbox, in other words – all come from somewhere. None of them are natural markers that we have simply stumbled upon. We thus need to be cognizant of whence these terms, categories and scholarly narratives emerged, including where, how and by whom. For this is ultimately where we all came from, at least intellectually. A greater attention to this will, I argue, permit for a modicum of theoretical reflection, even among those most reluctant. The reluctant genealogist, in other words, is not me but that person who is worried that attention to such matters will take away from the 'real' work of reading and analysing texts. An attention to genealogy *in addition to* (and not at the expense of) such work provides a more well-rounded analysis, one in which we can talk to our colleagues who, though they may work with different data, often work with similar sets of issues and questions.

Autobiographical reflection (of sorts)

Scholarship is based on a series of choices. We choose this religion to study as opposed to another. We choose this language or these languages to study as opposed to others. We choose this text or set of texts over others. We choose this village in which to do our fieldwork as opposed to that one. And so on. There are a few reasons – historical, religious, political, ideological, psychological and so on – that ultimately govern these choices, and it is surely worth reflecting on these reasons. This is where self-reflexivity comes in. We always have to have an internal dialogue with ourselves to ascertain why and how we are doing what we are doing. This returns me to a point I made earlier: if we are aware that the world does not self-categorize, we must realize that we are doing the categorizing, and that such categorizing is not necessarily a natural act, but ultimately an artificial one. Too often, however, we pass over this in silence and just assume that what we do is as natural as the world we encounter around us. Overlooked is the fact that it is ultimately us who transform stuff into data. We make rituals data. We make texts data. We make whatever cultural and social forms we happen upon and find interesting into data. We even make theories data. So, while this means that no datum is inherently important or significant, it also means that all data – no matter how small or seemingly insignificant – have the potential to be.

Those who engage in the types of critical reflection mentioned in the previous section are certainly not born that way. They are instead made, often in response to a much larger issue or set of issues encountered at formative moments in one's intellectual development. Trained as a scholar of Islam within the larger canopy of religious studies, much of my time in graduate school was spent learning languages, reading texts and trying to figure out the historical, social and intellectual contexts responsible for the production of such texts. My sole concern was writing a dissertation and getting a job, in that order. And get a job I did. Unfortunately, my first week on said job, at a large urban Canadian university, coincided with the events of 11 September 2001. That day proved to be fateful for the study of religion in general and for that of Islam in particular. While certainly aware of the more critical voices in the study of religion – I had after all read McCutcheon, J.Z. Smith, Lincoln and Dubuisson, among others in graduate school for my doctoral exam devoted to 'theory' – I was most interested in trying to transform my dissertation into a book.

However, that warm early fall day (at least in Calgary, Alberta) changed everything for me. In one fell swoop, the field of religious studies was now in the business of adjudicating between 'good' or 'authentic' forms of religious expression on the one hand, and 'bad' or 'inauthentic' ones on the other. Real Muslims and real Islam – and, by extension, real religions – could not motivate people to fly planes into buildings or commit other heinous crimes. At least this is the way that the field's dominant narrative had framed it. Rather than contextualize such events, I heard many colleagues remark that they were not religious acts, but political ones. That struck me as naïve, if not actually deceitful. Were we really supposed to justify our scholarly existence by claiming to be the arbiters of good v. bad religion?[1] While I had always had the difference between theology and the secular study of religion drilled into me since I had been a young undergraduate student, it now appeared as if a collective amnesia had set in and that distinction was simply jettisoned. Was the self-stated difference between religious studies and theology simply a thin papering over what was in fact a similar endeavour?[2]

Autobiographies without a more universal point quickly default to narcissism. I bring this up, in other words, with the hope that others will hopefully resonate with my situation. Certain events – whether global, local or personal – have the potential to remove the scales from our eyes. For me, it was when a tremendously violent act confronted a collective set of assumptions about religion, to wit, that it is experiential, that it is a force for good in the world, that it is distinct from the so-called political or the economic or whatever other sphere, that it is about the sacred, and so on and so forth.

Whenever someone – be it a colleague, a student, a politician or a reporter – says something about religion or a particular religion, more often than not and often unbeknownst to themselves, they peddle a series of well-worn tropes or metaphors. Religion, for example, is a force for good, and when people do bad things in its name it is assumed that such actions have been 'hijacked' into 'political' ones. But what, as Nietzsche always encouraged us to ask, is the nature of the relationship between metaphor and truth? For him, they were intimately connected to one another: 'truths are illusions of which we have forgotten that they are illusions, metaphors which have become worn by frequent use and have lost all sensuous vigour' (Nietzsche 1976: 47).

I want to focus on this quotation for just a little as it gets to the heart of my argument here. Truth, if in fact it even exists, is not something that does so naturally in the world; nor, moreover, does it do so in a manner that simply awaits our individual or collective uncovering. Instead, the world – and its so-called truths – has been brought into existence by and for us through a set of narratives, categories and metaphors that we have largely accepted as normative. We have mistaken, to invoke Nietzsche again, the metaphorical for the real and vice versa. It is thus contingent upon us, as scholars, to evaluate constantly our truths and illusions to see how and for what purposes they were created, and how and why they have come down to us.

Here the usual complaints may well arise. This type of theorizing, so the argument could go, leads nowhere. It is masturbatory. It does not involve getting our hands 'dirty' in traditions and texts and so on. If there is no ground, in other words, how can we possibly stand and upon what foundation can we possibly build things? Surely there must be a reality behind all these cultural constructions, so the critic of my approach here might respond. The chair upon which I sit is a chair. Sure, it may be called *la chaise* in French or *la sedia* in Italian, but it is still something upon which we all sit. All these terms in different languages nevertheless signify the same thing – a four-legged structure upon which people sit. But we could reply that not all cultures use chairs, nor is the way one sits in a chair necessarily the most natural way for the human body to repose. The statement also overlooks the fact that there are all kinds of 'chairs' – thrones, couches, loveseats, rocking chairs, benches, pews, folding chairs, recliners, stools, even toilets – all with different functions and serving different purposes. All of these can subsequently be subdivided or taxonomized. They are made with different details, for different purposes, and possess different ergonomic designs.

In Ancient Rome, men reclined, whereas women sat in chairs. In other cultures, however, it is only the head of the household that sits in a chair. In premodern Europe, the chair designated a privilege of state. It was only in the Renaissance that chairs became standard items of furniture for anyone, with many now able to afford to buy them. Chairs were not a standard staple of North American houses until the nineteenth century, and their production was greatly tied to other socio-economic conditions, such as the Industrial Revolution in Europe and then the rise of factories, general stores and mail-order catalogues. A chair is not just a chair. Nor is it a natural staple of the world. It is, instead, categorizable, historical, sociological, political, gendered and connected to various means of production.

If this is true for a chair, then I hope a reader might agree that this is equally true for pretty much every object that we think exists naturally in the world. If in fact it is true for every object, then it is equally true for all the terms and the categories we use, and the narratives constructed by such terms and categories. Applied to the Humanities, of which the academic study of religion is most certainly a part, it means that we possess, to return to Nietzsche's locution, a set of truths that are illusions, which are in turn produced by 'metaphors which have become worn by frequent use and have lost all sensuous vigour'.

It is incumbent upon us to wade through these metaphors, seeing what they have produced, illumined, marginalized and also excluded. To return briefly to those confusing days and months after the attacks of 11 September 2001, I might say that the whole debacle for me was tantamount to a confusion. A confusion of terminology. A confusion of categories. And, most significantly of all, a confusion of purpose. We failed as a guild. Religion is not inherently spiritual, ethical, sacred or high-minded. Instead, religion – as many of the chapters in this volume reveal – is a Western construct that has been used to cordon off and protect a certain group of mundane activities as special. This cordoning off, moreover, has been done for a host of political, social and economic reasons.

Anti-theory as theory

Theory is a term with a wide range of meanings. To some, it is synonymous with 'deconstruction', in which case it is seen as too critical, too cynical, or just too revisionary. To others it represents an indulgence, and that time should be better spent reading texts and solving some textual or other philological mystery. The quickest of glances at the structure and contents of the annual meeting of the American Academy of Religion (AAR) bears this out. It continues to work with an increasingly unfashionable world religions paradigm, albeit one that has grown to include sections and groups devoted to food, film and other aspects of popular culture.

To others, myself included, theory represents a way to breathe new life into traditional questions and topics. Far from deconstructive, theory or critical religion is a very constructive enterprise. Here it is important to remember that when, where, why and how we examine the things we do are just as important – if not more so – than what we study. This is another way of saying that we, as scholars of religion, do not find religion 'out there' as if it somehow exists naturally in the world. On the contrary, we conjure it into existence by the theoretical choices, methodological moves and rhetorical flourishes we choose. This is what the late Jonathan Z. Smith meant in his famous and oft-cited introduction to his *Imagining Religion*: 'there is no data for religion. Religion is solely the creation of the scholar's study' (1982: xi).

According to this phrase, it is us as scholars who are the meaning-makers. Theory attunes us to this fact. As such, every scholar of religion – even the most anti-theoretical and conservative – is ultimately a theoretician. Everyone, after all, engages in theoretical reflection, though they might well prefer to call it by another name. Even those who try to make the case that they loathe theory on account of it being too 'disruptive', too 'deconstructive', too 'faddish' or too 'meta', engage in theory. Anti-theory, in other words, represents but another form of theory.

Anyone who engages in a literature review, for example, engages in theory. When one chooses to work on one text and not another one, one engages in theory. Or when one compares 'x' with 'y' and not 'z', one engages in theory. Even the decision to translate a gerund as a verb in an ancient manuscript is a matter of choice and, thus, a theoretical decision. All these examples involve choice, and we need to be attentive to that choice. We all, in many ways, make the worlds that we study. In that world we decide what is important and what is not, what to include and what to leave out, what to emphasize and what to marginalize. Theory attunes us to such decisions. To invoke J. Z. Smith, once again, 'the student of religion . . . must be relentlessly self-conscious. Indeed, self-consciousness constitutes his [or her] primary expertise, his [or her] foremost object of study' (1982: xi).

Smith taught us – or perhaps better reminded us, since far too many of us have forgotten – that we need to be self-conscious, self-aware and self-reflexive scholars. There is, after all, nothing unique about the study of religion. It does not require a unique methodology that involves discovering, uncovering or otherwise deciphering kratophanies, hierophanies and the like. Since the study of religion has been caught up and historically hamstrung by a host of competing agendas that have, more often than not, involved showing the superiority of one form of Christianity over all the other religions on the planet, it is constantly necessary to be vigilant and attentive to past usages.[3] This is why genealogy is so important. Examining whence our terms originated, the uses to which they have been (and continue to be) put and the ideologies that travel in their wake is essential to the field.

Our analyses are only as good as the terms and categories that are in our possession. Since the secular and academic study of religion is, at most, 150 years old, it was preceded by two thousand years of theological speculation.[4] There is, then, much potential for terminological and taxonomical slippage. Therefore we must be vigilant. Engaging in theory is anything but indulgent. It is necessary. Terms like 'religion', 'orthodoxy', 'myth', 'ritual', 'comparison', 'origins' and 'extremism' – to name only a few – are neither objective nor value-neutral. This should be good enough an argument as to why theory is such a necessary component of religious studies.

The reluctant genealogist

Research agendas and questions do not simply pop onto our radar screens or emerge from nowhere. Facts are not natural, just waiting for us to stumble upon them. This is why a genealogical approach – with a healthy dose of self-reflexivity – is essential when it comes to the academic study of religion. Though we might be reluctant, it is incumbent upon us to do so to avoid past mistakes and falling into traditional modes of analysis. We have not only to understand why we are approaching our data, but how others have done so as well. If the latter attunes us to the words, categories and narratives that have traditionally been used to bring data to light, the former forces us to be keenly aware of how and why we are using them in the present.

In his highly influential 1976 *Keywords: A Vocabulary of Culture and Society*, the Marxist theorist Raymond Williams sought to show how 'academic subjects are not eternal categories' (1976: 14). Instead, Williams demonstrated that academic subjects consist of sets of vocabulary that are rarely reflected upon and rarely understood as being little more than historical artefacts. While the origins of a word may well cast light on its meaning, one finds that words originally meant something quite different than they do today or that, over time, there have often been political and ideological struggles over their 'correct' meaning and usage.

Our understanding of the contemporary usage of terms, Williams shows us, must be grounded in historical semantics, especially the profound shifts in meaning that terms and categories undergo over time. In this respect, some terms have actually come to represent the exact opposite of their original senses – think for example of the term 'secular', which originally was used to designate members of the clergy who *lived out* 'in the world' as opposed to those who *lived in* a convent or a monastery. We thus run into real difficulties when we assume terms to be static and then apply them willy-nilly to other temporal and geographic contexts as if they meant the same thing. Terms, in other words, derive meaning and significance from their historical contexts. Changing contexts both give terms new meanings and, in the process, illumine how subsequent semantic transformations are shaped by various political, social and ideological processes.

A genealogical attunement to terms – their origins and subsequent transformations, contortions and the uses to which they are put – is essential to prevent distortion and corruption in our research questions. Unless we are aware how terms change and transform, we risk using terms that have one meaning or set of meanings today to describe events, texts and so forth in which such terms might well have had different meanings, sometimes even radically different meanings.

Terms as mammoth as 'religion', not to mention those that designate individual religions (e.g. 'Islam', 'Judaism', 'Hinduism'), have been used differently by different social actors ever since their inception. Take, for example, the commonly used term 'monotheism' or 'monotheists'. Judaism, Christianity and Islam, so the dominant narrative goes, are the religions of monotheism. Scholars and students alike have no problem defining monotheism as 'belief in one God', differentiating it from so-called polytheistic religions (e.g. 'Hinduism', maybe 'Buddhism'), and subsequently identifying the shared traits of monotheists across time and geography. However, frequently overlooked is the fact that the term 'monotheism', like so many of our terms, is little more than a modern European invention. To call early Muslims or Jews or Christians, for example, 'monotheists' is to use a term developed much later to then make the historical and ethnographic information sensible in a particular manner. Most basically, the term does not exist in Syriac, and, though Greek by definition, it does not appear in Greek sources before the late medieval period.[5] This imposition of a specific sort of order therefore creates a host of structural, historical and epistemological problems for those intent on using the term as innocently descriptive.

The way scholars have used and continue to use this term is potentially problematic given the historical or genealogical uses just described. If this is true for monotheism, it is equally true for so many of the other terms that litter the field of religious studies.[6]

A hypothetical (of sorts) dialogue

Since a large part of this volume is, in the words of the editor, 'to offer an entry point into a rapidly growing literature of which more and more academics are aware but that many find difficult to penetrate', I thought it might be enjoyable and productive to imagine a potential dialogue between someone interested in genealogy and someone more conservatively minded and perhaps trepidatious of theory or critical religion. Although both represent ideal types, and the short dialogue is fictional, the encounter between GEN (our genealogist) and TRAD (our traditional colleague) could take place in any corridor, in any department, in any university and in any country. So, without further ado, I present an imagined dialogue to illumine some of the features raised above and to show why an attunement to critical religion is an important – perhaps the single most important – aspect of the academic study of religion.

GEN: I thought it might be useful to examine some of our differences with an eye towards me trying to convince you that an engagement with critical religion might benefit you.

TRAD: Sounds good. Go right ahead and try.

GEN: As scholars of religion, we need to be vigilant of the various discursive formations and structures of power that create field-wide blind spots. Such features, as Wael Hallaq has recently reminded us, 'always leave – by virtue of their very dynamism – openings, cracks, fissures, and fractures *antithetical to the paradigmatic structures*' (2018: 26; his italics). I would suggest that such openings, cracks, fissures and fractures provide us with a convenient way to give exclusions and silences an active presence, thereby illumining that which the status quo has rendered marginal and irrelevant.

TRAD: Wait a minute. These blind spots of which you speak have nothing to do with applying the latest in-vogue or faddish literary theory to what we do. The blind spots will either be lifted or auto-corrected by accumulating and reading more texts. The answer to the problem is not as you suggest, but resides in the manuscript tradition because, after all, the manuscripts do not lie.

GEN: This is a response that is rather typical in area studies. Indeed, I think it safe to say that a real tension that cuts across the field revolves precisely around this issue of texts. The scholar of religion – unlike say, the Arabist who studies Islamic texts or the Sanskritist who studies Hindu texts – uses the texts and other social productions as an *exemplum gratia* to illumine much larger systematic and structural issues in the field of religious studies. I think this is a crucial difference between you and I. Whereas I am trained in the academic study of religion, you come out of area studies. We both write for different audiences and have different research interests. While I certainly do not want to replicate what you do, I have learned considerably from your text-critical work over the years. I would also like to think that you might find what I do to be of value, and that you consider reflecting on why you read the texts you do, how you understand them and how they fit into a larger context of scholarly production.

TRAD: But many of you who are involved in critical religion are *too* critical, and do not take the beliefs of religious practitioners at face value. You then make it so that no one can say positive things about the tradition. Why should we not be able to write laudatory comments about the religious traditions we study, including the high ideals they embody, the inspiration they provide to the devout, and the many great ideas they have produced.

GEN: The critical scholar of religion is less interested in the contents of religion, than in the social conditions in which religious ideas are produced and disseminated, including their investment in, among other things, ideological power and legitimation. We ought to leave it up to theologians to provide their audiences with articulations of the high ideals of their tradition. That is not the scholar of religion's job. But we also note that the recoding of human speech as divine or sacred can create just as many problems as they solve. People murder in the name of religion, for example. Here our differences are clearly apparent. I write for those who work in any religion *in addition* to the specific religion or religions I study. My goal is not to uncover some hidden text or read as many manuscripts as I can to collate critical editions to illumine some aspects of some medieval literary tradition. This is certainly not to say that such work is not interesting. Far from it. It is to say, however, that my questions relate to method and theory, and how these two aspects have traditionally been used to bring data into focus.

TRAD: But if you want to understand a religious tradition, read the classical works from the religion! Method without content is just spinning theoretical wheels! This is the problem with those of you who make secondary literature the basis of your scholarship. Original ideas do not come from reading the scholarship of others, but from reading texts in their original languages.

GEN: This is the crux of the difference between you and me. In critical religion, everything is data. It is, to riff on the old anthropological saying, data 'all the way down'. No one should be able to decide what is data and what is not. For example, I do not see a difference between primary and secondary sources in the same manner that you do. Both seek to convince readers of the correctness of their opinions. Scholarship is not just about making connections or sets of connections between premodern texts. It begins with the acknowledgement, to quote Bruce Lincoln, that all texts – so-called primary and secondary – are human products. In his fourth thesis on method, he states:

The same destabilizing and irreverent questions one might ask of any speech act ought be posed of religious discourse. The first of these is 'Who speaks here?', i.e., what person, group, or institution is responsible for a text, whatever its putative or apparent author. Beyond that, 'To what audience? In what immediate and broader context? Through what system of mediations? With what interests?' And further, 'Of what would the speaker(s) persuade the audience? What are the consequences if this project of persuasion should happen to succeed? Who wins what, and how much? Who, conversely, loses?' (Lincoln 1996: 226)

TRAD: But you all are so critical, always trying to tear down the work of colleagues.

GEN: I am not critical to be mean. I only seek to point out some of the problems and assumptions that operate in the work of others. While I have no doubt that my work is predicated on certain assumptions, as self-reflexive awareness also requires me to confront them, I only ask the same of others. A good theoretical work, for me, begins with a problem that we encounter in our data. To demonstrate that our data is not unique and to show how it can be illumined by other traditions, it is then necessary to move out of our data and subsequently engage the work of those who study similar problems in different datasets. Such an engagement, in the words of J. Z. Smith, provides 'a range of terminology and notions on which we will continue to draw' (1987: 52). Such an approach shows us that we do not work in our own silos and that it is more often the case that scholars who work on a similar problem but with different datasets can come to our aid by encouraging us to reformulate our often specific questions and, thereby, hone our interpretive lenses. I also think that you misunderstand what I mean by 'critical'. I am not calling for a systematic deconstruction or dismantling of the field. Far from it. The goal of scholarship should never be simply about criticism and tearing down the work of others. On the contrary, it ought to be about honing our theoretical insights in order to make our analyses better. If we are not aware of the genealogies of our terms, we risk making mistakes.

TRAD: I take your point about knowing where terms come from. After all, I do read and study non-Christian texts, and I am often surprised how so many of our contemporary terms to describe those texts derive from Christian terms. Perhaps what you call theory, I call context. While I can see the importance of reflecting on such terms, you cannot convince me to not read texts.

GEN: I would not dream of transforming you into me or making you do what I do. The very fact that we can have this conversation and that you have reflected previously on how problematic some of the terms we use means that you are engaging in genealogy, albeit reluctantly.

Conclusions

This brief dialogue, I trust, reveals the terms of the debate when it comes to 'doing theory'. It is not a one size fits all, nor should it be. The study of religion must make room for the types of technical work that 'TRAD' does, just as it has to make room for more genealogical and theoretical studies. If 'TRAD' maintains that 'method without content is just spinning theoretical wheels', I might be tempted to reverse these: content with no method, like knowledge with no critical thinking, cannot produce results. It only leads to description, which should be the platform from which all analysis *begins*.

Critical religion – or theory and method, or 'doing theory' or whatever we want to call it – is less about slogans and more about critical attunement. Therefore, we can call it whatever we want. It is neither a name nor a school. It is, on the contrary, a critical orientation to one's material. This is why it is essential to be self-reflective about one's own approach. Why, for example, am I working on this topic as opposed to others? What is the goal of my study? If one wants, for example, to reform a religion from within, be upfront about this. This is surely much more productive than trying to argue historically that one's attempt at reformation somehow represents an authentic version of Islam. Or if one wants to make space within a religion for GLBTQ2S individuals, by all means do. However, it is important that one who seeks to do this is engaging in 'theology' and not 'history'.

The second important issue that theory raises, I have tried to argue here, is that of genealogy. Our terms, our categories and our narratives all come from somewhere. They are neither objective nor value-neutral. Instead, they have been created to bring certain features, and not others, to light. They deny and marginalize as much as they privilege. Within this context, data does not exist naturally in the world just waiting to be uncovered. Instead, we conjure our data into existence by the tools we use, the questions we ask, and the solutions we find plausible or not.

How does all of this relate to the current field of religious studies? Much of the field – contributors to this volume to the contrary – is stuck in the paradigm articulated by 'TRAD' above. That is, many take the reading and description of religious texts (broadly defined) as the goal of scholarship. Since we study religious lives, so the assumption goes, we cannot be critical of what they do or how they do it. However, the type of scholarship I am talking about here requires us to do something rather different, and not simply adopt (and then stretch) one local discourse – our own, those we study, or some combination of the two – to use as if it were a scholarly discourse capable of providing a systematic model for understanding the world around us.

In sum, much work remains to be done in the academic study of religion in general, and of the many religions that comprise it in particular. For me, this means engaging in the requisite historical and linguistic/textual skills on the one hand, and, on the other, being self-reflexive and genealogical. Everyone should be a self-reflexive genealogist, even if reluctantly.

References

Arnal, William E. and Russell T. McCutcheon (2013), *The Sacred is the Profane: The Political Nature of 'Religion'*, New York and Oxford: Oxford University Press.

Barton, Carlin A. and Daniel Boyarin (2016), *Imagine No Religion: How Modern Abstractions Hide Ancient Realities*, New York: Fordham University Press.

Chidester, David (1996), *Savage Systems: Colonialism and Comparative Religion in Southern Africa*, Charlottesville, VA: University of Virginia Press.

Chidester, David (2014), *Empire and Religion: Imperialism and Comparative Religion*, Chicago: University of Chicago Press.

Hallaq, Wael (2018), *Restating Orientalism: A Critique of Modern Knowledge*, New York: Columbia University Press.

Hughes, Aaron W. and Russell T. McCutcheon (2022a), *Religion in 50 Words: A Critical Vocabulary*, London: Routledge.

Hughes, Aaron W. and Russell T. McCutcheon (2022b), *Religion in 50 More Words: A Redescriptive Vocabulary*, London: Routledge.

Lincoln, Bruce (1996), 'Theses on Method', *Method and Theory in the Study of Religion*, 8 (3): 225–27.

Martin, Craig (2012), *A Critical Introduction to the Study of Religion*, London: Equinox.

McCutcheon, Russell T. (2003), *The Discipline of Religion: Structure, Meaning, Rhetoric*, New York: Routledge.

Nietzsche, Friedrich (1976) 'On Truth and Lie in an Extra-Moral Sense', trans. Walter Kaufman, in *The Portable Nietzsche*, New York: Viking Press.

Nongbri, Brent (2013), *Before Religion: The History of a Modern Concept*, New Haven, CT: Yale University Press.

Smith, Jonathan Z. (1982), *Imagining Religion: From Babylon to Jonestown*, Chicago: University of Chicago Press.

Smith, Jonathan Z. (1987), *To Take Place: Toward Theory in Ritual*, Chicago: University of Chicago Press.

Smith, Jonathan Z. (1990), *Drudgery Divine: On the Comparison of Early Christianities and the Religions of Late Antiquity*, Chicago: University of Chicago Press.

Smith, Leslie Dorrough, Steffen Führding and Adrian Hermann, eds. (2020), *Hijacked: A Critical Treatment of the Public Rhetoric of Good and Bad Religion*, Sheffield: Equinox.

Stroumsa, Guy G. (2010), *A New Science: The Discovery of Religion in the Age of Reason*, Cambridge, MA: Harvard University Press.

Tannous, Jack (2011), 'Review of *Muhammad and the Believers* by Fred M. Donner', *Expositions*, 5 (2): 126–41.

Wasserstrom, Steven M. (1988), 'Islamicate History of Religions', *History of Religions*, 27 (4): 405–11.

Wiebe, Donald (1999), *The Politics of Religious Studies*, New York: Palgrave.

Williams, Raymond (1976), *Keywords: A Vocabulary of Culture and Society*, Oxford and New York: Oxford University Press.

4

Classification matters
Why you should care about scholarship on the category religion*

Russell T. McCutcheon

I have written this chapter[1] with an intended audience in mind who might have better things to do than to stay up to date with the latest news from the academic study of religion – a field in which it is all the more challenging to stay current given that, in English alone, it goes by a variety of names, including religious studies, comparative religion, the history of religions, as well as the academic study of religion, the science of religion and, most recently for some, the critical study of religion (or simply critical religion). Now, for those who are just mildly aware of the field – and those with greater investments might have just perked up a bit at the mention of it being a *field*, inasmuch as there's an ongoing debate as to whether it is a cross-disciplinary field or a discipline, with North Americans generally favouring the former while many Europeans prefer the latter – it might be reasonable to assume that by 'debates' I mean the once-animated dispute over whether or not theology is

---

*An earlier version of this chapter was published in *On Making a Shift in the Study of Religion and Other Essays*, 63–75, Berlin: De Gruyter, 2021; originally written as a paper for the Interdisciplinary Study of Religions Seminar series at the University of Oxford on 13 March 2020. It is reproduced here, with some updates, with permission of the author and of De Gruyter.

properly considered to be a part of the study of religion (a dispute on which I was weaned while a graduate student, at the University of Toronto, in the late 1980s, what with one of my supervisors at the time, Donald Wiebe – himself a Lancaster PhD (1974), under the supervision of the late Ninian Smart – being among its most active participants). I say 'once animated' because it strikes me that, though it is easy to find some people still discussing it, this is no longer an issue that defines the field; for, all depending on with whom you speak, it might become obvious that, yes, that particular battle has been won and so, of course, theology is but one more component of the study of religion (take, for example, the American Academy of Religion, the largest professional association in the United States, and its explicit commitment to, as they – as well as many departments – routinely call it, 'religious studies *and* theology' [emphasis added]). Or, directing your query to yet someone else (such as myself, for example), you might instead learn that this classic way of dividing up the pie, theology versus the scientific study of religion, is rather misguided inasmuch as classical humanistic approaches to the study of religion – though not explicitly theological, they tend to see in religion a site where the enduring, and therefore timeless, human spirit is creatively and meaningfully manifested – are, in my view, no less ahistorical and normative than are those identified as outright theology (regardless of the brand), making it rather pointless to distinguish the two. And if you speak to those who, recalling a once but, in my assessment, no longer prominent understanding of science, aim for some sort of disembodied objectivity in their work, they'd likely lump my own work on the politics of classification systems in with those they'd refer to as theologians, thereby defining the field so narrowly as to exclude what many of us now actually do when we say that we're studying religion. All of this makes the once-prominent theology versus religious studies debate misleading at best. To rephrase: longstanding approaches to the field that see in religion but one more site where a disembodied and unique thing called human nature expresses itself, let alone more recent approaches that find in religion a special sort of cognitive puzzle to be solved by appeals to psychology, genetics and brain sciences, are, to my way of thinking, both just as troublesome as are approaches aimed at discerning how some timeless and universal, but utterly undefined, thing called the sacred is supposedly manifested (apparently of its own volition) first here and then there. This, of course, is an approach long associated with the work of the late Mircea Eliade, but it is one which, I'd argue, is just as prominent today in so-called lived or material religion approaches let alone many other subfields, as is evident in the introduction to Christopher Partridge and Marcus Moberg's new handbook on religion and pop music, where, despite modelling a so-called critical musicology approach, readers are nonetheless told that 'the sacred . . . concerns those ideas which exert a profound moral claim over people' as well as being found in 'manifestations . . . or "sacred forms", [that] comprise historically contingent expressions of particular cultures' (2023: 8). For, in all of these cases, scholars take a rather modern designator – the very word religion itself – and the things that we commonly use it to name, as obvious and self-evident, as if they are all naturally and thus properly distinguishable from other things in our lives. And it is this matter of distinction, and the practical implications that come with it, that has recently drawn the interest of a growing number of scholars. So, to return to where I started: those who haven't been carefully monitoring developments in the field might not be aware that far more than an argument over the place of theology has been taking place in the study of religion over the past few decades.

I'll therefore take the occasion of this chapter as an opportunity not just to summarize some of these more recent debates in the field but also to translate their significance to readers who, not unlike many of our colleagues, may assume that the study of religion is, predictably perhaps, all about studying religion (by which I mean describing and then comparing the worldwide diversity and similarities among people's beliefs and practices). What I hope will become apparent throughout is that, at least for some of us, an important shift over the last decade or two has been the realization that *the study of religion isn't really about religion at all*, whatever that may or may not be defined as being (since there are almost as many definitions of religion as there are definers, no?). Instead, freed initially by a strong critique of what we used to call sui generis religion (that old but powerful idea that religion was utterly unique and therefore couldn't be understood correctly as *anything but religion* – the topic of my first book, in fact: McCutcheon 1997), some have by now concluded that the study of the things commonly designated *as* religion is but an example, citing the late Jonathan Z. Smith's preferred phrasing – useful in studying *people*: what they say, what they do, how they organize, and what they leave behind after they're done saying and doing and organizing. And among the curious things that some of those people do is to make claims about a subset of their sayings, their doings, their relics and their organizations being somehow set apart from all others, something marked by calling them 'religious'. Thus – and again, for some of us in the field today – the study of religion offers an opportunity to study how people distinguish, classify, rank, organize and thereby come to know and act in the worlds that classifying something *as* religious helps to establish and then represent as persuasive and authoritative – a system no doubt linked to other common and everyday distinctions as us/them, in/out, private/public, safe/dangerous, citizen/foreigner, allowed/disallowed, and, yes, sacred/profane. And so, with all of that having been said, I would hope that this chapter's title now makes just a little more sense, for not only do I, along with many other scholars to be sure, think that classification systems matter – that is, have practical consequences, making them far more than just mere names that we only later attach to things – but also that those who are not deeply immersed in at least some current developments in the study of religion may come to see it as a particularly good place to illustrate and explore this point, making plain, once again, that the study of religion isn't really about religion.

Now, again appealing to those with just a passing acquaintance with the field, the position that I've just outlined may sound rather counterintuitive. After all, many of us likely just assume that we all know what religion is, feeling quite comfortable using the term to carve up our day-to-day world at what we generally presume to be its joints (recalling that famous line from Plato's *Phaedrus*, 265d–6a); and so, like that associate justice of the US Supreme Court talking about obscenity long ago, we all more than likely think that we know it when we see it. (I'm here citing the words of Potter Stewart, of course, in the well-known 1964 case of Jacobellis v. Ohio, which reversed a lower court's conviction of a movie theatre manager who had been charged with possessing and exhibiting obscenity by showing Louis Malle's then-provocative 1958 film, 'Les Amants'.) Thus, a newspaper with a religion section that's set apart from the local political or sports stories, not to mention the personals and the want ads, surely makes good sense to many of us, as does the ability for a town council to treat a bowling alley, a pub or a hospital as somehow different from a mosque, a church, a temple or a synagogue – with the latter grouping undoubtedly striking many of us as naming the members of an obviously common class of items, given something that they apparently all share (with us coming up with the name 'houses of worship' to name them all). In fact, our knowledge of religion – dare I call it folk knowledge and risk inviting you to see yourselves and your own common-sense practices as our object of study? – is so firmly established that we might greet as absurd anyone who wishes to argue that just because we're accustomed to calling certain things religions, this taxonomic habit doesn't make them any more religious than anything else.

What should by now be clear is that my hope is to persuade readers that such a counterintuitive approach is not absurd at all. Quite to the contrary. Say we start from the position that sees not religion but the *discourse* on religion – which encompasses both the word itself along with the vocabulary associated with calling something a religion (by which I include such signifiers as faith, belief, experience, tradition, myth, ritual, magic, superstition, etc.) as well as the practices and institutions that help us to take this thing we call religion for granted as an item of our intellectual and social landscape. Starting from the position that sees not religion but the *discourse* on religion as a fairly recent historical occurrence of practical effect allows us to ask a whole new set of questions about how people like us continually create, govern and police the usually taken-for-granted environments in which we live our lives, arrange our affairs, distribute our resources, and establish and contest our identities, doing so by designating and then treating certain things in the past or present as religion.

In order to make this argument, I'll presume that a once (and, no doubt for some, still) dominant version of the field is known to you – the one in which the study of religion is understood as descriptively chronicling, at a variety of places and times, the many variants (aka manifestations or expressions) of an inherent trait of the human, usually represented as an internal feeling or private experience that, sooner or later, is expressed outwardly by means of those things commonly called myths, rituals, and traditions (see my detailed critique in McCutcheon 2021: 11–60). Being comparative at its heart – hence the choice of comparative religion for the field's early name in the English-speaking world – scholars in this vein aimed to look beyond the evident differences to find the universal sameness that they presumed to be the basis for all religion, which, in turn, was assumed to provide insight into our most basic and thus universally shared humanness. Now, some of you may already know that comparative religion, as it was once called, was a colonial exercise of the late nineteenth century, something identified by a variety of recent scholars. But what you may not have considered is that today's still-prominent world religions class and textbook genre, not to mention current calls to enhance so-called religious literacy, sometimes via what is known as Religious Education in the public school system (see Jasper and l'Anson in this volume), can be understood as a survival, in the classic anthropological sense, of that much-earlier age of expansion, when reports from euphemistically labelled 'explorers' and 'missionaries' concerning the alien and exotic customs they encountered in the colonies made their way back to curious minds in European centres of learning, reports that challenged the leading thinkers of the time (not to mention the politicians and the people once in charge of the business world) to figure out how 'us' and 'them' were (or, as they so often concluded, were not) related to one another. With the invention of the category of world religions (first originated by later-nineteenth century Dutch and German theologians, but quickly adopted by others, all the way to us today), our intellectual predecessors were able to distinguish what they understood as merely national or ethnic religions from those that they thought had successfully spread worldwide (making their way from 'them' to 'us', as it were). Thus, a modern, global, organizational concept was born that, though the rationale of its use has certainly changed over the past century or more, still allows us to group together otherwise diverse and separated (whether in space or time) people, places and things in terms of what we interpret as their universally shared philosophically idealist content – simply put, because we seem to have decided that people first of all *experience* and then *believe* things (about such things as gods and ancestors, about something ethereal that outlasts the individual's body, about the beginning of the universe and the end of time, and about the reason we're all here – what Douglas Adams succinctly summed up as life, the universe and everything). Then, second, because we've apparently concluded that these same people then act out their prior beliefs in unique public ways (via such things as ceremonies, rituals and myths), it's seen as not just worthwhile to group together all the similar-looking systems that result from these two assumptions (and thus something called Hinduism is not just born but can be spoken of in the very same breath as something called Judaism or Islam) but, as part of that same sorting and grouping activity, we've also decided that it's a good idea to separate them all, as a group, from what we see as the far more ambiguous world of politics and history, given the generally agreed upon timelessness and purity of the former and the contingent messiness of the latter.

So, presuming that, like most members of our own society, you're up to speed on the common usage of the general term religion, or using the more particular term world religions, let alone the way that we make claims about the supposedly uniform identity, across changing time and place, of the members of that family (e.g. Buddhists believe X, Christians do Y and Sikhs wear Z, etc.), what you may not know is that, beginning an academic generation or so ago, some scholars started to rethink these almost self-evident assumptions and conclusions in rather significant ways (Owen 2011 is a useful example of the shift some began to make). Now, by this I don't mean the once influential work of the late Wilfred Cantwell Smith (who died in 2000, having played a foundational role in both McGill's programme in our field, in Canada, as well as Harvard's in the United States – an approach that some rather sloppy scholars have mistakenly thought that I support). Although his early 1960s project did indeed critique the category religion, it did so in order to replace it with a term that, or so he argued, was even better for naming the unique thing that he somehow already knew to be in need of a name. For those unaware of his work, Cantwell Smith, in a book entitled *The Meaning and End of Religion* (1962), argued that our common, Latin-derived word, religion, inappropriately named what he claimed to be two separate things: the initial experience or, as he preferred to call it, faith in transcendence, as well as the tradition that resulted and accumulated only later, deriving from the eventual expression of that prior faith; calling it all religion, or so he concluded, incorrectly conflated the original cause with the secondary effect. Calling into question Cantwell Smith's undefended assumption that there was some self-evidently distinguishable kernel inhabiting the heart of that class of objects known as religions, the scholars whom I have in mind went looking elsewhere for their inspiration – finding it in the work of social theorists interested in how groups are formed. I'm referring to a scholarly tradition into which I place myself, one that resulted, eventually, with the work of Tomoko Masuzawa in the United

States (such as her still important 2005 book *The Invention of World Religions*) as well as the current work of such people as Naomi Goldenberg in Canada, Tim Fitzgerald, Malory Nye, Suzanne Owen and Richard King in the UK, Teemu Taira in Finland, or Brent Nongbri, now in Norway, not to mention some of the authors collected together by Christopher Cotter and David Robertson (the founders of the Religious Studies Project podcast, by the way) in their 2016 edited volume, *After World Religions*. Although it's not difficult to find scholars who criticize our current use of the world religions category for being too narrow and thereby excluding other things that they somehow know to rightly need a place within it (such as so-called Pagan religions or indigenous religions), the group that I'm describing takes a rather different approach, one that is nicely summed up by the subtitle of Masuzawa's book: *How European Universalism Was Preserved in the Language of Pluralism* (2005). For, unlike Cantwell Smith and even some current critics of the world religions model, these scholars are not looking for the correct or a better way to name the thing formerly known as religion but, instead, are interested in our very tendency – noting that it is a very specific 'we' who betray this tendency, by the way, given that the word or concept of religion is hardly universal among humankind – of assuming that a clearly delineated subset of human claims, actions and organizations *ought* to be distinguished from all others by being represented as somehow having austere, serene or pristine origins or contemporary uses. Accordingly, the scholars I have in mind are not interested in merely substituting words like spirituality, worldview or lifeway for this term religion. (I think here of the interest of Vaia Touna (2017), my colleague at Alabama, in the practice of labelling certain things in the ancient world *as* religious.) Starting instead from the assumption that *all* human claims, practices and institutions are inextricably part of situated history (by which I mean, building on the work of the late French scholar, Roland Barthes, the world of contingency and happenstance, where no social actor possesses the omniscience of a novel's narrator and all claims and associations are contestable and invested), these scholars became intrigued that social actors sometimes invoke the voice of another, as in attributing some practice to 'tradition', let alone 'the gods' or maybe even 'the law', but inevitably doing so in their own voice, since it's the only one that we've got. (I think here of the 1970s US comedian Flip Wilson (d. 1998) and his once-iconic character Geraldine, who, having made a transgression of some sort, regularly exclaimed, 'The devil made me do it'.) This double-speak, if we can call it that (or perhaps ventriloquism is a more apt analogy?), struck some scholars as a way of disowning the situation and interests that routinely animate our claims, not unlike how someone grading essays might draw attention to a writer's use of the passive voice, which removes agency and thus accountability from the narrative, such that saying 'someone was hit by a car' seems to imply that the car somehow did it on its own. Seeing the representation of invariably historical claims and practices as if just some of them could be grouped together as uniquely distinguishable from all others as itself being an effective authorizing technique that, if it works, transforms the contingent into the necessary and the debatable into the authoritative, the scholars to whom I'm referring concluded not only that Geraldine's attribution of agency to the devil (if you recall Flip Wilson's routine, mentioned just a bit ago) was – pretty obviously, I guess – a handy way to dodge the implications of her own choices, but also that the designation of certain claims, practices and institutions, whether now or in the recent or distant past, *as* religious, *as* sacred or *as* spiritual *has the same privileging effect* for the claims, practices and institutions so named. For, at least as it has developed in European- and then North-American-derived, modern liberal democracies, the term, though commonplace in folk discourse, is actually a technical legal category, one that is enshrined in governance documents and which therefore comes with a variety of practical benefits, such that an uncontested claim that some disclosure, item, action or group is religious results in a privilege for those engaging in it – such as the widespread practice of classifying such institutions as churches, at least for the purpose of taxation, as non-profits instead of as businesses.

Now, you may have caught that I just made reference to something happening *if* claims worked and *if* they go uncontested, something that reminds us that, should we always see them as historically situated, such claims should be understood as *always* being contestable, inasmuch as they originate from but one of almost innumerable positions that an interested and invested social actor might occupy – something not all that apparent when we hear someone say, 'God demands', 'The Constitution says . . .', or even 'Tradition dictates . . .'. But, again starting from the assumption that what we study is always human, and thus contingent and situated through and through, means that we, as scholars, will continually look for the authorizing mechanisms that allow *this* to be seen as persuasive over *that* – that is, the devices whereby the many ways of doing something are policed and narrowed to *just these* practices and *just these* institutions or, in a word, the production of those continually tweaked conventions that we come to represent as authoritative, uniform and timeless *traditions*.

If you've stuck with me so far, and if the sort of work that I've been describing is either somewhat or completely new to you, then you may need a practical example or two to see the relevance of this shift in scholarship that I've been describing. Hearing that the very designation or treatment of something *as* religious, *as* sacred, is one among many socially formative techniques of governance used to make a certain sort of mundane, day-to-day life possible and persuasive can sound rather abstract; and, given how firmly committed many of us are to instead understanding these designations to be inherently linked to some unique feature of the items so named, well, as already indicated, this alternate position can seem counterintuitive, at best, or maybe even a little absurd. For who would be prepared to see, let's just say, a church as just another social institution within a community, one among many others, all of which are working to normalize certain sorts of social relations, in competition with other institutions which are themselves trying to establish yet other ways of arranging social life . . .? (Come to think of it, those organizations called churches are awfully interested in such seemingly mundane things as who you can marry, when you can have sex, when children should be treated as adults, etc.) So, I could invite you to consider, for example, a 1984 US Supreme Court decision in which the court decided that it was allowable for public funds to be used to set up and maintain what was pretty obviously an explicitly Christian nativity scene in the downtown shopping district during the Christmas season (the case of Lynch v. Donnelly 465 US 668). Why? Although the US Constitution's First Amendment makes pretty clear what some, echoing the text of a letter written by Thomas Jefferson, have called a wall of separation between church and state (a wall that, in practice, is far more porous than you might at first imagine), the crèche was characterized by the justices as being more *economic* than *religious*, given that it was part of a wider (dare we say secular?) effort to attract shoppers to the downtown, 'to let loose with their money', as a witness, quoted in the Court's decision, had phrased it. But instead, I'll cite some more recent and maybe more relevant examples in which the social management taking place via the category religion (a way that our societies rule things as being either in or out of bounds) may be a little more familiar and thus a little curious to you.

So consider Asma Uddin's 2019 book, *When Islam Is Not a Religion: Inside America's Fight for Religious Freedom*. Anyone familiar with European and North American news over the past few decades – not to mention other parts of the world, such as what's going on, since about 2014, in China with the Uyghur population, let alone the ways in which Islam has been represented over the past several hundred years throughout Europe – will know that politicians, journalists and intellectuals alike have expended considerable energy to normalize a certain type of Islam (one that is seen to be in step with so-called liberal democratic values, such as tolerance) in opposition to a type that is seen to be in direct (and, at times, violent) competition with the so-called West. (That the West/East distinction is itself among the management tools used in these disputes should be obvious to anyone who read, and retained, their Edward Said, by the way – making it a no less socially formative, and not merely descriptive, designation. Sadly, though, I see this distinction often used today by scholars, with little to no nuance.) Thus the terms 'political Islam' and 'Muslim extremism' were born, as normative ways to distinguish certain sorts of Muslims from others, under the presumption that Islam, being a religion, ought properly to inspire only inner emotions and quietist dispositions; variations from that norm, whether Muslims in Europe or the Middle East or even Buddhists in Indonesia, are candidates for the designation 'terrorist', inasmuch as their practitioners are portrayed as 'appropriating' or, more popularly, 'hijacking' the religion in question. Uddin's book, focused on cases in the Unites States, examines wholesale efforts to discount Islam as a religion, such as movements to deny building permits for mosques in various parts of the country, such as the case of the Islamic Center of Murfreesboro, Tennessee, which, back in 2010, sought to expand its facility. Given the manner in which the so-called free exercise clause of the US Constitution's First Amendment is understood to ensure that government remove itself from its citizens' religious lives – 'Congress shall make no law respecting an establishment of religion or prohibiting the free exercise thereof . . .' – losing the designation of religion would lead to the loss of some pretty obvious benefits for Muslims in the Unites States, such as the equal protections clause of the Constitution (i.e. the Fourteenth Amendment) no longer applying, let alone possibly changing their status with regard to human rights protections, making it possible to legally discriminate and deny services to them. As already referenced, this all hinges on the role this word religion plays in the US government's founding document, prompting us to distinguish between how people might use the term religion in daily life as opposed to how it functions as a governing category in law. Uddin's book, then, is a handy catalogue of recently devised tactics, on the part of some, to manage Islam within the Unites States by representing it instead as a dangerous political ideology intent on undermining the rule of law.

But what I find most interesting is how, in an interview with this author that was posted at the Religious Studies Project (on 24 June 2019), the interviewer seems incapable of understanding the category 'religion' to function in precisely this manner – something more than apparent to those who went to court to stop the expansion of the Islamic Center's facility, by the way, since they saw undermining the linkage between Islam and its status as a religion as an effective way to oppose their neighbours' different way of life. Instead, I'm guessing that the interviewer more than likely assumes that the word religion names some obvious feature or aspect that Islam, of course, shares in common with all of those other things that we call religion. For, while discussing the 2010 court hearing in the case of the Islamic Center of Murfreesboro's desire to expand its building, Uddin said:

> in the course of that six-day hearing it was argued very explicitly . . . and there's always been a long time when these arguments have implicitly been made that Islam is not a religion, but these words were actually stated in court. And the argument was, essentially, that all the different protections

that houses of worship get under the law do not apply in that case because Islam is not a religion. (Religious Studies Project 2019)

To which the interviewer, Benjamin Marcus (himself at the Religious Freedom Center in Washington, DC, working on religious literacy initiatives) replied, sounding somewhat incredulous, 'And I assume that . . . Did the judge say anything, provide any good questions . . . that would try to undermine that argument? Or did the judge just let that go forward unchallenged?' Here is the moment where I think we see the practical, governance effects of the category religion in a liberal democracy bumping up against the common-sense understanding of religion that operates in much of our day-to-day lives, for the interviewer just naturally seems to assume that the judge *should* intervene in such an argument – 'I assume that . . .' he starts off, after all, making plain the expectation that a judge *ought* to be undermining or challenging this position (though he catches himself and revises his initial declarative statement by reinventing it as a question). And after Uddin outlines some of the 'outrageous questions' posed in that courtroom to defendants by the critics of the mosque, Marcus adds, 'Wow! So what do you find most alarming about this move to redefine Islam as something other than a religion?' Now, while you may all probably agree that Islam is a religion, I would hope that you would not greet all this with a 'Wow!' but, instead, see in both your own classificatory agreement as well as this one episode from Tennessee two instances of social actors strategically using what is at hand – in this case, a designation with practical, legal consequences – to achieve a variety of social goals (whether your own or those of but one of Murfreesboro's rather conservative subgroups), thereby seeing the category religion as an organizational tool that, when awarded, brings benefits and, when withheld, denies protections. To repeat: although you may wish those privileges to extend to the Muslim members of the city of Murfreesboro, this does not mean that it is not worth understanding how the tug and pull of social life within a group is negotiated and managed *by means of this common designation*. (Aside: the new Murfreesboro Islamic Center opened on 10 August 2012, after the US federal government's Department of Justice intervened, and on 2 June 2014, the US Supreme Court declined to take the opponents' request to appeal, putting an end to the legal dispute.)

And so, as I noted earlier, studying religion is not really about religion at all; instead, as made pretty evident in this case from the American South, studying how this category religion is used, in seemingly mundane day-to-day situations, is all about how societies establish and contest themselves.

As a second example – with a nod to the US Supreme Court decision involving the nativity scene that I mentioned just a bit ago – consider those occasions when the benefits come *not* from bestowing but, instead, from withholding the category religion. Now, so far I've proposed that, in liberal democracies such as our own, the category, once entrenched in law, as it often is, provides a mechanism to privilege certain sorts of claims or behaviours among others. But that's only half of the story, because, as with all privileges, such benefits come at a price. The question is whether a community is willing to pay that price in exchange for the perks that being designated as a religion entails. I think here of historic commissions that exist in many towns, those bodies that decide on which neighbourhoods or even which buildings will be awarded a status that sets them apart from all others, inasmuch as they are said to represent the history of the community. While such designations are generally seen as prizes to be won, they also mean that changes to your home, whether repairs or renovations, must now meet the expectations of a committee, concerning such things as allowable exterior paint colours or types of roof shingles. (I recall here the 27 April 2011 tornado that tore through my own city and, at least as compared to us and the damage to our little home at the time, the difficulties and limitations that a friend had in fixing their home, given that, unlike our own, it was on the city's so-called historic register.) While this might be a small price to pay for the additional home value entailed in such listings, it nicely illustrates that no benefit is free of cost – so too in the case of the category religion; for once this designation is bestowed, a variety of practices might be allowable – practices that, in regular social life, might not – but one can only engage in them in a rather strictly policed manner, concerning when and where and who gets to do it (whatever the it is). Sure, in the United States, the Afro-Caribbean syncretistic tradition known as Santeria was designated as a religion in another famous US Supreme Court decision (1993's Church of the Lukumi Babalu Aye, Inc. v. Hialeah, 508 US 520), but that doesn't mean that members can indiscriminately kill (i.e. sacrifice) chickens, anywhere and anytime they like. No, but they *can* do it as part of their ceremonies, at specific times and in specific places, free from the sorts of animal cruelty and food handling laws that might govern slaughtering chickens otherwise.

So if benefits and costs attend such designations, it might be incorrect only to assume that being called a religion is beneficial; perhaps, as suggested in the case of the nativity scene, the benefit sometimes comes from *not* being a religion (for, in that case from Rhode Island, the dominant group in the city got to have seasonal symbols displayed at the public's expense, but only when they were understood as economic instead of religious). And so, with historic commissions in mind, especially given that they are sometimes called heritage sites (I think here of everything from the English Heritage Trust, a charity that runs a variety of historic sites throughout the country, to the small town of, say, Cleveland, Mississippi, whose Heritage Commission ensures that, according to their website, the '[p]roperty owners within Crosstie Historic District enjoy the advantages of increased economic value and a built environment protected from unsympathetic changes'), I turn to my second example: the manner in which things others might routinely call 'religious' can be strategically redefined as 'heritage' or even culture when dominant groups within communities seek to banish something called religion from public space but without undermining their own interests. What I have in mind here can be exemplified in a wide variety of places, from the heritage signified by the wooden crucifix, complete with a crucified Jesus on it, that still hung for some time above the speaker's chair in the legislature of the Province of Quebec, in Canada, despite the pending secularism legislation introduced by the provincial government. Known as Bill 21, it bans public employees from wearing overt religious symbols during work hours. (It was reported that this and other crosses, hanging in Quebec courts, would come down once the bill becomes law, in June 2020 – and it did; it is a bill, by the way, that has been strongly criticized by others in the country.) I could easily add to this list: as but one example, consider the German region of Bavaria, where crosses are now considered part of their cultural heritage and not as religious symbols, thereby allowing the government to mandate that, as of June 2018, Christian crosses be placed prominently in all public offices while other people's religious symbols are banned from the public space. That some church leaders see this as a crass appropriation by the state of their own religious symbols adds complexity to the example, of course, demonstrating nicely that the authority that results from our efforts to set things (and people) apart is itself contestable. But my larger point concerns how this artful redefinition (by the invention of such qualified designators as 'conspicuous religious symbols', which function similarly to 'political Islam') allows a dominant group to display only its treasured identity markers, at a taxpayers' expense that's shared by all, while still allowing them to portray themselves as tolerant and thereby respecting that much celebrated liberal value of religious diversity – all by, at least in this case, artfully withholding the designation religion from their own treasures.

I know that this is only two brief examples – though there are so many more that we could draw upon, such as the current practice of attributing religious motives to one's desire to, for example, deny services to customers with whose lifestyles one disagrees, so as to steer clear of otherwise relevant anti-discrimination laws or how people can designate their refusal to give their children vaccines as being based on a 'sincerely held religious belief'. (I think here of recent efforts in the United States to overturn Obama-era protections and instead allow 'faith-based adoption organizations' to deny LGBTQ couples the right to adopt children – efforts in the United States that, with former President Trump once again taking office, we may see gain momentum, what with recent signals that protecting a dominant group's rights to express their views may be taking priority over protecting the rights of minorities – all of which is explored in the new final chapter to the second edition of McCutcheon 2025.) What I hope to have demonstrated by means of these examples is that the category has utility in this modern world of ours, *not*, as many might at first think, for naming something ethereal and thereby inherent to the items being named as such but, rather, for walling things off from one another, so as to promote or demote them in relation to other things in society, all depending on the social interests of the speaker. Making this shift in how we understand this category to work – from assuming that it names some prior religious identity to seeing it as identifying for a variety of socially formative purposes – is part of what Daniel Dubuisson, on the opening page of his most recent English book, *The Invention of Religions* (2019), has called a 'veritable scientific revolution . . . in the departments of "Religious Studies" in many North American universities along with some of their British counterparts'. That this revolution is largely unknown to people outside the field is something that I've sought to correct here, by trying to make evident that how we name and organize our worlds not only matters – something that's pretty evident to almost anyone when they consider themselves to have been mis-identified in some manner – but that this can be illustrated by our usually taken-for-granted habit of giving so-called religious names to things that can be understood in a variety of other ways (inviting us to consider precisely what is to be gained by adding that adjective 'religious' as a qualifier to their names). That the category religion is up to something, making it not just a neutral descriptor of obvious spiritual and thus apolitical, otherworldly states and dispositions, is all I've hoped to persuade you of – and I mean here *all* of its uses, and not just some that we judge (and dismiss) as crass or insincere – something you might recall the next time you see the term in even its most benign uses, thereby making you just a little curious about what all might be going on when we extract things from our everyday, mundane and historical lives by ascribing to them religious names, sacred identities and thus timeless and uncontestable value.

References

Cantwell Smith, Wilfred (1962), *The Meaning and End of Religion: A New Approach to the Religious Traditions of Mankind*, New York: Macmillan.
Cotter, Christopher R. and David G. Robertson, eds (2016), *After World Religions: Reconstructing Religious Studies*, Oxford: Routledge.
Dubuisson, Daniel (2019), *The Invention of Religions*, trans. Martha Cunningham, London: Equinox.
Masuzawa, Tomoko (2005), *The Invention of World Religions, or, How European Universalism Was Preserved in the Language of Pluralism*, Chicago: Chicago University Press.

McCutcheon, Russell T. (1997), *Manufacturing Religion: The Discourse on Sui Generis Religion and the Politics of Nostalgia*, New York and London: Oxford University Press.

McCutcheon, Russell T. (2021), *On Making a Shift in the Study of Religion and Other Essays*, Berlin: De Gruyter.

McCutcheon, Russell T. (2025), *'Religion' and the Domestication of Dissent, or How to Live in a Less than Perfect Nation*, 2nd edn, New York and London: Routledge.

Owen, Suzanne (2011), 'The World Religions Paradigm: Time for a Change', *Arts and Humanities in Higher Education*, 10 (3): 253–68.

Partridge, Christopher and Marcus Moberg, eds (2023), *The Bloomsbury Handbook of Religion and Popular Music*, 2nd edn, London: Bloomsbury.

Religious Studies Project (2019), 'When Islam Is Not a Religion', Podcast Interview with Asma Uddin and Benjamin Marcus, 24 June. Available online: https://www.religiousstudiesproject.com/podcast/when-islam-is-not-a-religion/ (accessed 8 January 2025).

Touna, Vaia (2017), *Fabrications of the Greek Past: Religion, Tradition, and the Making of Modern Identities*, Leiden: Brill.

Uddin, Asma T. (2019), *When Islam Is Not a Religion: Inside America's Fight for Religious Freedom*, New York: Pegasus Books.

5

The Ideology of Religious Studies then and now

The author's view*

Timothy Fitzgerald

I have rarely revisited *The Ideology of Religious Studies* (*IRS*) since its publication in 2000 (see, however, Fitzgerald 2017). *IRS* is a ragged ensemble of arguments on a wide range of issues aimed against a complex target. The long-range target was and is liberal capitalism, and the illusions of possessive Individualism (Macpherson 1962).

The more proximate targets are various agencies that seemed to me to be serving to normalize or naturalize liberal capitalism (religious studies, phenomenology of religion, the World Religions paradigm, liberal ecumenical theology, and the social sciences more widely). By ragged I do not mean that there are no connections between the overlapping arguments. I mean that I was less critically aware of the inconsistencies than I am now. Viewed from twenty years on, *IRS* was an early stage in a longer-term project that is still evolving.

---

*This chapter was previously published as an article in *Implicit Religion* 22, no. 3–4 (2019): 268–90; part of a special issue edited by Teemu Taira and Suzanne Owen under the title 'Twenty Years of *The Ideology of Religious Studies*' (available online: https://journal.equinoxpub.com/IR/issue/view/1796). See the other articles in that issue for various scholars' reflections on the significance of critical religion and on the state of the field over recent decades. This chapter is reproduced with permission of the author and of Equinox Publishing.

Since *IRS* I have had time to clarify in my own mind what I meant by 'liberal capitalism'. What follows is consistent with *IRS* though more developed in subsequent publications. By 'capitalism' I meant a) the system of practices constituted from an ungrounded belief in the 'natural' and inalienable right of the Individual to accumulate private property (possessive Individualism) with minimal responsibility for the remainder (negative liberty); b) the narratives, fictions and rhetoric that since the late seventeenth century have served to legitimize and normalize this vast system of organized plunder; and c) those constitutional, juridical, financial, bureaucratic and academic institutions that serve and promote this belief and its operations globally. The ambiguous term 'liberal' became attached to 'political economy' during the eighteenth century, misleadingly associating possessive Individualism with tolerance, flexibility and generosity. This became reified as 'liberalism' in the nineteenth century at a high point of Imperial dominance. Liberal political economy and classical economics operate to provide the various forms of capitalist exploitation – 'accumulation by dispossession' – with a mask of scientific objectivity, normality and respectability.

The invention of generic religion and its binary opposite, the non-religious secular, is fundamental in generating the illusion that today's dominant system of exploitation and inequality is sane, rational, normal, natural and the only possible game in town.

Motivations for writing *IRS*

So *IRS* is a critique of liberal capitalism, and the institutions and values that make endless property accumulation appear as normal, inevitable, rational and the sign of a successful life. *IRS* was concerned with the operations of the religion and non-religion binary in making the colonial globalization of liberal capitalism appear like a benign civilizing mission rather than global armed robbery.

There is therefore a moral commitment to my work which some readers may feel is inappropriate for academic work in the social sciences. After all, the professional academic is ideally neutral and objective, and does not impose his or her subjective moral preferences on the matter at hand.

On the other hand, this distinction between subjective values and objective facts is itself part of the configuration that requires critique. In *IRS* I touched on the significant functions that the empty, contested category 'the Individual' has in validating a range of ideologically productive binaries, from the mind-matter dualism of Descartes and the Kantian transcendental ego to the possessive (mostly male) Individual *homo economicus*, the carrier of natural inalienable property rights in liberal and neoliberal political economy.

Liberal capitalism and the valorization of competitive self-interest is a destructive and ugly unleashing of desire, greed and fear which has been given a *faux* 'Science' appearance and wrapped in discourses on the brutal struggle for existence in the context of an insentient and unforgiving 'material nature'. 'Religion' as a term and a category has a crucial function in this normalizing process. This anti-capitalist critical spirit is still a motivation for writing, and it is strongly connected with extended critique, not only of 'religion' but the wider ensemble of related categories.[1]

However, I was also motivated by a desire to recoup a topic of study, an area or domain or field or territory, by way of ethnographic representation. There were good reasons for this, some of them obvious and pragmatic. I wanted to talk about what I had discovered in India and in Japan, and I wanted to use that to open up religion and religious studies to critique. I needed another job to be united with my family. I needed something to teach and be expert in. I needed to be offering something 'concrete' and 'constructive' like a new idea about how to formulate a common ground of research within the humanities and social sciences. There was the desire to present my work as ethnographically 'factual', in the sense of closer to the ground, more immediate, more closely observed or better evidenced.

Another reason why writing *IRS* felt and feels like a personal commitment is because I had been brought up and schooled to be proud of British imperial history, and I inherited racist stereotypes about India and Japan and much of the world. And now I had friends among people designated as 'untouchable' in Maharashtra. And I was living and working in Japan, married to a Japanese woman, with bilingual children, was learning Japanese myself, and working in a Japanese university that in some ways treated me more generously than a British equivalent. I felt empathy and friendship with my father-in-law who had been trained as a kami kaze pilot but whose life had paradoxically been saved by the Nagasaki bomb. He was no different from an old soldier in any country who wanted to play his part in defence of his own country.

My readings of Indian and Japanese history also changed my views. It is not that I think Japan or India are great examples of 'democracy'. But then nor is Britain. 'Democracy' is another unclear and contested category, typically exemplified by the oscillations of the two-party parliamentary systems. In this restricted sense of 'democratic', Japan has a democratic constitution, written under the auspices of the US occupation force after WW2. However, there is a more deeply-rooted ethos of senior-junior relations that permeates all Japanese institutions. Living in Japan and learning more about the problematic historical situation that faced the literate male elites there when American warships were entering Edo Bay during the 1850s has made me more critical of the idea that imperial powers such as Britain, France, Holland or the USA are or ever were good examples of 'democracy'.

There were other personal factors of motivation too. One was disappointment at the failure of the Christian churches to stand against selfish individualism, which I took to be the reverse of the Christian message of loving one's neighbour. This is one reason why I felt impatient towards the self-satisfied complacency of the liberal ecumenicists and the world religions experts and their inventions. This was part of the shedding of the Christian faith I had been raised with.

There are other, deeper, personal motivations, which are difficult to speak about. One was the series of mental breakdowns that occurred to me between the 1960s and the mid-1980s. These almost destroyed me and have never really 'gone away'. I wanted to explore this disintegration of self as a metaphor for the disintegration of empire that was occurring during the time of my upbringing and schooling. I was supposed to internalize the narratives of British imperial grandeur while the violent processes of de-colonization through national liberation movements were occurring. From the reader's point of view, developing this narrative might have felt like an unwelcome intrusion of the subjective and personal into the objective and public. Speaking for myself, I would say that this is a threatening collapse of the sense of subjectivity that derives from being brought up and schooled at a time when imperial ideology was being stripped of credibility, leading to a radical loss of trust in the authority of received tradition.

Two different antagonistic projects in *IRS*

I now think there are two different projects in *IRS* that are tangled up. Recognizing this may help to understand the different kinds of reaction to *IRS*. I want to try to separate out these two entangled projects analytically.

One project is the *extended critique* that makes the idea of factual representation problematic. Whose facts? And who has the right to represent who? This radical questioning has serious implications for both ethnographic and historical representation. *Extended critique* follows the logic where it goes. This does not only have implications for religious studies and the 'religion' category, but also for sociology and 'society', for anthropology and 'culture', and for science and 'nature'. If methodologically we should pay attention to the category 'religion' itself, and not the supposed empirically observed objects ('religions') that we imagine the term corresponds to, then why should 'politics', 'culture', 'society', 'nature', 'science',[2] or 'economics' and all other supposedly non-religious domains be different? Extended critique questions the discursive production of secular knowledge itself, and therefore the secular university and the secular state. The extended critique of religion and related categories takes us into radically unknown territory.

The other project is *limited critique*, which draws back from the implications of a fully extended critique. This kind of critique is safer. It limits critical deconstruction to 'religion' and tries to save other categories such as 'culture', 'politics' or 'society'. This limited critique means that religious studies can in some sense survive, though as part of a larger inter-disciplinary arena. In the case of *IRS*, this is a more *positive* attempt to find a different grounding for the study of religion within 'culture', as in cultural anthropology and culture studies. Here I tried to re-instate 'culture', which I now think was a mistake. I also mistakenly tried to reinstate 'politics' in the tripartite scheme of ritual, politics and soteriology.

The *extended* critique in *IRS* amounts to, or at least implies, a critical deconstruction of Anglophone or more widely Europhone categories and their modes of deployment. It is to question our dominant collective representations. To critique religion is logically to critique the non-religious secular, and to critique the non-religious secular is to critique all those imaginary domains that are classified as secular. It is to recognize the ideological significance and implications of the purely imaginary separation of religion from non-religion. Tracking the historical emergence of the discourse on generic religion must also logically be to track the historical emergence of these other reified categories that construct our belief in modern liberal (or socialist) secular scientific progress. This extended critique targets the configuration of categories that operate together in binary forms to legitimize and normalize capitalism and its rhetorical associations with such contested and indefinable signs as liberty, liberalism, progress, individualism, utilitarianism, materialism and liberal political economy. This configuration constructs a view of human nature, a myth of progress and well-being by way of markets and private ownership, and a legitimization of colonial interventions, invasions, foreign impositions and theft of land, resources and labour.

In *IRS* this radical project of extended critique is not fully conscious, nor consistently executed. I was not critically aware of what I was doing or what the implications might be. Since then I have come to realize that what we call 'modernity' or 'The Enlightenment' was and is itself an imaginary invented from a whole range of associated imaginaries, and these have become the common sense of our world. This includes our experience of space, time, matter and causation. The growth of a literate male elite with few rights in the seventeenth century led to a flowering of rhetoric on liberty, nature, inalienable rights of private property and representation, the progress of nations, and free markets as the solution to poverty and inequality. The new sources of wealth have been derived from the creation of landless poor in Europe, America, Africa, Asia and globally.

There was an idea in the back of my mind while writing *IRS* which has become more explicit since then. To mention it here may help the reader to understand its composition. To systematically unpick these complex and contested categories that behave like unitary signs could be viewed as a 'meditation' practice. It is a deconstruction of 'self'. The mention of the term 'meditation' would embarrass many secular academics who tend to place such a practice in the religion or spiritual classification, along with 'prayer' and 'worship', and to compare it unfavourably with 'Science'. It is 'navel gazing', effeminate, and not proper empirical knowledge of secular reason. What would a university look like if we went there to 'meditate' instead of producing knowledge? This would not be attractive for many academics or students. Realizing the emptiness of the categories that organize so much of our 'knowledge' of the world would leave one feeling lost and without any orientation. This would be a more radical kind of 'postcolonial' consciousness than the kind implied by Edward Said's excellent but partial critique of orientalism, which fails to identify the religion-secular binary as postcolonial remains (Fitzgerald 2016). It would amount to the critique of all those institutions and forms of knowledge that support the illusions of 'material nature' and liberal (and socialist) secular modern progress.

This is to get somewhat ahead of *IRS*. At the time of writing it, I had not quite arrived at this point. In *IRS* I critically analysed many texts of different kinds to show how the religion-secular transcendental binary operates in a wide range of different contexts. I wanted to show how people in religious studies, anthropology, sociology and other disciplines contributed largely unconsciously to the mystification and normalization of liberal capitalism and the global ambitions of its colonizing practitioners by imagining 'religion' as an ahistorical and universal phenomenon. My purpose was to show the contradictions and the mostly unconscious rhetorical techniques for disguising the relation between the study of religion and the reproduction of the wider ideological formation. However, this has implications for the very idea of a secular university and its purposes. This would threaten not only the survival of religious studies departments, but the entire system of classification that supports secular social and natural science.

The other project is more limited and tries to find a more secure way of conceiving the work done in religious studies departments. If not religion, then what? The study of 'culture', as in cultural anthropology and cultural studies, seemed a fruitful way to go. One of the expressions I used was 'theoretically informed ethnography'. For this project, while continuing to critique other people's representations by closely examining their texts, I was simultaneously offering alternative representations. I was also deploying personal narratives and 'data' gathered in my travels and my workplace. I was questioning sociology and 'society', and yet the book has many sociological abstractions that I would now weed out. There are lots of expressions such as 'Hindu ideology', 'constructing a collective identity', 'the core elements of the social order', 'cultures', 'tradition' and 'traditional thought', 'western and non-western', 'social structure', 'economic domain', and others. In this way, while arguing that 'religion' should be the object of our attention and therefore should be suspended as a descriptive and analytical category, I was not fully in control of that methodological practice, recycling other problematic terms such as 'culture' or 'politics' or 'society' for descriptive and analytical purposes (representation) and thus contradicting my own critique.

I think the parts in the later chapters of *IRS* (eleven and twelve), where I try to find another home for religious studies in a merger with cultural studies and cultural anthropology, were worth the attempt but ultimately a mistake as they stand.[3] Anthropology has too many of its own problems, and they are not dissimilar to those inhering in religious studies.

Representations of religion in 'India'

I had good practical reasons for going to do research in India in 1983–4. I had managed to get a full-time lecturing job at a college of higher education. This was around the time I was finishing my PhD, which was in philosophical theology. My remit was to teach Hinduism, Buddhism, and Theory and Method. About half my students were training to be school-teachers. I had begun thinking critically about the World Religion paradigm and its flaws while doing my BA degree at King's College, London. The course that I had taken in Social Anthropology with Nancy Tapper (now Lindisfarne) had awoken me to the difference between the kind of textual representation from which Hinduism and Buddhism were constructed by orientalists, and the participant observation and ethnographic methods of anthropology.

The artificial abstractions called religions, such as Hinduism, were often based on texts compiled and edited by scholars in European centres. The Bhagavad Gita is undoubtedly a great work, but how does it help us to understand caste, or the Republican Constitution, or the ordinary lives of people living mostly in Indian villages? Would anyone in an average village have a clue what Hinduism meant? Given that we are often reminded that eighty per cent of Indian people live in agricultural villages, what relevance would the cerebral, literate, theological or philosophically-inclined texts have for the vast majority of Indian people? And meanwhile would I have been able to explain to the students the things that many of them wanted to know: Who can marry whom? How does clan, subcaste and caste work in practice? Why do women wear a red dot in the middle of their forehead? What kind of food do people in villages eat? Who can eat with whom? Is 'untouchability' still a factor and how does it work? Do renouncers still renounce and how do they live? Can women also be renouncers? What is an ashram? What is *sati* or *suttee*?

The students were expecting the World Religion paradigm approach and yet they were also critical of it. The vast construct Hinduism was based largely on translated Sanskrit texts placed in a speculative historical sequence. I found the term 'Brahmanism' more apt than 'Hinduism' because clearly the European scholars who invented Hinduism derived much of their knowledge from Brahmins and other high caste informants who traditionally had a monopoly on Sanskrit. The orientalists placed the Brahminical ideas in a historical development sequence to fit the dominant European constructions of historical time and geographical space. It started with the Indus Valley civilization, then the Vedas, then went to the Vedanta and the Upanisads, then to the Smriti law books, then to Epics – the Mahabharata and Ramayana, and then on to the Puranas. These were all given approximate dates for their composition, the dates being BC or AD (or CE). Quite a lot of time was spent reading the Bhagavad Gita. Then there were the different theological or philosophical interpretations of Vedanta by Sankara, Ramanuja and Madhva. And inevitably, time restrictions meant that vast periods of Indian history were traversed in quick time or skimmed over. The Mughal Empire? Mentioned in passing! The East India Company? Mentioned in passing! We spent some time on modern reform movements and especially the influence and philosophy of Gandhi. The latter was a kind of Saint hero for the World Religion ecumenicists. Hinduism texts sometimes mentioned 'caste' in the context of the classical *varnashramadharma* divisions, and went a bit further when discussing Gandhi and the problem of untouchability.

This does not mean that reading and translating the texts such as the Vedas, Upanishads, the Bhagavad Gita, the Ramayana and the Mahabharata, the Puranas, the authoritative law books and much else is a waste of time. On the contrary, these texts provide compelling ways to think about cosmology, about personhood, about suffering and the causes of suffering, about order and disorder. They can provide an alternative ground from which to reflect back on ourselves and our own ways of dealing with the serious issues of life and death. Reading such texts can expand the imagination, provide a space from which to question our own normality, and can help one escape a narrow Christian or Liberal Secular indoctrination. I really enjoyed teaching some of these texts – the Gita for example, because in its own terms it makes compelling sense. However, texts require contexts. For example, as a secular academic I can read translations of the Gita made by specialist experts and

I can teach them to undergraduate students in UK. But few villagers in India could or would have read the Gita, and probably never heard of it. Villagers would know their proper place in the ritual hierarchy of things and persons, but few would have read the Brahminical Sanskrit lawbooks such as the Manu Smriti. So where exactly is the putative religion Hinduism located? Perhaps more in secular universities in Euro-America than in Indian villages.

Another point that needed clarification was the relation between indigenous institutions based on hierarchical principles exemplified by the dichotomy between pure Brahmins and impure Untouchables, and the colonially imposed values of liberal capitalism: liberty, private property, representative democracy, centralized bureaucratic administration, and secular constitutional nation-state. It was in this context that I began to think about how the religion-secular binary operated in the Indian context.

As a result of these intellectual, theoretical and pedagogical needs I applied for funding and went to India for four months alone in 1983–4. My project was to study Ambedkar Buddhism.[4] Of course I was reading a lot of anthropology of India, especially Louis Dumont but certainly not only his work.[5] When I returned and began teaching again, I felt a bit more authentic in the sense that I had at least spent months travelling and meeting people in India, and when a student asked me about caste and subcaste for example, I could give quite detailed descriptions and could name many of the caste groups cohabiting villages in rural Maharashtra. The experience of being alone in India had frightened me. I had been having mental breakdowns for several years anyway, and being in India challenged me in all sorts of ways, both expected and unexpected. On the whole it strengthened me. I came to accept the proposition that British colonial rule, far from being a glorious period of civilization symbolized by Queen Victoria, the Empress of India, had left this vast sub-continent in a dreadful mess.[6]

I had a much better understanding of the vastness and complexity of 'India'. I also now could understand and explain much better than previously what anthropologists meant when they talked about 'the caste system', the opposition between purity and pollution in practice, what 'dominant caste' means and so on. I also discovered about Gandhi and his rivalry with Dr B. R. Ambedkar, the leader of the untouchables (Dalits and Buddhists). Ambedkar and his movement also helped me to understand the conflict between Brahmanical principles of caste hierarchy and the prominent liberal colonial principles of representative democracy that Ambedkar himself, as First Law Minister in the Nehru government, had incorporated into the Republican Constitution. How could members of castes defined as untouchable by the dominant Brahmanical orthodoxy become 'equal' citizens of a modern secular republic?

It should also be mentioned that I made friends in Maharashtra, mostly with Dalits and Buddhists, several of whom were middle-class academics who spoke good English, and who were committed to the Ambedkar movement. They were able to explain a great deal to me. I felt committed to them in turn, but I knew that I could escape the consequences of commitment because I could return to my relatively well-paid job in England. Nevertheless, trying to understand this movement was a good vehicle for exploring wider issues. It increased my understanding and made me explore my own consciousness in relation to the British colonial history.

I have no doubt that my teaching got better, the students felt greater confidence in my understanding. However, there was always a tension between the expectations set up by the World Religion paradigm and the closer-to-the-ground methods of ethnographic representation. My experience of travelling in Maharashtra and other parts of India strengthened my scepticism not only about 'Hinduism' but the very idea of 'religions' and 'world religions'. In particular, the movement of Dalits and Buddhists and the writing of their great leader Dr Ambedkar seemed to make it impossible to separate the 'religious' from the 'political' and the political from the 'economic' elements. Furthermore, I was powerfully struck by 'the ritualization of everyday life'. It was in this context that I thought of the tripartite scheme of ritual-politics-soteriology. I was looking for a way to look at a specific movement in Maharashtra – Ambedkar Buddhism – and to represent it in terms that were more faithful to what I had seen, heard, read and been told.

So, my motives for attempting ethnographic representation were practical, pedagogical, self-developmental and theoretical. They were also about solidarity – by teaching about Dr Ambedkar and the Dalits and Buddhists I was raising consciousness about their collective suffering and desire for liberation from poverty and structural inequality. My motives were also concerned with escaping the flawed and distorting World Religion paradigm, and being able to face my students and tell them honestly that I had at least taken the trouble to spend time in India, had seen a lot of stuff that people there had helped me to understand, and was better equipped to say that the ecumenical construct Hinduism is best understood as an essentialization, a reification, and a Europeanized version of the dominant Brahmanical ideology.

However, this was not the kind of ethnographic representation that comes from spending months and years in a village or urban locality. In fact, it was not essentially different from well-informed research journalism. I even met the Dalai Lama on my travels. Talking at different times to Tibetan Buddhists and also to the occasional Theravada Buddhist monk (usually from Sri Lanka or other parts of South East Asia), as well as the Buddhist followers of Ambedkar, I realized how different Buddhists are from each other, how closely tied to their own collective identity – 'ethnicity', 'caste', 'nation' or 'lineage' – and how difficult it is to essentialize 'Buddhism' as though this is a coherent and clearly distinguishable 'religion'.

One thing that I did notice from my reading in the Indian anthropological literature was that anthropologists uncritically persisted with the application of Europhone categories such as religion, politics and economics. Yet these are the globalizing categories of liberal capitalist modernity. It occurred to me that social or cultural anthropologists were deploying categories for objective description and analysis that had been imported by the colonial powers to reorganize India and to make it a 'modern' and 'rational' private property society and secular nation-state.

Representations of religion in 'Japan'

These issues were all alive for me when I went to live with my family in Japan in 1988, where I worked in a university, mostly as an English teacher, but also as a research faculty member. Here we were tied to Japan by work, income and family (my wife, Noriko, is Japanese). Whereas in India I had been something between an anthropologist and a serious research journalist, in Japan I was defined by family, institutional and national ties. I was a taxpayer, a householder and a working colleague of Japanese academics. Here again I was impressed by the 'ritualization of everyday life'. It was hugely different from the ritualization of life in India, but it nevertheless problematized the very idea that the everyday customs and presentation of self in everyday life could be divided between the religious and the non-religious aspects of life. And here I switched my attention from the religions 'Hinduism' and 'Buddhism' to the so-called Japanese religions such as 'Shinto', 'Buddhism' and 'Confucianism'. There were also other categories such as 'Folk Religion' and 'Christianity'.

There was also an anthropology of Japan and a religious studies sector in Japan. I read a great deal of literature on the 'religions of Japan' written by Japanese and non-Japanese experts. Here again I found an uncritical willingness to continue to organize representations in the terms and categories that had been imposed on Japan since the Meiji period by US power. Academic writers in religious studies seemed determined to insist that 'religion' and religious sentiment (religiosity!) were self-evident in Japan, despite that when interviewed most Japanese people denied that they were religious. The Japanese people were in effect being told: 'You really are religious people, but you don't know it! You need a Euro-American intellectual to point this out to you!' In my own interviews I found that most Japanese simply denied that 'religion' or *shukyo* had much part in their lives. Many Japanese identify 'religion' with 'Christianity' imported from America and Europe. A few thought

'Buddhism' might qualify. However, as far as they were concerned, visits to temples and shrines and participation in festivals had nothing to do with 'religion' but were 'our Japanese customs'.

I was animated by such questions as: Is it true that Japanese people are 'really religious' even when it is very difficult to find anyone – even academics – to agree to any such thing? In what sense are Buddhism, Shinto or Confucianism really distinct 'religions', and to what extent are these distinctions imposed by secular constitutional requirements and academic assumptions? Are temples and shrines 'religious' institutions, while the Japanese state, the corporations and the schooling system are 'secular' institutions? I argued that the ritualized values of everyday Japanese practices do not follow this either-or binary choice, and that all these institutions (schools, corporations, universities, family households, small businesses, craft specialists, temples, shrines) reproduce a form of life and consciousness according to largely shared principles.

I was therefore looking for a more basic and veridical level of representation. I wanted to be able to tell a coherent story about India and Japan to my students. I had not fully awoken to the deeper level problem: What, if anything, is being represented? A good ethnographic study of a specific community can convince the reader that the narrative is more concrete, and thus more veridical, because it is close-to-the-ground and based on personal face-to-face experience. I consequently felt the compulsion to observe and represent as an anthropologist might. And this led me into at least two *cul-de-sacs*. One was to try to save politics from a similar critique as the one applied to religion by formulating the ritual, politics and soteriology tripartite analytical tool. The other was to try to merge religious studies, cultural studies and cultural anthropology on the grounds that we are all studying 'culture' in the sense of theoretically-informed ethnographic studies. This at times is couched in terms of convergence and inter-disciplinary overlap. At other times it sounds as though I am reducing 'religion' to 'culture'.

If I had been fully and critically awake, I ought to have been more consistent in my application of the same deconstructive logic to the categories of 'politics', 'culture' and 'society' as I was applying to 'religion'. Instead the practical problem of finding a way to reformulate religious studies blocked a more consistent view that Religious Studies, Cultural Studies, Sociology, and Cultural and Social Anthropology are also, in their own ways, serving the same configuration of mystifying colonial categories. This gets dangerously close to delegitimizing the whole of the Humanities and Social Sciences. (It also has implications for the idea of the Natural Sciences.) What is all this problematic knowledge for? What is its purpose?

I think *IRS* at least raises for careful consideration the question why we need such a vast plethora of academic textual representations when they are typically and continually contested by competing specialists, and yet rarely read by anyone outside a limited portion of the academic community. The endless proliferation of journals is a case in point. What does all this knowledge amount to? Even more to the point, how could any degree of accurate communication be conducted when academia, both Japanese and foreign, were insistent in ordering their knowledge production in terms of Western colonial categories which are misrepresenting what many Japanese people think and say?

My sceptical conclusion now is that the supposedly factual content of this vast expanding library of representations is less important than the bare insistent reproduction of the categories themselves. The incessant reproduction of a paradigmatic configuration of values embeds a form of classification, and makes a historically peculiar order of power based on a supposed right to unlimited private property accumulation seem inescapably normal. Why do religious studies academics not study the global banking system that has facilitated the processes of accumulation by dispossession since the seventeenth century? If all these experts are studying religions, social structures, secular nation-states, political domains, economic systems and cultures, then they, or we, are performing rituals that reproduce and re-authorize 'our' system of collective symbolic representations. These are the same values and categories that were developed to give an air of legitimacy to a colonially-imposed, Euro-American capitalist agenda of centralized nation-states managing the interests of male private property accumulation. How could the hierarchical principles that operated in all Japanese (or Indian) institutions be articulated in relation to the 'liberty', 'equality' and Individualism of liberal political economy?

Anthropologists *can* be highly critical of the problems of translating Europhone categories and deploying them as representations of non-European forms of life. There is a lot of interesting debate in anthropology on the deployment of binaries such as male and female, nature and culture, wild and cultivated, raw and cooked, pre-logical and logical. There has been a significant debate between substantivists and formalists in identifying the supposed 'economic domain' that economists imagine to be there. There is also a minority literature on the definition of religion, and many anthropologists have asserted that most of the people in the world do not have a word for religion (or politics or economics or society) and do not make any distinction between natural and supernatural. However – and I include Durkheim and *l'ecole sociologique* in this critique – most anthropologists deploy Europhone categories such as religion, secular, politics, economics, society, nation or culture with surprisingly little critical reflexivity. And the resistance on the part of anthropologists to reading the critical religion stuff is almost absolute.

I think what was effective about *IRS* and perhaps ahead of the field was that I was not only destabilizing religion, but also secular, politics, society, culture and nation. I did not do this completely or consistently. These terms often re-appear through the back door. I was not fully in control of that in *IRS*.

Anthropology, ethnographic representation and 'writing culture'

Critique of categories that appear benign and useful but which on closer inspection have an ideological spin to them makes the very idea of representation problematic. I was making representations and claims about Japan and India in order to critique the existing representations. In order to show that the idea of Indian religions and Japanese religions are ideologically distorted representations, I thought I needed to present an alternative. This then led me to look for a less ideological ground for representation in the notion of 'culture' understood as theoretically-informed ethnographies, a kind of minimum field that could be shared by religious studies, cultural studies, and social and cultural anthropology. It was probably more like 'thick description' pioneered by Clifford Geertz.

How can we represent anything accurately – ourselves or others – when so many of our general categories are untranslatable, and even in our own language mislead us? Terms that appear as ahistorical, pristine, definitive and self-evidently universal, such as religion, secular, politics, nation or society, are historically recent categories, old words given new contexts and therefore new meanings, contested rhetorical deployments. These ideas constituted – and yet were also constituted by – the narratives of progress, liberty and Individualism, and served and consolidated the interests of a capitalist world order. Old words have been invested with new meanings and yet appear as the smooth continuation with the past. Categories that appear as neutral representations of what we find in the world turn out on closer inspection to persuasively *construct* a picture of reality. Our collective and personal consciousness is heavily dominated by empty abstractions that appear concrete, and that unconsciously operate and organize our knowledge. Since *IRS*, I have researched other problematic inventions such as 'history', 'nature' and 'The Enlightenment'.

In *IRS* I wanted to represent what I observed as the customary practices in India and Japan, and to demonstrate that they are both 'religious' and 'secular', and therefore neither. I needed to do this in the first place because I wanted to critique capitalism and colonialism. I wanted to destabilize religious studies as a mystifying agency and yet I also wanted to save the possibility of an empirical studies of 'something' that could be accepted as real. I thought it was more productive to advocate a merger of religious studies with anthropology and cultural studies by theorizing 'culture' than to follow the logic of extended critical deconstruction.

So, the problem was to find a way to represent or re-represent Indian or Japanese customary practices in order to prove my point – that religion and related categories are colonial impositions that reorder indigenous institutions and practices to suit the interests of global capital. I used descriptive and analytical representations of Indian and Japanese customary practices to show that the religion-secular binary had been rhetorically developed[7] to transform the world to suit capitalist interests while clothed in the rhetoric of progress, objectivity, correspondence with the real facts as distinct from the superstitious fictions of tradition.

This is the major contradiction in *IRS*. I still don't know how it can be resolved. I was so intent on showing why religion is a problem as a word and an idea that I had to find some alternative ground that avoided deploying religion as a descriptive and analytical category. I was looking for a common methodology and the possibility of a shared body of knowledge along the lines of theoretically-informed ethnographies. The problem is that disciplines such as Cultural Studies and Social and Cultural Anthropology are also caught in circularities. They were and are, like religious studies, largely comfortable with uncritically reproducing religion discourses as though it is obvious that religion is a universal. This simultaneously constructs the non-religious secular base that legitimates the supposedly objective knowledge of anthropology as an academic discipline. Therefore, critique of anthropology from within the discipline is circular and cannot be adequately accomplished.

On the other hand, I imagined that these disciplines were in the front line of critical reflection on ethnocentrism, ethnographic representation and the problems of translation. There is a highly critical tradition in anthropology that I cite and quote a great deal that supports the critical deconstruction. I now realize that, despite this critical tradition, anthropology and its various more empiricist or positivist branches continue to operate a rhetorical system for the reproduction of colonial categories.

I had not fully realized the extent to which Sociology, Anthropology and Cultural Studies also rest on wobbly foundations. Even in my reading of Robert Brightman's thought-provoking article 'Forget Culture: Replacement, Transcendence, Relexification' (1995) and also Bernard McGrane's excellent book *Beyond Anthropology* (1989), an article and a book which review many of the problems with 'culture', 'human nature' and colonial origins in anthropology, I still wanted to emerge at the other end with something that could be useful for reconceiving 'the field'. The problem is that there is no 'field' outside what a body of opinion claims it to be. I think the point I made that religion and culture are indistinguishable is correct. The error in retrospect was to limit the problem of representation to a replacement of religious studies with cultural studies, or ambiguously their merging with anthropology, as if this would solve the wider problem of representation.

While we in religious studies were interrogating our central category 'religion', they in cultural anthropology were interrogating their central category 'culture' in the 'writing culture' genre. There is a stream of anthropological critique from which religious studies could gain. There are the blurred genres of Geertz, his combination of fiction and fact in 'faction'. There are the subsequent critical discussions in the 1970s and 1980s of culture, ethnography, coloniality and representation, in texts such as Roy Wagner, *The Invention of Culture* (1975); Marshall Sahlins, *Culture and Practical Reason* (1976); James Clifford and George Marcus, editors, *Writing Culture* (1986); George Marcus and Michael Fischer, *Anthropology as Cultural Critique* (1986); James Clifford, *The Predicament of Culture* (1988). (See also Tim Ingold (2000; e.g. chapter 4) on anthropological constructions of 'nature' and 'culture'.)

Perhaps in *IRS* I should have expanded the discussion of culture and the problems of representation. If I had done, I think the more radically sceptical project of extended critique would have asserted itself with greater consistency. Anthropology would have appeared less the solution and more part of the problem. I would have become more clearly sceptical of the idea, the purpose and the possibility of ethnographic representation. The critical reflections by a minority of anthropologists, albeit highly influential, on their own disciplinary origins, practices and institutions was also an attempt to reformulate anthropology. In addition to their moral ideals of justice and fairness, which I take seriously, they wanted to save their jobs and departments much as we wanted to save ours – which is reasonable. Having considered the matter more over the years since *IRS* was published, I now think that anthropology as a clear and distinct idea or practice that can be classified as an objective 'science' is deeply problematic, along with religious studies. What we can do is a form of hermeneutics, provided that there is some co-productivity in the hermeneutical practice.

In a fairly recent publication Richard Handler cites Dell Hymes's edited volume *Reinventing Anthropology* (1972), a collection that already included these themes:

> Deemphasizing the study of exotic 'others' at the periphery, anthropology should focus more on disempowered social categories of the center. Augmenting the traditional orientation downward toward the powerless, it would also 'study up' toward the groups that wielded power ... Ideologically, it would move beyond the liberal posture of relativistic tolerance toward one of radical engagement in the struggles of the powerless against the holders of power. Methodologically and epistemologically, it would reject

the positivistic assumption that cultures or cultural behavior could be observed as 'objects' in the external world and, instead, would recognize the essential reflexivity of participant observation and the inherently problematic character of the knowledge generated by the ethnographic process. (Hymes 1972: 321; quoted in Handler 2015: 53–4)

There is much in this perspective of productive self-critique that I might have drawn into my argument in *IRS*. Critical anthropologists are deeply uncomfortable with the colonial origins of anthropology, and the sometime collusion between anthropologists, colonial administrators and powerful private property interests. Furthermore, colonial others are not only those who have been the victims of colonial power 'out there' on what has been imagined as the periphery, but should include 'disempowered social categories of the center'. This is tacitly an acknowledgement that the same forces – or classes – that were colonizing the globe in 'other cultures' were at the same time colonizing the powerless in the metropolitan centres. An example that illustrates this point for me: the enclosure movements in Europe since the sixteenth century should not be viewed as different and unrelated to the theft of land and the colonial reorganization of peoples and their institutions in America, Asia and Africa. What Marx called 'primitive accumulation' or 'accumulation by dispossession' is an inherent part of liberal capitalism, at home and abroad.

Handler's summary of the spirit behind 'writing culture' suggests speaking truth to power. Instead of 'the liberal posture of relativistic tolerance', anthropologists should engage radically in transforming the world. I deeply appreciate these sentiments, and they reflect the spirit with which I wrote *IRS*. I now fear this radicalism is insufficient. How can a highly paid professor of anthropology or religion with secure employment in a prestigious liberal secular university and with access to research funds generated by a liberal capitalist regime of power genuinely engage 'in the struggles of the powerless against the holders of power'?

The 'crisis of representation' to which he refers goes deeper than even he realizes. Handler rightly critiques the reification of 'cultures' as though they were 'objects in the external world'. This implies a critique of empiricist and positive illusions of objective representation, as though the anthropologist who writes the ethnography is merely an objective observer and is not indirectly implicated in the conditions of exploitation that he or she claims to be reporting on. Where then is the critique of 'religion', the excluded term that makes the non-religious secular a possible idea in the first place?

I am unclear that the critical anthropologists go far enough. I think there is more to 'the inherently problematic character of the knowledge generated by the ethnographic process' than even this critical wing of anthropology can acknowledge. For one thing, he is not arguing that anthropology is inherently implicated in imperial reproduction simply by being a flourishing part of secular university education.

The wider legitimations for secular education have always included the idea that secularity is objective, neutral and free from a 'faith perspective', or free from the bias of 'religious indoctrination'. This distinction between the subjective faith bias of religion and the objective knowledge production of secular reason operates to protect and fund anthropology. The anthropologists who write these generous sentiments towards the down-trodden are sometimes people with big salaries and secure jobs guaranteed by funds that come either from the tax payer or from some private corporate source.

This situation is shared by religious studies as an institutionalized, secular practice. The origins and commitments of social science disciplines, their sources of funding, their 'non-religious' status, imply deep entanglement with the liberal colonial and neo-colonial establishment. But how far can we really claim to be radically supportive of the people who are globally exploited by the processes of accumulation by dispossession when we ourselves are still 'owned' by wealthy, secular, Euro-American universities? And if 'factual representation', 'field work' and ethnographic writing are so problematic, as indeed they are, then what possible meaning and purpose can 'cultural anthropology' continue to claim?

There is another point of contact with 'writing culture' that makes more sense to me in relation to the extended critique that I now advocate. It is one thing for me to advocate transforming 'religion' into 'culture' or religious studies into cultural studies. However, when we come to realize that religion, culture, society, politics, nation, liberty, progress and many other general categories form a self-sustaining system of ideological classification, then their status as objective descriptors is highly problematic. If my argument – that discourses on religion are inseparable from the construction of a totalizing liberal and neoliberal paradigm – is correct, then the question 'what shall we put in their place?' can be seen as an opportunity rather than a threat. We need to find a new language that frees us from the burden of abstractions that construct the 'modern', like 'religion' or 'politics' or 'economics' – which are themselves transcendental or metaphysical operators – and that grounds us more in community and collective consciousness. We need a new form of expression.

Stephen Tyler indicates a shift from factual representation to poetry:

> a post-modern ethnography is a cooperatively evolved text consisting of fragments of discourse intended to evoke in the minds of both reader and writer an emergent fantasy of a possible world of commonsense reality, and thus provoke an aesthetic integration that will have a therapeutic

effect. It is, in a word, poetry – not in its textual form, but in its return to the original context and function of poetry, which by means of its performative break with everyday speech, evoked memories of the ethos of community and thereby provoked hearers to act ethically. (Tyler 1986: 125–6, quoted also in Marcus 2015)

The idea of ethnography that is more like 'poetry' productively confuses one's presuppositions. Note that Tyler and Marcus mean 'poetry' in the sense of a mode of democratic communication that valorizes aesthetics, ethics, community, therapy (perhaps they mean healing through processes of negotiation), and a performative break with everyday speech. The term 'poetry' might act as a place-holder for the project of developing a language and style of exposition that grounds us more in a shared egalitarian, anti-colonial ethos, instead of objectifying and essentializing 'knowledge of other cultures' in categories that normalize capitalism and maintain the dominant system of unequal power.

Now, when I read through chapters eleven and twelve of *IRS*, I can see in hindsight that I did not do it right. Perhaps there is no right way. On the one hand we need to represent ourselves and others, and yet at the same time it is not clear that anything objective is being represented. There may be an analogy here with the relation between map and territory. We need maps as abstract representations of a territory in order to find our way through it. We need the map to know what the territory is, and where its boundaries are situated. There is no ready-made territory waiting to be mapped. In a sense the map constructs what we take to be the territory being represented. Different maps describe different territories. One might say that 'map *is* territory'.

Religion and its non-religious opposite does not map onto the Japanese or Indian realities. Rather I ought to say: 'does not map onto Japanese or Indian maps.' Their maps, like ours, are generally produced by the dominant male elites. Ours is a colonial map drawn up by colonial officers. The latter is intended to take the place of the former, and the indigenous population are instructed how to use it. A constitution is perhaps a kind of map. It imposes a cognitive map and thus reconfigures what counts as 'reality' and what counts as the superstitious past of religious myth. But what are the Japanese or Indian realities, and who can claim to know them or represent them? Whose reality? We get caught up in circularity, and we find that there is no prior ground to be represented.

I wanted to show why the discourse on religion, religions and world religions, while appearing to give us a useful and objective descriptive and analytical tool, imposed a conceptual grid on colonized sites that reorganized the indigenous customary practices along a fictional axis of progress and development. The religious studies discourses operated within a wider matrix of representations that constructed religions as voluntary and private faith that had nothing to do with non-religious secular government, politics, the state or the realities of material nature disclosed by science. Yet many characteristics of the indigenous practices, institutions and values resisted this binary separation. The Europhone binaries that supported the separation of religion from non-religion, such as natural and supernatural, faith and knowledge, private and public, irrational and rational, metaphysical and empirical, spirit and matter, fiction and fact, are each as problematic as all the others in the series, and merely displace the definitional problem from one indefinable pair to another.

It is not only Religious Studies that is the problem, but for me it was an obvious place to start. I came to admit too late that anthropologists are generally as reluctant as everyone else to interrogate the cognitive hegemony implicit in deploying their key categories as though they are good for universal representation. I now have a more sceptical view of the very idea of 'representation', and I speculate that we are *driven* to think by the internalized, normalized, rhetorical operations of the dominant configuration of categories *rather than choosing* to think thus. This has led me to consider general categories as being empty signs operating in an automatic signalling system. They operate us more than we operate them. But at the time of writing *IRS* I was not fully conscious of this.

I have spent the last twenty years attempting to iron out the faults and take forward the logic of the critique of religion, and applying it equally to these other categories. This helps to explain why I became less and less interested in constructing representations, and more and more interested in critically deconstructing them. We could call this critical hermeneutics. This has meant studying their range of deployments and tracking down their historical origins. This meant returning from Japan to the UK, figuratively and literally, and researching the colonial history of my own country so that I could see both ends of the colonial relationship. But this was not the situation at the time of *IRS*, when I was both critically deconstructing religion and related categories while also trying to get at a valid level and method of representation.

Conclusion

Despite these contradictions I do not think that my attempts to save these other categories and construct a legitimate ethnographic groundwork for reporting on India and Japan was a waste of time. The rather tortuous attempts to put religion in the melting pot but to save these other terms from the same fate had the effect of destabilizing these others as well. I anticipated arguments that could be used against me. In order to defeat them I anticipated counter-arguments along the lines 'if religion can be critiqued and rendered inoperable, then why not culture, politics, nation or society?' I now believe that the more important practice is the critical historicization of a wider range of categories that construct our knowledge, our subjectivities and our careers.

So, on the one hand *IRS* has a great deal of destabilizing analysis not only of religion as a category but also of politics, culture, society, etc. This is I think the valuable part of *IRS*. It stirred up assumptions and presuppositions and made people think more critically of the way categories operate, the problems of defining them, and their discursive function in the normalization of secular reason. On the other hand, I couldn't carry through with the insight that politics, society and culture are as problematic as religion. It seemed too nihilistic. How would I fulfil my role as academic informer and teacher of religious studies with a special interest in Japanese and Indian phenomena if I think that religions, societies, cultures, political domains, social structures, economic systems and nation-states are abstract fictions, reifications confused for objective reality? The logical outcome of such an idea would be that not only religious studies and its reification of religion, but also the social sciences in general, and their reifications of politics, society, nature and culture (and many other categories such as 'the economy') were all engaged in a 'built-in' system of empty signs. Not only Religious Studies but the Social Sciences also can be seen as the ritual reproduction of the order of liberal capitalism under the guise of neutral, harmless, fair-minded, objective representation. *IRS* virtually broaches such an idea but also draws back from it.

Twenty years ago, I was not seeing this with consistent clarity. I could see that 'religions' were misleading representations that reified some customary practices and beliefs through decontextualization, and marginalized others. I saw that the invention of the discourse on generic religion was also the invention of the discourse on secular reason and enlightenment progress. However, I drew back from the full implications of this in order to protect an area of study. This places me in a moral dilemma. The dilemma is choosing between expanding employment opportunities and the survival of religious studies departments on the one hand and following the logic of critique on the other. This inability to make a clear analytical distinction between two antagonistic projects at the time of writing hopefully helps to explain the different kinds of reactions to *IRS*.

References

Brightman, Robert (1995), 'Forget Culture: Replacement, Transcendence, Relexification', *Cultural Anthropology*, 10 (4): 509–46.

Clifford, James (1988), *The Predicament of Culture: Twentieth-Century Ethnography, Literature, and Art*, Cambridge, MA: Harvard University Press.

Clifford, James and George E. Marcus, eds (1986), *Writing Culture: The Poetics and Politics of Ethnography*, Berkeley: University of California Press.

Fitzgerald, Timothy (2000), *The Ideology of Religious Studies*, Oxford: Oxford University Press.

Fitzgerald, Timothy (2016), '"Postcolonial Remains": Critical Religion, Postcolonial Theory, and Deconstructing the Secular-Religious Binary', in Jyotsna G. Singh and David D. Kim (eds), *The Postcolonial World*, 169–83, Abingdon: Routledge.

Fitzgerald, Timothy (2017), 'The Ideology of Religious Studies Revisited: The Problem with Politics', in Steffen Führding (ed.), *Method and Theory in the Study of Religion: Working Papers from Hannover*, 124–52, Leiden: Brill.

Handler, Richard (2015), 'Between History and Coincidence: Writing Culture in the Annual Review of Anthropology, ca. 1982', in Orin Starn (ed.), *Writing Culture and the Life of Anthropology*, 52–71, Durham, NC: Duke University Press.

Harrison, Peter (2015), *The Territories of Science and Religion*, Chicago: University of Chicago Press.

Hymes, Dell, ed. (1972), *Reinventing Anthropology*, New York: Pantheon.

Ingold, Tim (2000), *The Perception of the Environment: Essays on Livelihood, Dwelling and Skill*, Abingdon: Routledge.

Macpherson, Crawford Brough (1962), *The Political Theory of Possessive Individualism: Hobbes to Locke*, Oxford: Clarendon.

Marcus, George E. (2015), 'The Legacies of Writing Culture and the Near Future of the Ethnographic Form: A Sketch', in Orin Starn (ed.), *Writing Culture and the Life of Anthropology*, 35–51, Durham, NC: Duke University Press.

Marcus, George E. and Michael M. J. Fischer, eds (1986), *Anthropology as Cultural Critique: An Experimental Moment in the Human Sciences*, Chicago: University of Chicago Press.

McGrane, Bernard (1989), *Beyond Anthropology: Society and the Other*, New York: Columbia University Press.

Sahlins, Marshall (1976), *Culture and Practical Reason*, Chicago: University of Chicago Press.

Tyler, Stephen A. (1986), 'Post-Modern Ethnography: From Document of the Occult to Occult Document', in James Clifford and George E. Marcus (eds), *Writing Culture: The Poetics and Politics of Ethnography*, 122–40, Berkeley: University of California Press.

Wagner, Roy (1975), *The Invention of Culture*, Chicago: Chicago University Press.

PART III

Applying critical approaches in the field

6

The projection of 'religion' upon Japan by the United States since the 1850s

Mitsutoshi Horii

Introduction

This chapter has a practical aim, which is to demonstrate how turning the category 'religion' into an object of analysis, rather than a tool of analysis, enables us to see the world in a different way. This chapter focuses on the discourse on 'religion' at the level of international diplomacy and statecraft. It examines the norms and imperatives which govern the discourse on 'religion' in US-Japan international relations. The critical examination of 'religion' is far more than mere pedantry in the abstract theoretical discourse: it aims to unveil the 'real' and lasting impacts of conceptual categories upon human lives. Our categories of understanding are not natural. They are invented by people for specific purposes. When they retreat into the background of our consciousness, they naturalize and authorize specific norms and values which these categories were made to serve in the first place. This chapter brings our categories of understanding to the forefront of our consciousness and discusses the projection of the category 'religion' onto Japan in the historical context of US-Japan relations.

Denaturalizing 'religion'

The genealogies of 'religion' have been studied by many scholars (e.g. W.C. Smith 1963; Bossy 1982; J.Z. Smith 1998; Harrison 1990; Dubuisson

2003; Fitzgerald 2007a; Nongbri 2013). Although these works are extremely important, in this section I am going to refer primarily to Timothy Fitzgerald's *Discourse on Civility and Barbarity: A Critical History of Religion and Related Categories* (2007a) for the sake of the argument that follows. In this book, Fitzgerald examines the historical development of the term 'religion' in the Anglo-American context, with considerable references to North American constitutionalism from the late seventeenth century. This is particularly relevant to this chapter because it was the Americans who first brought the idea of religion to Japan in the mid-nineteenth century and later redefined it in 1945.

Fitzgerald (2007a) highlights the following four points, which are particularly important for the analysis of the United States projection of 'religion' upon Japan. First, during the time of the European Enlightenment and Protestant Reformation, the term 'religion', at least in England and other Protestant areas, meant Protestant Truth in the sense of Christian civility. This was conceptualized against the idea of pagan barbarity and was also used against Catholics. It denoted the ideological totality of Christian confessional church states. Fitzgerald (2007b) calls this old idea of religion 'encompassing religion'. Second, during the era of European colonialism from the sixteenth to the nineteenth century, indigenous people in colonized lands were often believed by colonizers to be people without 'religion' in the sense of Christian civility. This sense of 'religion' can be found in both Protestant and Catholic usages of the term. For example, Jonathan Z. Smith (1998: 179) refers to an example from *A Treatyse of the Newe India*, Richard Eden's 1553 English translation of part of Sebastian Müenster's 1544 *Cosmographia*. The quotation goes: 'At Columbus first coming thether, the inhabitants went naked, without shame, religion or knowledge of God.' Smith also refers to Pedro Cieza de León's 1553 *Crónica del Perú*, in which the north Andean indigenous people were described as 'observing no religion at all, as we understand it'. Müenster was a Lutheran and de León was a Catholic. In both cases, the apparent absence of 'religion' was believed to be the sign of the barbarity of natives. In the sixteenth-century context, this made European colonizers think that indigenous people were not full human beings. There were some contexts, however, where the term 'religion' was applied to categorize various beliefs and practices that colonial explorers encountered all over the world. Nevertheless, this kind of use was ironic, because it still implied that the true religion was Christianity, while other 'religions' were in fact all fallen ones, which were simultaneously termed 'paganism' and 'idolatry'.

Third, this old semantics of religion was dramatically transformed in the late seventeenth century by North American constitutionalism, where the idea of religion became conceptualized as 'private' belief located in the inner realm of individuals. This idea of 'religion' contrasted with the ideas of 'politics', 'political society', 'civil government' and the like, which were imagined to be 'non-religious' 'public' space. Fitzgerald (2007a) identifies a number of writers who influenced American Constitutionalism. John Locke, William Penn and Benjamin Hoadly were among the most influential. Among them, the most influential writer is John Locke. According to Fitzgerald (2007a: 22): 'Locke's purpose seems to be to subvert the dominant and orthodox understanding of civil government as a relatively distinct branch of God's providence within the overall encompassment of Christian Truth, and to persuade his readers to imagine it as different in kind, that is, as essentially different, as a different ontology'. The Lockean religion-politics separation 'fit the interests of a growing number of Dissenting and nonconformist men and women who conceived of their salvation in new Calvinistic ways, many of them escaped to America, and whose prosperity depended on success in colonial trade and the need for cheap labour and markets' (Fitzgerald 2007a: 37). It authorized American colonists' desire for independence from Anglo-European church states. This new orthodoxy demanded rights to own land and to endlessly accumulate private property. It promoted the myth of self-maximizing individuals and self-regulating markets. Authorizing this new orthodoxy required the creation of a new government and constitutions. Historically, the Lockean myth of private property justified the dispossession of the Native American in North America and various kinds of colonial land policies in other parts of the world.

Fourth, from the late seventeenth century up to the late eighteenth century, the Lockean religion-politics distinction was still a marginal discourse. As the Unites States became a hegemonic power by the nineteenth century, however, this new conceptualization was exported back to Anglo-European colonial powers. Since then, the Lockean religion-politics binary has been utilized in the context of Western European and Anglo-American (thereafter, Euro-American) imperialism, so as to authorize and naturalize values and norms of modern nation-states. One of the countries to which the Lockean separation of religion and politics was exported was Japan. Euro-American nation-states give constitutional rights to whatever beliefs and practices they formally recognized as 'religious'. Once individuals or institutions are identified as 'religious', they are free to practice their own 'religion' as long as it does not violate law and order. This in turn means that whatever is classified as 'religion' is not allowed to take part in the operation of the liberal democratic government. In other words, 'religion' is a category of governance (Stack, Goldenberg and Fitzgerald 2015).

Historically, it was in the process where the state (in the form of parliament) gradually separated from the church that the term 'religion' became associated exclusively with the church, rather than the state (Cavanaugh 1995). In the wider European context, including the Church of England, the invention of the term 'religion', as separate from the state, appeared in the sixteenth and seventeenth centuries when the dominance of the state over the church was established (Fitzgerald 2007a; Cavanaugh 2009: 57–122; Nongbri 2013). Whereas the US Constitution in effect proclaims the dominance of the state over the church by making 'religion' a special case, in England it was a gradual struggle as the church-state (the confessional state) slowly became the state-church. The term 'religion' currently attached to the Church of England, for example, is the product of a past power struggle with the emerging modern nation-state.

More recently, the modern liberal democratic states came to identify themselves as 'secular' and use the category 'religion' to cordon off specific beliefs and practices. By calling rival value orientations 'religion', the states prevent them from entering the power structure, keeping them at the margins of society. The religion-secular binary is used to clear the space for the state's orthodoxy. Imagining the non-rational illusion of private 'religious' belief authorizes and naturalizes the state's orthodoxy as its binary opposite 'the secular', which is represented as the 'public' realm of natural reason and objective facts.

Jonathan Z. Smith famously claimed that 'religion is not a native category'. He went on to say: 'It is not a first-person term of self-characterization. It is a category imposed from the outside on some aspect of native culture' (Smith 1998: 179). Smith is correct that 'religion' is *not* a native category in the sense that it was imposed by European colonizers upon the non-European parts of the world where the concept of religion did not exist. In the same critical spirit, however, it is possible to argue that 'religion' *is* a native category of Western Europe in the sense that it 'is a Western folk category that contemporary Western scholars have appropriated' (Saler 2000: ix). It is a concept historically developed within cosmologies and ways of life particular to Western Europe.

The issue that is problematized in the following paragraphs is the ways in which this particularity of 'religion' has been universalized. The indigenous conceptual map of Western Europeans, which was transformed from an all-encompassing category to a binary category, has been utilized to navigate different parts of the world since the fifteenth century. It does not correspond with other indigenous conceptual maps in the world outside Western Europe and its settler colonists' communities. When Euro-American powers colonized and subjugated many parts of the world, the Western European conceptual map was transformed into a universal standard. Ruling elites in other parts of the world were not only threatened by Euro-American powers, but also aspired to westernization and modernization. The cosmology of the powerful was taken as the universal truth. In the case of Japan, by the late nineteenth century, the cosmology of Euro-American empires was taken as the universal truth by the ruling elite. Non-Euro-American ruling elites and intellectuals all over the world rewrote their own conceptual map according to the Euro-

American demarcations. In this process of redrawing conceptual boundaries, 'religion' became regarded as one of the ostensibly universal categories.

American projection of 'religion' upon Japan in the mid-nineteenth century

The interaction between Euro-American nation-states and Japan was extremely limited throughout history up to the mid-nineteenth century. Japan traded with Portugal and Spain in the sixteenth century. However, the Japanese territorial authority closed its border in the seventeenth century. From then until the mid-nineteenth century, it had traded only with the Dutch and the Chinese specifically at the designated port of Dejima in the eastern edge of the country. A radical transformation was triggered in 1853 by the arrival of the US expedition commanded by Commodore Matthew Calbraith Perry (1794–1858). This is also known as the Perry Expedition. Japan was forced to open some of its ports to the United States and subsequently to other imperial powers.

This section examines the projection of 'religion' on Japan by the United States in the mid-nineteenth century. The term 'religion' was used in relation to Japan in three related but different senses. First, it still carried the older all-encompassing idea of Christian Truth, as opposed to 'pagan barbarity'. Second, when multiple 'religions' in Japan were imagined, they were assumed to be inferior to Christianity. Third, the term 'religion' was also conceptualized in the Lockean sense of private belief as opposed to the non-religious, civil government. The United States (mis)recognized the religion-state separation in the Japanese ruling structure, but assumed it to be an inferior kind compared with the one in the United States. In the same breath, the United States employed the idea of freedom of religion to demand the decriminalization of Christianity in Japan.

Encompassing religion

The US Expedition to Japan and the wider mid-nineteenth-century US public shared the encompassing idea of religion as Christian civility in their discourses on Japan. For the US government, the objective of the Perry Expedition was to establish commercial relations with Japan. In this context, 'Commerce and civilization were commonly believed to progress hand in hand' (Neumann 1954: 248). At that time both 'commerce' and 'civilization' were closely associated with 'religion' in the sense of Christian (Protestant) Truth: 'One of the most frequently made claims for the expected results of Perry's mission was a religious one, an association befitting an age in which commerce was described as the "handmaiden of the gospel"' (Neumann 1954: 251). In this light, Protestantism was symbolically inseparable from the civility of the Unites States, as contrasted with 'barbarous' Catholics and pagans. In the mid-nineteenth-century public discourse, it was assumed that 'the civilization of Japan lacks all the elements which it would have derived from religion' (*The North American Review* 1856: 241). In this sentence, Japan was believed to be ignorant to the civilizing power of Protestant Truth. Even when Japan was believed to have 'religion', it was regarded as 'the grossest paganism' (*De Bow's Southern and Eastern Review* 1852: 555), whose darkness was to be eradicated by the true religion of Protestantism. The opening of Japan to commerce was believed to be the first step in this mission.

The chief translator of the Perry Expedition, Samuel Wells Williams, wrote to his brother (dated 16 July 1853) that the United States' demands for the shogunate, which were stated as 'good treatment for all Americans visiting or wrecked on the shores of Japan, a port at which to get coal for our steamers and provisions for the vessels coming after coal', were only the 'ostensible reasons' for the US government to have sent its powerful squadron all the way to Japan (F.W. Williams 1889: 197). He believed that 'the real reasons are glorification of the Yankee nation, and food for praising ourselves' (197).

Importantly, these statements in Williams's letter to his brother were followed by attestations of his belief in the God-given national mission of the United States. Williams continued: 'Behind them and through them lie God's purposes of making known the Gospel to all nations, and bringing its messages and responsibility to this people, which has had only a sad travesty of the truth as it is in Christ Jesus' (F.W. Williams 1889: 197). He shared with his contemporaries the belief that the so-called 'seclusion policy' of Japan was 'not according to God's plan of mercy to these peoples' (197). It was assumed that the US government was on a divine mission to liberate the Japanese people from such an 'unnatural' state of being. He declared that Japan 'must acknowledge the only living and true God, and their walls of seclusion must be removed by us, perhaps, whose towns on the Western Pacific now begin to send their ships out to the opposite shores' (197).

Prior to this letter, in his diary entry on 4 July 1853, Williams had already expressed the same conviction: 'I am sure that the Japanese policy of seclusion is not in accordance with God's plan of bringing the nations of the earth to acknowledge of His truth, and, until it is broken up, His purposes of mercy will be impeded – for His plan is made known to us, and we have no knowledge of any other' (F.W. Williams 1889: 192–3).

Then, in the same entry, he professed his grief that the Japanese were idolaters and that their first historical encounter with Christianity had occurred through the medium of Roman Catholicism. He believed that only the civilizing power of the true religion, the Protestant Truth, could save the Japanese nation from its 'ignorance and seclusion' (F.W. Williams 1889: 193). For him this was 'the law of God' (193).

Williams was not alone in expressing this belief in the Christian civilizing mission. Many of his contemporaries shared the same sense of America's divine mission to open up Japan to Christianity. These included Townsend Harris, who arrived in Japan in 1856 as the first US consul to Japan. While Harris was staying in Edo (present-day Tokyo), he conducted his own Christian services with the assistance of his Dutch-American interpreter Henry Heusken. This rather solitary Christian practice had, for Harris, a significant meaning in terms of his belief in the divine role of American civilization. In his diary entry on 6 December 1857, Harris noted in his personal journal: 'Assisted by Mr. Heusken I read the full service in an audible voice, and with the paper doors of the houses here our voices could be heard in every part of the building' (Cosenza 1930: 465). He was excited that this was 'the first time that the English version of the Bible was ever read, or the American Protestant Episcopal Service ever repeated in this city' (465). Reflecting the historical fact that Christians in Japan had been punished severely, he professed that the Christian service he had just performed was the 'first blow' which was 'struck against the cruel persecution of Christianity by the Japanese' (466). The American projection of 'religion' onto Japan in the mid-nineteenth century was an integral part of America's Christian imperialism, powered by its self-belief in its divine mission in the world. The opening up of Japan was believed to be in accordance with God's plan. Harris stated in the same diary entry: 'I shall be both proud and happy if I can be the humble means of once more opening Japan to the blessed rule of Christianity' (467–8).

Plural 'religions' in Japan

The official report of the Perry Expedition (compiled by Francis L. Hawks, [1856] 2005) contains a section on 'Religion' in Japan in its Introduction. The report describes 'religion' and 'religions' in Japan, in both singular and plural forms. It agrees that there were at least three 'religions' in Japan: Shinto, Buddhism and Confucianism. The report also adds that Catholicism was brought to Japan by the Portuguese but was driven from Japan a long time ago (Hawks [1856] 2005: 33). The idea of 'religions' in the plural form indicates the belief that these multiple 'religions' share the same essence which is conceptualized as 'religion' in the singular form, as the title of this section suggests. However, what is also implicit in this taxonomy of Japanese 'religions' is the assumption that these 'religions' are all fallen ones. The report tacitly assumes that the true religion is Protestantism, while other 'religions' are regarded essentially as 'superstitions'. This is reminiscent of the older meaning of 'encompassing religion' discussed above.

The idea of multiple 'religions' appeared on the European conceptual horizon in the seventeenth century (Josephson 2012: 12), and was entangled with a hierarchical idea of nations and civilizations in which Europe and America were placed on the top. According to Tomoko Masuzawa (2005: 47):

> This older system divided the nations of the world into four categories rather unequal in size, value, and stature. There are Christians, Jews, Mohammedans, and the rest. This last, the rest, were variously termed pagans, heathens, idolaters, or occasionally, polytheists – terms that could be used more or less interchangeably.

In this discourse, Japan belonged to 'the rest'. Thus, Japan was imagined as an uncivilized land of 'pagans', 'heathens' or 'idolaters'. When one said something about 'religions' in Japan, it would have been a polite way of meaning 'idolatry' and 'paganism'. The narrative on Japanese 'religions' in the official report of the Perry Expedition, for example, echoes this taxonomy of nations and civilizations. It uses the term 'religions' in the Japanese context to denote what were generally regarded as 'idolatry' or 'paganism'. The narrative of the multiple religions in Japan from the report is grounded in the hierarchical taxonomy of nations and civilizations, on top of which Protestant Christendom stands.

Lockean 'religion'

The official report of the Perry Expedition also projected the newer Lockean idea of 'religion' upon the Japanese ruling structure. The report projects the idea of polity – which includes the notions of 'government', 'civil polity' and 'politics' – upon Japan as a separate entity from 'religion' (Hawks [1856] 2005: 22–33).

As discussed above, the report's idea of multiple 'religions' in Japan consists of Buddhism, Shinto and Confucianism. The origin of grouping Buddhism, Shinto and Confucianism into one category can be traced back to the Sino-Japanese concept of 'three teachings' (Chinese *sanjiao*; Japanese, *sankyō*) (Josephson 2012: 15). In China, the idea of three teachings was originally formulated in the Tang Dynasty (618–907) to denote Buddhism, Confucianism and Daoism. When the idea of three teachings was imported to Japan, it was transformed into a reference to Japanese Buddhism, Confucianism and later Shinto. This was then translated by European writers as 'three religions'. When the concept 'teaching' was translated as 'religion', it was assumed that 'three teachings' should be distinguished from the idea of polity.

The Sino-Japanese idea of 'teachings', however, is radically different from 'religions'. Interestingly, the chief translator of the Perry Expedition, Williams, can tell us about the meaning of 'teaching(s)' in Chinese in the mid-nineteenth century. Williams was an expert in Sinology, and his publications indicate that the mid-nineteenth century Chinese notion of teaching(s) (*kiáu* 教) had a much broader meaning than the Lockean concept of religion as private faith. The definition of *kiáu* in Williams's 1856 dictionary is: 'To instruct, to teach, to show how; to command, to order; precept, principle, rule; doctrines, tenets; a religious sect, a school, or those who hold to the same opinions' (S.W. Williams 1856: 144). It also denotes a kind of hierarchical harmony between the old and the young, and between ruler and subjects (S.W. Williams 1874: 372).

In the Japanese language, the same ideograph is read *kyō*. It is also pronounced *oshie*. As *kiáu* does in Chinese, the Japanese notion of *kyō*/*oshie* refers to the generalized idea of teaching or teachings. However, *kyō*/*oshie* seems to have moved away from the strong hierarchical connotation which is apparent in its Chinese meaning. According to Josephson (2012: 7): '*oshie* was used in a broader sense to cover not only pedagogy but also systematic knowledge in general.' Therefore, *kyō*/*oshie*, which was represented in the forms of Buddhism, Shinto and Confucianism, meant for the Japanese a kind of systematic knowledge constituting the basis for public morality and the outward form of state ritual (Josephson 2012: 161). In this sense, it was likely that such things as the constitutional systems and state ceremonies in Europe and America would have been categorized as *kyō*/*oshie* by the Japanese (161). In this light, the distinction between 'three teachings' and polity, which the report of the Perry Expedition made, does not appear to have existed in the mid-nineteenth century Japanese order of things.

In the section on the Japanese 'polity', the report describes 'two Emperors' in Japan: 'the one secular, the other ecclesiastical' (Hawks [1856] 2005: 22). The report called the former 'the *Mikado*' (the Emperor), and the latter 'the *Ziogoon*' (the Shogun) (23–30). It claimed that the *Mikado* had 'not a particle of political power' and was 'politically insignificant' (25) whereas the *Ziogoon* was 'the ruling head' (26) and associated with 'political power' (25). Here the report projected the Lockean politics-religion distinction upon the Japanese ruling structure, drawing from the US constitutional principle of the separation between the state and the church. The *Mikado* was classified as the 'spiritual' (23–4) (thus, by implication, 'religious') authority, while the *Ziogoon* was believed to be the 'secular' (23–4) and 'political' authority. The *Ziogoon*'s government was regarded as a Japanese equivalent of civil government. Thus, the US authority regarded the *Ziogoon* as the legitimate ruling authority with which the US government should negotiate.

Here the projection of the religious-political distinction prevents observers from seeing structural dynamics between the Shogun and the Emperor in the mid-nineteenth century. When the US squadron arrived in Tokyo bay on 8 July 1853, the shogunate was ruled by Tokugawa Shogun, Ieyoshi. However, he died on 23 July while the shogunate was dealing with Perry. Ieyoshi's successor was Iesada, who signed the first treaty with the United States in 1854. Importantly, the shogunate drew legitimacy from the imperial house. At the time of Perry's arrival, the imperial house was headed by the Emperor Komei. The Shogun is a military appointment confirmed by the emperor; 'the shogunate was commonly seen as the subject of imperial authority' (Ravina 1999: 25).

When the shogunate was negotiating with Perry over the treaty, the shogunate was troubled by the imperial authority. In the face of the Euro-American military might, the shogunate decided to open some of Japan's ports to foreigners to avoid any military conflicts. However, the Emperor Komei was adamant about maintaining the closure of Japan from the Euro-American powers. The shogunate managed to obtain agreement from the Emperor on the condition that it would be only a temporary opening for a few years before resuming the closure of the ports (Fujita 2013: 211–12). In spite of these disagreements, however, both the shogunate and the emperor maintained their unity (Fujita 2013: 214–49). They remained functionally interdependent.

One of the main functions of the Emperor was to give prayer to deities, as well as ordering major shrines and temples to conduct rituals. This could be conceptualized as 'religious' in the modern sense of the term. However, this is an integral part of Japanese polity. The ruling order of Japan was often called *matsurigoto* (政 or 政事). The guiding principle of this governing order was the service to the upper chains of command in the ruling hierarchy (Maruyama 1988). It was also characterized by the complex system of ritual performance of submissions, which maintained the peace of the hierarchical order (Roberts 2012). Service was directed from the subordinated upwards, to lords, the Shogun and the Emperor. Importantly, it did not end with the Emperor as he was also expected to serve the power above him. That was the deities. Thus the Emperor's prayer was an integral part of the polity.

The shogunate's ruling structure, and its relation to the Emperor, cannot be conceptualized in terms of the religion-politics binary. Nevertheless, US observers saw the Japanese polity through a lens coloured with the religion-politics distinction and they (mis)recognized 'religion' and 'politics' in the Japanese polity. This projection of the religion-politics binary upon Tokugawa Japan, however, did not result in the recognition of Japan as a 'civilized' nation. In Perry's report, Tokugawa Japan was classified as a 'kingdom', and its polity was regarded as 'feudalism, or something very similar to it' (Hawks [1856] 2005: 16). Hinting at Japan's apparent backwardness, it claimed that the Perry Expedition could contribute to Japan's 'progress', which had thus far been 'rendered impossible' (21). The report further stated: 'We may venture to hope, even in the partial communication with strangers allowed to the Japanese by the late treaty with our country, the first step has been taken in breaking down their long prevalent system of unalterable laws and unchangeable customs' (21).

The Meiji Restoration and the invention of 'religion' in Japan

The arrival of the US Navy squadron caused panic among the Japanese ruling class. The display of the US's military might in the form of steam gunships was threatening enough for the Tokugawa shogunate to open its ports. In the following years, Japan signed the so-called 'unequal' treaties with the United States, the UK, the Netherlands, France and Russia. On the other hand, the Emperor Komei's anti-foreigner position encouraged those forces that were against the opening of Japan to grow and became radicalized. They also evolved into anti-shogunate forces. However, the Emperor's determination to maintain the historical unity with the shogunate protected the latter from vicious attacks. The situation radically changed when the Emperor Komei died in 1867, and the fourteen-year-old Emperor Meiji was enthroned. Anti-shogunate forces gained momentum in the absence of an authoritative emperor who could defend the shogunate's legitimacy. The Shogun 'returned' the right to rule to the Emperor Meiji, partly to avoid a full-scale civil war. Then, in 1868, the anti-shogunate forces established a new Meiji government, by 'restoring' the Emperor as the sovereign of Japan. This event is now called the Meiji Restoration.

Throughout this transitional period, Japanese officials and intellectuals were urged to study Euro-American knowledge. All parties involved in this process, both pro-shogunate and anti-shogunate camps, appeared to have agreed on the supremacy of 'the West' and the importance of learning Western knowledge and technologies (Ravina 2017; Auslin 2004). Under the Tokugawa rule, scholars were ordered to study international law, diplomatic protocol and the professional work of interpreting. The subsequent Meiji government, which inherited 'Western learning' from the Tokugawa shogunate, transformed Japan into a constitutional centralized nation-state, powered with modern industrial capitalism (Ravina 2017; Vries 2020). This programme of westernization was called 'enlightened civilization' (*bunmeikaika* 文明開化) (Howland 2002).

Meiji leaders sought to build a nation-state by emulating 'what they understood as Western best practice' (Ravina 2017: 7). They were also looking for a new orthodoxy which authorized and naturalized the centralized nation-state system and industrial capitalism. The Tokugawa system of ideological formations was now redundant, but the new domain of territorial control had to be filled with a new orthodoxy to give legitimacy to Meiji statecraft. For this purpose, the government decided to employ symbolism and rituals from Shinto tradition to authorize the new nation-state of Japan.

It was during the early Meiji period (1868–1912) when the 'historical consciousness' of an indigenous entity called Shinto clearly took shape, as if it had existed in Japan since ancient times (Kuroda 1981: 19). In pre-Restoration Japan, what constituted the customs and beliefs of the Japanese people 'was the kenmitsu Buddhist system including its components, such as Shinto and the Yin-yang tradition, and its various branches, both reformist and heretical' (20). This was a 'comprehensive, unified and self-defined system' in Japan in pre-modern times (20). It was from the kenmitsu system that Shinto was extracted to be an independent entity and was represented as 'indigenous'. This process was achieved 'both in name and in fact with the rise of modern nationalism' (19) by the so-called nativist scholars in the second half of the nineteenth century, during the decline of the Tokugawa shogunate and the establishment of a centralizing, imperial government in its place. According to Thal (2002: 101): 'worship of the kami emerged from the activities of scattered scholars and priests to coalesce into a widely recognized entity called Shinto central to the political and intellectual life of the emerging nation-state'. The construction of Shinto was 'never intended to represent or codify the amorphous faith of the people seen in innumerable, localized, and highly diverse cults of kami' (Hardacre 1986: 53). Instead it 'gradually transformed local folk Shinto shrines into political instruments for inculcating emperor-centred patriotism and values of social harmony' (Garon 1997: 65) and simultaneously for 'inculcat[ing] in the people a willingness to follow the state's commands regarding taxation, conscription, and a host of other matters' (Hardacre 1986: 53).

Importantly, this reified realm of the 'Meiji constitutional regime' (Thomas 2019) was defined as separate from 'religion'. By the 1880s, the Euro-American concept of 'religion' had been translated into Japanese in a definitive way with a newly invented word *shūkyō* (Josephson 2012). It began to be utilized as a technology of governance (Maxey 2014). By separating itself from 'religion', the Meiji government represented itself as a civil government in a Lockean sense. In legal and constitutional discourse, the concept of *shūkyō* only included 'Buddhism', 'Christianity' and the so-called 'sectarian Shinto' (which had divorced from the state-authored Shinto institution). The category of 'religion' was used by the government to domesticate its possible rival powers. Maxey (2014: 3) summarizes this as follows: 'Efforts to shield the state from competition with Christianity, from Buddhist disaffection, from internecine conflict among Shinto priests . . . led to the political construction of religion as a category to be rendered distinct from the state'. They were specific institutions and value orientations which could threaten the new state orthodoxy.

First, Christianity was long feared by the Japanese rulers as a potential cause of major revolts (e.g. Paramore 2009; Ion 2009), while Euro-American powers demanded freedom to practice Christianity in Japan. In other words, the older idea of religion as Christian Truth and Protestant civility, which drove Euro-American power to Japan, was transformed into mere private belief, in the Lockean sense. In this way, Japanese authorities attempted to domesticate Christianity.

Second, Buddhist temples, as reminiscent of the Tokugawa ruling structure, were redefined as private associations which dealt with matters of belief that are located within the inner realm of individuals. This generated a sense of rivalry among Buddhist elites directed towards Christianity. There was a series of intellectual and institutional efforts to re-present Japanese Buddhism as a civilizing force, equal or superior to Christianity (e.g. Snodgrass 2003; Krämer 2015).

Finally, 'sectarian Shinto' was the category which encompassed those self-identified Shinto groups that separated from the Meiji state's Shinto institutions. It was the product of doctrinal disputes within the Shinto tradition, which could disrupt the utilization of Shinto symbolism and rituals by the state for nation building (e.g. Zhong 2016). Thus, the category of religion was utilized to contain these disputes as a matter of personal belief.

By classifying these three groups as 'religions', the Meiji government guaranteed their constitutional freedom, but importantly on the condition that they were not disrupting the public order. In other words, by classifying them as 'religion', the Meiji constitutional regime domesticated its rivals under its authority. Importantly, the category 'religion' was reserved only for these three 'religions'. Other value orientations and practices outside the 'religion' category were regarded as 'evil teaching' (*jakyō*) or 'pseudo-religion' (*giji-shūkyō*). They were likely to be classed as 'superstition' (*meishin*), which was perceived to be a threat to public order. This was because officials and intellectuals regarded these as backward beliefs and practices that went against the national drive towards 'enlightened civilization'. It must be noted that the development of this classification scheme was parallel to the expansion of Japanese colonial territories in East Asia. This typology was in fact utilized by the Japanese colonial administrators as a tactic of governance in Japanese colonies, most notably in the Korean peninsula, in the early twentieth century (see Isomae 2012: 235–63; Anderson 2017). Colonized people's beliefs and practices were classified according to this Japanese scheme so as to legitimize Japanese colonial rule. More specifically, in Japanese-occupied Korea, the Japanese colonial authority recognized as 'religion' only Christianity, Buddhism and sectarian Shinto. Thus various beliefs and customs among the local population in Korea were largely classified as 'superstitions', so as to be subject to the colonial authority's control.

Meanwhile, the idea of (state-sponsored) Shinto as non-religion was controversial from its inception. Japanese intellectuals and officials were aware that Shinto had often been regarded as a religion in the Euro-American world. It was against this Euro-American assumption that the Japanese government had to be adamant that Shinto was non-religion and Shinto shrines were non-religious national institutions. In 1912, for example, a Japanese statesman and jurist, Nobushige Hozumi (1912: xii) claimed:

> In Western countries, we see everywhere stone or bronze statues of great men, which not only serve as ornaments of towns, but are also made objects of veneration. . . . All the difference, if any, comes from this – that they erect statues and we establish shrines.

In other words, Hozumi tried to explain to a Western audience his and likeminded Japanese officials' views on Shinto shrines as national objects. In this sense, Shinto shrines in Japan before 1945 embodied striking functional commonalities with other national structures such as the Cenotaph in London or the Lincoln Memorial in Washington DC.

Post-1945 reclassifications

The Meiji regime's classification scheme of 'religion' and 'non-religion' was counterintuitive for Euro-American observers. For example, they regarded the emperor and Shinto as 'religious' in addition to Buddhism, Christianity and sectarian Shinto. This was reflected in the way the Japanese ruling order was reclassified after the Second World War under the Allied Occupation between 1945 and 1952. The emperor was allowed to be a 'secular' entity after he was stripped of his ostensible 'divinity' to redefine him as a mere human being, while 'Shinto' was classified as a 'religion'.

The brutal Pacific War ended when Japan surrendered to Allied forces in August 1945, and the Allied Occupation of Japan, predominantly led by the United States, started in September of the same year. This was followed by the reclassification of Japanese social categories – especially the categories of 'religion' and 'politics'. In this process, pre-war Japanese state orthodoxy was denounced as being contaminated by 'religion', while the realm of religion was extended considerably to include a variety of value orientations and institutions that had previously been excluded from the category.

The term 'State Shinto' played a key role in the deconstruction of the Meiji constitutional regime under the Occupation. It authorized the reclassification of the Meiji constitutional regime (which utilized Shinto symbolism and rituals) as 'religion'. For example, the 'U.S. Initial Post-Surrender Policy for Japan', issued on 6 September 1945, used the term 'State Shinto' in its assessment of the Meiji constitutional regime, so as to regard it as 'ultra-nationalistic and militaristic organizations and movements . . . [which] hide behind the cloak of religion' (National Diet Library 2003–4a). The term 'State Shinto' was also the key concept in 'The Shinto Directive', issued on 15 December 1945 (SCAP [1945] 1960). Its objective was 'to free the Japanese people from . . . a religion or cult officially designated by the state' (SCAP [1945] 1960: 85), which was 'State Shinto'. This classification had been confirmed explicitly in 'The Shinto Directive Staff Study', issued on 3 December 1945 (Woodard 1972: 322–41), which expressed the view that 'there is no doubt that State Shinto . . . is a religion' (328).

During preparations for the Shinto Directive, Daniel C. Holtom's works on Shinto were referred to most extensively (Woodard 1972: 322–44). Holtom was probably the most influential scholar of Shinto in the Anglophone world in the first half of the twentieth century. He 'connected Shinto with nationalism, imperialism, and militarism, explaining that Shinto . . . had been perverted by militarists. He credited Shinto with imbuing prewar society with chauvinistic patriotism and unswerving loyalty to the emperor' (Hardacre 1991: 135). By 1945 the term 'State Shinto' had been invented by Americans – owing to the influence of Holtom's scholarship – and it played a key role in the Occupation's deconstruction of the Meiji constitutional regime and reclassification of it as 'religion'.

Between 1868 and 1945, the Japanese state had constructed the three categories of 'non-religion', 'religion' and 'superstition'. As soon as the Allied Occupation of Japan began, 'religion' and 'superstition' were merged into a single category of religion. For the category of superstition, the faith groups which previously existed outside the formal category of religion could now be given constitutional freedom. By 1952, those groups, which would have been regarded as 'pseudo-religion' or 'heretical teaching' in pre-war Japan, were legally certified as 'religions' under the new Religious Corporation Law. Subsequently, these groups came to be known as 'new religions' in post-war Japan. As for the category of 'non-religion', it was still associated with the realm of statecraft. Shinto was siphoned out from Japanese statecraft after its reclassification as 'religion'. Then the emptied Japanese statecraft was quickly filled with the modern Euro-American belief in freedom and democracy.

Borrowing John Dower's (1999: 347) expression: 'The old shell was then refilled with Anglo-American and European democratic ideals – and more'.

In this process, the Meiji constitutional regime was portrayed as a deviation from the Lockean principle of separation of religion and politics. Japanese pre-war polity was represented as a dangerous mixture of 'religion' and 'politics', which was termed 'State Shinto'. Thus the Occupation authorities claimed that the ostensibly 'religious' element in pre-war Japanese 'politics', that is Shinto, must be removed and replaced with liberal democratic ideals. 'Democracy' was represented as the state of nature, which needed to be 'revived' in Japan. This belief had already been explicitly expressed before Japan surrendered. For example, the Potsdam Declaration, issued on 26 July 1945, had already stated: 'The Japanese Government shall remove all obstacles to the revival and strengthening of democratic tendencies among the Japanese people' (National Diet Library 2003–4b).

This realm of democracy, which was supposed to be 'revived' and strengthened in post-war Japan, was institutionalized by the proclamation of the new constitution. In the beginning of February 1946, the Supreme Commander for the Allied Powers, General MacArthur, instructed 'his staff at general headquarters to prepare a new constitution for Japan. In ten days, they produced a draft in English, and presented it to the Japanese government for adoption' (Inoue 1991: 1). This American draft was quickly approved by the parliament. According to Dower (1999: 388): 'By the time the draft constitution came before the Diet [in June 1946], the most ultra-nationalistic and reactionary politicians had already been purged . . . seats emptied by the occupation's purge had been filled by the appointment of an unusually learned and cosmopolitan group.' These more liberal-minded politicians welcomed the American discourse of democracy.

The American categorization of the Meiji constitutional regime as a 'religion' functioned to naturalize and authorize the notion that the Japanese people, including the ruling elite, were all deceived by the military leadership who had claimed that Shinto was a 'non-religion'. The American term 'State Shinto' authorized the claim that the Japanese state misused the 'religion' of Shinto. In addition, other American terms such as 'ultra-nationalism' and 'militarism' were also actively employed by politicians, intellectuals and the media under the Occupation. All these terms quickly constructed the new shared assumption that the pre-war Japanese state committed a crime by mixing 'politics' and 'religion' so as to produce 'ultra-nationalism' and 'militarism', which led the nation to utter ruin.

However, this kind of narrative may discursively conceal the root causes of the war (unequal international diplomacy, colonial power struggle, racism, etc.) by simply associating Japan's involvement in the war with the 'irrationality', 'fanaticism', 'extremism' and 'illusion' of the Japanese military. At the same time, the same discourse naturalizes the ideology of the Allied Powers (namely, 'freedom' and 'democracy') as 'secular', 'rational' and 'non-religious', as if it is in accordance with natural reason. In the same light, it also authorizes the violence committed by the Euro-American Allied Powers, by characterizing it as a 'rational' and 'calculated' 'political' decision as opposed to the 'irrational' 'religious' 'fanaticism' of Japanese state violence. This is not to justify the state violence committed by Japan. However, the state violence committed by the victor (i.e. the United States) seems to have been naturalized by these triumphant narratives, which demonize the ostensibly 'religious' 'politics' of pre-war Japan.

Conclusion

In the mid-nineteenth century, Japanese intellectuals insensibly learnt the ways of life in Europe and North America. They initially tried to understand the mid-nineteenth-century Euro-American world by utilizing mid-nineteenth-century Japanese conceptual tools. However, they soon abandoned their indigenous conceptual tools and started equipping themselves with the Euro-American ones. In the face of overwhelming military might and the material wealth of the Euro-American world, Japanese intellectuals took Euro-American conceptual tools as universal. Japanese elites believed that by using the same tools, Japan could have the same might and wealth as Euro-American powers.

'Religion' is one of these nineteenth-century Euro-American conceptual tools that was believed to be universal. It is important to keep in mind that 'religion' is not a universal category, but indigenous to Western Europe. It was the might of Euro-American empires that made Western European folk categories such as 'religion' appear as if they were naturally occurring all over the world. In the late nineteenth century, the Japanese elite started using 'religion' and they created 'religions' in Japan by putting specific institutions and traditions into this category. They learnt that this conceptual tool was useful to establish a new orthodoxy. By categorizing rival value orientations and institutions as 'religion', and defining itself as 'non-religious', the new state orthodoxy was authorized and naturalized as if it was the factual reality or order of things.

After the Second World War, however, the pre-war state orthodoxy became 'religion'. The conceptual tool of 'religion' was effectively utilized by the Allied Occupation authorities to eliminate the orthodoxy of the pre-war Japanese state. When it was regarded as a 'religion', a new orthodoxy was put in place as a 'non-religious' value orientation. This was liberal democracy.

When the might and wealth of Euro-American empires generated existential fear and irresistible aspiration all over the world, the indigenous categories of Western Europe became universalized. This historical accident, however, does not change the fact that 'religion' is an idea native to Western Europe. When the Perry Expedition projected 'religion' upon Japan, people in the United States and Japan had very little understanding of each other. As long as we see the world in terms of 'religion', we may still be wearing glasses tinted with the nineteenth-century Euro-American imperial worldview. In the twenty-first-century world, where we seem to have a much greater understanding between different modes of human lives, it may be time to take the old glasses off, and try to see what we can see. Our naked eyes may well still be tinted with something else, and they have their own limitations, but at least we can see the world differently. And hopefully we can benefit from this new perspective.

References

Anderson, Emily (2017), *Belief and Practice in Imperial Japan and Colonial Korea*, London: Palgrave Macmillan.

Auslin, Michael R. (2004), *Negotiating with Imperialism: The Unequal Treaties and the Culture of Japanese Diplomacy*, London: Harvard University Press.

Bossy, John (1982), 'Some Elementary Forms of Durkheim', *Past & Present*, 95: 3–18.

Cavanaugh, William T. (1995), '"A Fire Strong Enough to Consume the House": The Wars of Religion and the Rise of the State', *Modern Theology*, 11: 397–420.

Cavanaugh, William T. (2009), *The Myth of Religious Violence: Secular Ideology and the Roots of Modern Conflict*, Oxford: Oxford University Press.

Cosenza, Mario Emilo (1930), *The Complete Journal of Townsend Harris: First American Consul General and Minister to Japan*, New York: Japan Society.

De Bow's Southern and Eastern Review (1852), 13 (July–December): 541–63.

Dower, John W. (1999), *Embracing Defeat: Japan in the Wake of World War II*, New York: The New Press.

Dubuisson, Daniel (2003), *The Western Construction of Religion: Myth, Knowledge, and Ideology*, Baltimore: The Johns Hopkins University Press.

Fitzgerald, Timothy (2007a), *Discourse on Civility and Barbarity: A Critical History of Religion and Related Categories*, Oxford: Oxford University Press.

Fitzgerald, Timothy (2007b), 'Encompassing Religion, Privatized Religions and the Invention of Modern Politics', in T. Fitzgerald (ed.), *Religion and the Secular: Historical and Colonial Formations*, 211–40, London: Routledge.

Fujita, Satoru (2013), *Bakumatsu no Tennō*, Tokyo: Kōdansha.

Garon, Sheldon (1997), *Molding Japanese Minds: The State in Everyday Life*, Princeton: Princeton University Press.

Hardacre, Helen (1986), 'Creating State Shintō: The Great Promulgation Campaign and the New Religions', *Journal of Japanese Studies*, 12: 29–63.

Hardacre, Helen (1991), *Shinto and the State, 1868–1988*, Princeton: Princeton University Press.

Harrison, Peter (1990), *Religion and the Religions in the English Enlightenment*, Cambridge: Cambridge University Press.
Hawks, Francis L. ([1856] 2005), *Commodore Perry and the Opening of Japan*, Stroud, Gloucestershire: Nonsuch Publishing Limited.
Howland, Douglas (2002), *Translating the West: Language and Political Reason in Nineteenth-Century Japan*, Honolulu: University of Hawaii Press.
Hozumi, Nobushige (1912), *Ancestor-Worship and Japanese Law*, Tokyo: Maruzen Kabushiki-Kaisha.
Inoue, Kyoko (1991), *Macarthur's Japanese Constitution*, Chicago: University of Chicago Press.
Ion, Hamish (2009), *America Missionaries Christian Oyatoi and Japan 1859–73*, Toronto: UBC Press.
Isomae, Jun'ichi (2012), *Shūkyō gainen aruiwa shūkyōgaku no shi*, Tokyo: Tokyo Daigaku Shuppan.
Josephson, Jason (2012), *The Invention of Religion in Japan*, London: University of Chicago Press.
Krämer, Hans M. (2015), *Shimaji Mokurai and the Reconception of Religion and the Secular in Modern Japan*, Honolulu: University of Hawai'i Press.
Kuroda, Toshio (1981), 'Shinto in the History of Japanese Religion', *Journal of Japanese Studies*, 7: 1–21.
Maruyama, Masao (1988), 'The Structure of *Matsurigoto*: The Basso Ostinato of Japanese Political Life', in Sue Henny and Jean-Pierre Lehmann (eds), *Themes and Theories in Modern Japanese History*, 27–43, London: Athlone.
Masuzawa, Tomoko (2005), *The Invention of World Religions*, Chicago: University of Chicago Press.
Maxey, Trent E. (2014), *The 'Greatest Problem': Religion and State Formation in Meiji Japan*, Cambridge: Harvard University Press.
National Diet Library (2003–4a), 'U.S. Initial Post-Surrender Policy for Japan (SWNCC 150/4/A)', *Birth of the Constitution of Japan*. Available online: https://www.ndl.go.jp/constitution/e/shiryo/01/022_2/022_2tx.html (accessed 20 December 2024).
National Diet Library (2003–4b), 'Potsdam Declaration', *Birth of the Constitution of Japan*. Available online: https://www.ndl.go.jp/constitution/e/etc/c06.html (accessed 20 December 2024).
Neumann, Williams L. (1954), 'Religion, Morality, and Freedom: The Ideological Background of the Perry Expedition', *The Pacific Historical Review*, 23 (3): 247–57.
Nongbri, Brent (2013), *Before Religion: A History of a Modern Concept*, New Haven, CT: Yale University Press.
Paramore, Kiri (2009), *Ideology and Christianity in Japan*, London: Routledge.
Ravina, Mark (1999), *Land and Lordship in Early Modern Japan*, Stanford: Stanford University Press.
Ravina, Mark (2017), *To Stand with the Nations of the World: Japan's Meiji Restoration in World History*, Oxford: Oxford University Press.
Roberts, Luke (2012), *Performing the Great Peace: Political Space and Open Secrets in Tokugawa Japan*, Honolulu: University of Hawaii Press.
Saler, Benson (2000), *Conceptualizing Religion: Immanent Anthropologists, Transcendent Natives, and Unbounded Categories*, Oxford: Berghahn Books.

SCAP (Supreme Commander for the Allied Powers) ([1945] 1960), 'The Shinto Directive', *Contemporary Religions in Japan*, 1 (2): 85–9.
Smith, Jonathan Z. (1998), 'Religion, Religions, Religious', in Mark Taylor (ed.), *Critical Terms for Religious Studies*, 269–84, London: University of Chicago Press.
Smith, Wilfred Cantwell (1963), *The Meaning and End of Religion: A New Approach to the Religious Traditions of Mankind*, New York: Macmillan.
Snodgrass, Judith (2003), *Presenting Japanese Buddhism to the West: Orientalism, Occidentalism, and the Columbian Exposition*, Chicago: University of Chicago Press.
Stack, Trevor, Naomi Goldenberg and Timothy Fitzgerald, eds (2015), *Religion as a Category of Governance and Sovereignty*, Leiden: Brill.
Thal, Sarah (2002), 'A Religion That Was Not a Religion: The Creation of Modern Shinto in Nineteenth-Century Japan', in D. Peterson and D. Walhof (eds), *The Invention of Religion: Rethinking Belief and Politics in History*, 100–15, London: Rutgers University Press.
The North American Review (1856), 83 (172): 233–60. Available online: http://www.jstor.org/stable/25104748 (accessed 11 September 2020).
Thomas, Jolyon Baraka (2019), *Faking Liberties: Religious Freedom in American-occupied Japan*, Chicago: University of Chicago Press.
Vries, Peer (2020), *Averting a Great Divergence: State and Economy in Japan, 1868–1937*, London: Bloomsbury.
Williams, Frederick W. (1889), *The Life and Letters of Samuel Wells Williams, LL.D.: Missionary, Diplomatist, Sinologue*, New York: G. P. Putnam's Sons.
Williams, Samuel W. (1856), *A Tonic Dictionary of the Chinese Language in the Canton Dialect*, Canton: The Office of the Chinese Repository.
Williams, Samuel W. (1874), *A Syllabic Dictionary of the Chinese Language*, Shanghai: American Presbyterian Missionary Office.
Woodard, William P. (1972), *The Allied Occupation of Japan 1945–1952 and Japanese Religions*, Leiden: Brill.
Zhong, Yijiang (2016), *The Origin of Modern Shinto in Japan: The Vanquished Gods of Izumo*, London: Bloomsbury Academic.

7

Religionization of minorities and culturalization of Christianity

How to study boundary cases?

Teemu Taira

Introduction

In 2016 it was reported that the Dutch Chamber of Commerce granted the status of church association (*kerkgenootschap*) to the Church of the Flying Spaghetti Monster (*Kerk van het Vliegend Spaghettimonster*). The group had been trying for it for a while, but when they got the result they desired, they celebrated with a bowl of pasta. This was a small victory for Dirk Jan Dijkstra who in a previous year was denied permission to wear a colander in his passport photo. Soon after the recognition, the municipality of Emmen rejected his renewed application on the basis that the status of church association does not mean that Pastafarianism is a religion. Dijkstra sued the municipality and the Groningen court examined the issue. The court decided that Pastafarianism is a life stance but not a religion, so religious exemption is not a valid justification to wear a colander in a passport photo, although Pastafarians had succeeded in obtaining such permission from the municipalities of Leiden and The Hague.

Further south, in Italy, Finnish-born Soile Lautsi, a member of the Union of Rationalist Atheists and Agnostics, questioned whether crucifixes hanging in classrooms violate religious freedom. The Italian court rejected the case first. Then the European Court of Human Rights decided in 2009 in Lautsi's favour that crucifixes are religious symbols and should be removed from the classroom. However, two years later the Grand Chamber of the European Court of Human Rights overruled the previous verdict in favour of Italy with votes fifteen to two. The decision was based on the argument that crucifixes, though they may be considered religious, are 'passive' Christian symbols that refer to Italian history, heritage and culture (Beaman 2015: 42–5).

The first case is an example of what I call 'religionization' of minorities, and the second, 'culturalization' of Christian majorities.[1] In the first case, a group gets their voice heard by presenting themselves as a religion and demanding that religious exemptions should apply to them. In their case, the strategy was partly effective – they won the status of church association – but lost the right to wear a colander in a passport photo. In the second case, a Christian majority won their case only through a long negotiation in which a symbol that has been typically understood as a religious one – and in this case the symbol could be taken as a prototype of 'religious symbol' in general – was classified as part of culture (i.e. non-religious or sufficiently non-religious).

If there is anything that synthesizes contemporary negotiations over whether a group, symbol or practice is 'religious', it could be the processes of the 'religionization of minorities' and 'culturalization of Christian majorities'. It is appropriate to stress already at this point that there are individual exceptions to the general process, but this simply underlines that it is crucial to understand the situated, contextual and often strategic nature of classification.[2] Rather than aiming to flood evidence in favour of the suggestion or to falsify the claim, the purpose of this chapter is to offer a methodological framework for studying such processes. Therefore, this chapter provides a methodological framework and general guidelines for doing case studies on the category of religion by paying special attention to contemporary society where many actors are involved in debates where the boundaries of 'religion' are negotiated. 'Religion', like most categories, is amenable to constant historical change, however slow and moderate it may be. It is therefore relevant to consider what type of approaches are needed for studying such cases, especially in our present-day societies.

Before going into the methodological framework for studying 'boundary cases' related to 'religion', and two Finnish examples of 'religionization' and 'culturalization', this chapter first explicates why 'religion' (rather than religion) is an important object of study and how the chosen approach relates to other studies focusing on the category of religion.

What's wrong with 'religion' and what should we do about it?

One of the common complaints by scholars of religion is that there is no consensus on what religion refers to – and that there has never been one. Religion is a fluid and flexible concept whose almost infinite malleability makes it possible to talk about practically everything as religious. It is difficult to justify why one would label something as religious and something as 'secular' or 'cultural' or something else, or why one definition is better than the other. Furthermore, it is a term that is difficult to apply to languages which are not influenced by Latin. What is more, several scholars have argued that exporting the modern Western concept of religion to the rest of the world has been one of the many ways in which colonialism and imperialism – both in the concrete material sense of domination and also in a more immaterial sense of colonizing the life-world of others – has taken place.

Many students of religion are familiar with the views I have just summarized briefly. I also assume that many are familiar with the obvious reactions saying 'Aren't all concepts problematic? Why pick on religion only? But we need concepts if we wish to talk about the world!' I argue that it is our duty as scholars of religion to pay serious attention to the category of religion, not to protect it from critical scrutiny. If we do not do the critical work, no one will, because people in other fields have shown very little interest in historicizing and deconstructing 'religion'. This does not mean that only religion is a problematic concept. All concepts are problematic in some ways, but only some are used in organizing power relations and distributing privileges in society. Religion is one of them.

This project of examining discourse on religion is not essentially connected with either a realist or anti-realist standpoint, despite the tendency to think so. Some scholars have framed the issue about the category of religion being about 'realism versus anti-realism' where defenders of the analytical utility of 'religion' are considered realists or critical realists, and those critical of 'religion' are regarded as anti-realists (e.g. Schilbrack 2014, 2017). However, one can well be a realist and say that 'religion' is not part of my analytical vocabulary in a similar way that 'phlogiston' is not part of anyone's scholarly vocabulary anymore, so being critical of the analytical utility of 'religion' does not yet say anything about whether one is anti-realist in general or not. Rather than accepting such framing, I argue that the category of religion can be explored without finding it necessary to posit oneself as realist or anti-realist. One may think like Richard Rorty, who suggests that 'we must repudiate the vocabulary our opponents use' – referring to realism and anti-realism – 'and not let them impose it upon us' (Rorty 1999: xviii). Instead of asking whether or not religions exist, his question is whether 'religion' is a good term for our coping with the environment, or whether or not we might create new vocabularies (Rorty 1991: 5–6).³

Two of the main reasons why I am not too keen on using religion in my own vocabulary – at least not without caution – are that, first, it divides the world artificially and often unhelpfully into different spheres, one religious and the other non-religious, and second, that it is a term used in allocating and distributing resources in society. If we use the term, we should do so reflectively and self-consciously – this is one option. We can also choose not to use it in our own analytical vocabulary and focus on studying how other people use the category. I have used the term 'religion' in some of my publications, and if one wants to use it heuristically in specific research designs in order to solve some problems, then it can be valuable.⁴ But one should not assume that there is anything other than a heuristic role for it. Moreover, using the term itself is often needless, because one can be more specific (Goldenberg 2018). If you study rituals, beliefs or something else, be specific and say so. It is also quite easy to talk about Evangelical Christians or Sikhs or whatever you study, and avoid the word 'religion' if it does not have added analytical value for obvious comparative or other purposes.

The solution I am focusing on in this chapter is slightly different: it suggests that it is relevant to study how other people use and negotiate the category of religion. One could study how people demarcate boundaries between the categories. One could ask what people aim to achieve with their classification. What 'work' does 'religion' do? And more generally, how does society organize itself with the category of religion?

The term 'religion' is not always contrasted with the same terms. Its 'other' differs from one context to another, but in the modern world they can be divided into classes. The first consists of terms classified as the non-religious secular where the actual 'other' may be, for instance, 'politics', 'science', 'economy', 'arts', 'culture', 'heritage' or simply 'secular'. These are perhaps the most typical opposites in a modern understanding of the category of religion. This, however, has not always been the case; for instance, in pre-modern English language documents, 'religion' meant something like Christian Truth and it included both 'ecclesiastical' and 'secular', where 'secular' was commonly used in the expression 'secular priesthood', referring to priesthood outside a monastery (Fitzgerald 2007: 133, 172).

The second 'other' is something that is both non-religious and 'non-secular' at the same time, although much closer to 'religion' than 'secular' in a modern imaginary. 'Religion' can be seen as different from 'superstition', 'cult', 'magic' or 'spirituality'. In such contexts, the difference between religion and the secular is not the focus, but the hierarchical distinction within non-naturalistic systems. We have plenty of examples from colonial contexts in which 'religion' was considered part of us, or even part of the colonized locality that colonizers supported, whereas 'superstition' or 'magic' characterized either the colonized locality or a selected part of the locality (see Horii in this volume). This binary has worked in relation to social class position, too, where lower classes have 'superstition' and ruling classes have 'religion'. Or in examples where urban people are said to have 'religion' and rural folk have 'superstition'. Some so-called New Religious Movements have frequently been labelled as 'cults' – something that resembles (what we consider) religion but is not considered really a religion, at least an acceptable one. 'Religion' is also seen as different from 'spirituality' (see Owen, Sutcliffe in this volume). Again, this is not the same as a religion versus secular binary, because 'spirituality' is typically not regarded as part of a naturalistic, secular outlook. It is somewhat different from superstition and cult as well, because many self-identify themselves as 'spiritual' as in statements such as 'I am spiritual but not religious', whereas 'superstition' and 'cult' are usually designations employed by outsiders.

These binaries ought to be treated as primarily rhetorical devices, rather than analytical concepts for separating two different modes of relating to the world. These examples are potentially interesting areas of study one could examine in detail. I am focusing on the first (secular) 'other' in the remaining part of this chapter in order to highlight more specific processes of 'religionization' and 'culturalization'. Before that, the specificity of my emphasis should be located within the existing studies on the category of 'religion'.

Mapping studies on 'religion'

For many, research begins with the definition of religion, but here not defining religion is the starting point for studying 'religion'. This means that the scholar brackets the question of whether something is or is not a religion, and explores how others construct religion and for what purposes. Then one ends up studying classification and discourses related to the category of religion. One of the organizing questions is, then, how boundaries are drawn between 'religion' and something else. Then one ends up theorizing what work the category of 'religion' does in society and how it is part of power relations more generally in different societies, at different times.

Indeed, there have been plenty of studies doing exactly this, many of them focusing on the period from the seventeenth century to the early twentieth century, and particularly the nineteenth century. This scholarship has paid attention to the constructions of 'religion' in particular traditions and areas and also in the scholarly tradition itself.

There are also some developing attempts to provide an argument that might unite many of these examples, such as Naomi Goldenberg's (2015; also in this volume) idea of how those things that have been labelled as religions can be understood as vestigial states: entities that have been rivals or competitors to nation-states and may also become such in the future. While Goldenberg's idea seems to apply to some examples quite nicely, highlighting the differences between arguments is still worth the effort. For that purpose, a very simplified list of arguments should help us to navigate in this scholarly terrain. The four main arguments outlined below are ideal types. The given examples of studies have emphasized one of the ideal-typical arguments particularly well, but this does not mean that there is no overlap between the arguments or that the authors of studies mentioned necessarily defend such a position throughout their *oeuvre*. The four arguments are as follows:

1. The modern category of religion has been crucial in the constitution of modern secular nation-states. Labelling something as religion is, then, about castrating utopian ideas by classifying them as private and non-political. This argument has been put forward in Arnal and McCutcheon 2013. Similar views can be found in McCutcheon 2003 and 2005, and support for this position can be detected in Leora Batnitzky's (2011) views on how Judaism began to be conceived as a religion in eighteenth- and nineteenth-century Prussia (see Yadgar in this volume).

2. Groups and institutions labelled as religious are allowed to socialize their adherents relatively independently of the nation-state in the name of religious freedom and by portraying such work as a 'private matter', for example. This gives them a lot of ground in society, because when 'religiously' socialized people operate in a so-called secular sphere, they bring their preferences with them. This argument highlights the circulation of power through a local compromise where groups labelled religious have special roles and privileges: their role is limited by the state (as 'private matter') but they also gain something ('private matter' allowing them to keep on transmitting their preferences and values somewhat unchallenged). Craig Martin's *Masking Hegemony* (2010) is the most explicit example of this argument, using the US situation as his case.

3. The modern category of religion has been a tool for dominating colonized people and also a means by which the Western conceptual system has been exported almost globally and implemented in local cultures. Scholarship is full of variations of this idea, so it can be said

that this third argument is the most common one (e.g. Chidester 1996, 2014; Dubuisson 2003; Fitzgerald 2000, 2007; King 1999).

4. In cultural encounters between the West and the Rest, some actors in non-Western localities have also been interested in implementing the category of religion in their society because they have something to gain from it. One of the studies highlighting this is Jason Ānanda Josephson's *The Invention of Religion in Japan* (2012) which argues against an approach that neglects the agency of local actors in colonial settings.

The first two arguments take the formation and functioning of the nation-state as a focal point of their analysis, whereas the third and fourth highlight colonialist and imperialist settings. In the first and third arguments, those who are labelled as religious lose their ground vis-à-vis other social actors, whereas in the second and fourth those who are labelled as religious gain something. This is an empirical question of what really happens in particular contexts, so we should not assume in advance that one of these is generally correct and others are not. The historical constraints on the development of the category of religion may increase the likelihood of some of these, but they do not guarantee the result in every case. Furthermore, all four can be partly true at the same time, but one (or more) of these may be highlighted on the basis of a researcher's questions and interests.

What is typical for the examples mentioned above is that very few of them focus on present-day societies. Most are interested in the emergence and historical constitution of the modern discourse of religion and its functioning in different geographical settings. Many of these studies pay attention to the nineteenth century, which undoubtedly was a crucial period in the development of modern discourse of religion. The history of the category of religion, however, did not end in the nineteenth century. Discourses on religion are not stable; they change over time. Discourse 'moves, in its historical impetus, by clashes', as Roland Barthes (1977: 200) once remarked. Furthermore, knowing simply the origin of the discourse is not enough if the present formation is of our interest. As Foucault (2002: 28) noted, 'discourse must not be referred to the distant presence of its origin, but treated as and when it occurs'.

In my own work I have focused on present-day societies and negotiations about the category of religion in Europe (Taira 2022). This is not because the present day is theoretically more important to study than, say, the nineteenth century; rather, it is my more general interest in the post-World War period that has directed my choices in selecting cases. I have been particularly interested in studying cases in which the religiosity of a particular group or practice is asserted, contested and negotiated. I have called them boundary cases because different actors have to clarify what counts as religious and what does not, and no one can be sure about the outcome of the negotiation. In some cases, different actors have even had to revise their understanding of what religion consists of. This is why I have paid attention to some small and marginal groups, but these are not studies of marginal groups for the sake of them being marginal; I have examined how the society operates with the category of religion by choosing case studies which typically (but not always) involve small groups. This approach does not differentiate whether or not the groups or practices in question are considered jokes or taken seriously by sincere believers. Journalists, lawyers, experts and other voices may bring that aspect into the debate, particularly when addressing Pastafarianism and Jediism, or to a lesser extent with Wicca and Druidry for instance. However, for a scholar it is simply an aspect of the discourse to be analysed, if relevant for the case. What is common to these cases is that minorities aim to be included in the category of religion and get whatever benefits are available for them if they are classified as religions. Recently I have started to study the same phenomenon from the majority side too, and then the issue is not usually the wish to become recognized as religious but to reclassify a practice or a symbol that has been previously understood as religious as 'cultural' or 'part of heritage' or 'tradition'.

I have come to synthesize my argument on what is going on in present-day societies, especially in the Western world, as 'religionization' of minorities and 'culturalization' of Christian majorities. In other words, one of the best ways for different minorities to get more resources, attention, or cultural or social capital is to start presenting themselves as religious, while Christian majorities increasingly attempt to maintain their hegemonic status by classifying their symbols and practices as cultural (or part of heritage). The question animating the rest of the chapter is, then, how can such processes be examined through boundary cases?

Practical methodological framework for boundary cases

For pedagogical reasons, I will dissect the process into analytically separate but practically overlapping 'steps'. In order to reflect on the research process after finishing it, I have detected five general steps that have been relevant in my previous case studies.

Step one: Find a relevant case. One should find a case where there is a conflict over classification. Following news media and paying attention to public institutions and courts is helpful in finding one. Often such conflicts take place in legal contexts, but even then they usually include one or more other institutions, such as schools, parliament, military, healthcare providers or media outlets. Sometimes such conflicts are discussed in the media without a decisive court case. Typically, the conflict arises when small and not-so-well-known groups or practices are involved, such as pagan groups, Jediism, yoga, Scientology or Pastafarianism.

Step two: Learn the context well. Even when the basic parameters of the case appear simple, one cannot assume one understands the context in advance. One should know something about the group involved and also about the status of the group within the wider field of tradition it identifies with. In legal contexts, one should know how the law has been applied previously and how the legal process functions. When I studied the charity registration case of the Druid Network in England and Wales (Owen and Taira 2015), I was able to do it jointly with Suzanne Owen because she knew the field of Druidry in Britain much better than I did. She had access to the Druids' discussion forums and she was already in contact with key figures who initiated the charity registration process. We both needed to learn more about charity law and how these processes usually proceed. We also had to explore several previous charity law cases in order to understand the reasoning of the charity commission. In addition, we studied how British charity law itself has emerged and developed, although we did not say much about it in the final product. At that time, I was researching British media, so I was stronger on that part. I had also published about a similar process in Finland regarding Wiccans (Taira 2010), so I knew how to apply the basic framework and what kind of actors and aspects (e.g. charity law, field of Druidry, media, expert voices) might be relevant to include in the study. The study would have been difficult without our complementary expertise and our interest to learn more about the context.

Step three: Formulate questions and choose relevant concepts. After getting to know the basics of the case, one needs to specify one's questions and select fruitful concepts. As should be clear by now, I do not approach cases from a point of view that attempts to decide whether X is or is not a religion. Rather, I ask why someone wants something to be classified as religion; how someone attempts to do it; who contests the attempt and why. These questions are specified according to the case. I tend to operate with concepts such as interest, discourse, effects, power and so on. We all need analytical concepts, but it is up to us to decide whether religion is one of them, and here I am proposing a model in which it is not.

Step four: Select appropriate data and decide which actors are relevant. There are several possibilities of where to focus after identifying a case. It is often possible to examine the interconnectedness of different actors. For instance, the struggle is not always between a group and the state or law; people sharing the same identification (Druidry, for example) have disagreements about the classification and its relevance, and that is possibly interesting as an object of study. Negotiations are often covered in the media, and in some cases the media takes an active role in them. This too can be studied. Even scholars are sometimes involved, either directly as expert witnesses and consultants, or indirectly, when their views are sometimes referred to in the processes or their authority is used to support certain positions. If the amount of material is limited, it is possible to address all of these in one article-length study. Otherwise, one has to make an informed choice. This step is often strongly connected with the previous step as the initial selection of concepts and data may be refined after progress in either step is made. Although the data do not speak to us without us having concepts and questions, we can certainly change or refine both as we go on, making them co-constitutive in the end.

Step five: Theorize the case as part of larger socio-cultural processes. This step may be considered somewhat vague, because it does not specify in advance which processes are relevant. However, this is one of the ways in which the selected case can be made relevant for those who may not have initial interest in it. As a Finn who sometimes writes about Finnish cases, I cannot assume that all international readers know much about my cases or have special interest in Finnish curiosities. Step five may help. In practice, this theorizing ensures that one is not simply content in describing and analysing the selected case but sees it as part of larger social change or as an example of something more general or 'some fundamental issue in the imagination of religion' (Smith 1982: xi). This is like the Marxist understanding of the preference for 'concrete' over 'abstract': the abstract is not connected with anything else, whereas making something concrete means weaving the connections between separate dots and offering a more thoroughly contextualized analysis. Some examples of such analysis are Lawrence Grossberg's (1992, 2010) views on radically contextual cultural studies embodied in the concept of articulation, as exemplified in the works of Stuart Hall and Lawrence Grossberg (for an introduction to the theory and method of articulation, see Slack 1996). These are just examples of available options; the final choice of the most appropriate conceptual toolkit and context should be made case by case. Thinking about how this and that piece might be connected – thus increasing the effectivity of articulated parts – is an attitude I tend to maintain by considering how analysed cases are part of larger processes and contexts.

I shall show briefly how I have applied these ideas and steps in two cases, the first highlighting what I call religionization of minorities and the second exemplifying the culturalization of Christian majorities.

Religionization of minorities: Registration of People of the Bear

People of the Bear (*Karhun kansa*) – a small group founded in 2010 to rehabilitate pre-Christian Balto-Finnic folk beliefs and rituals – applied for the status of registered religious community in Finland and they received an initial rejection letter in 2013. The rejection was based on an expert committee statement arguing that People of the Bear is not a religious community according to the criteria of Finnish law on religious freedom. The law itself provides some criteria for religion but not a detailed definition as such (and this is very typical of laws concerning religion internationally). It says that in order to count as religion, the group should be 'based on a creed, religious texts regarded as sacred, or another specified and established basis for activities regarded as sacred', as stated in section 7 of the Finnish Act on the Freedom of Religion. People of the Bear submitted a revised application and almost a year later their application was approved by the same expert committee. (For a detailed analysis of this registration case, see Taira 2022: 69–91.)

We have now identified an interesting boundary case. We have access to official documents (which is not very difficult in Finland as long as you visit the Finnish Patent and Registration Office in Helsinki and make a request to have a look at the documents) and there are previous studies about similar cases, such as my study regarding the unsuccessful and contentious application process of Finnish Wiccans (Taira 2010).

What could be studied in this particular case? In my view it is not very innovative to examine whether People of the Bear qualify as a religion according to some scholarly definitions, but it is fascinating to study how the expert committee reasoned and, in the end, changed their view; it is interesting to study how the applicants constructed their religiosity in their two applications; it is relevant to study how the media covered the case; it is significant to study how scholars were involved in the public debate concerning the registration system after the initial rejection – even the Minister of the Interior responded to me twice in the mainstream media after my public comments concerning the case, and this probably had something to do with the success of the revised application.

Furthermore, it is possible to explore how People of the Bear's stated identification as part of 'Finnish faith' relates to other groups claiming to practice the same religion. There is one similar group, *Taivaannaula*, which has been operating for a longer time but never applied for the status of religion. Often it is the case that if one group gets the status of religion, it becomes a spokesperson for that identification in the public sphere. At least initially it looked like this was happening in favour of People of the Bear. However, it was also significant for this case that nowadays *Taivaannaula* strictly denies their religious nature and more recently they have even dropped the term 'Finnish faith' from their own vocabulary in order not to be associated with ethno-nationalist groups, leaving People of the Bear the only recognized group to identify with that term.[5]

There are various material and symbolic benefits to becoming a registered religious community. Such communities may get the right to conduct legally valid marriage ceremonies; they may be included in religious education in schools; they can apply for financial support from the state; and they may get general recognition or approval in the society by becoming a religious community. These are all strong motivators driving different minorities towards presenting themselves as religious.

In the case of People of the Bear, they have gained permission for a few named specialists to conduct legally binding marriage ceremonies. They have not become part of religious education in schools and they have not received financial support from the state. They have gained a good amount of predominantly positive media presence. But there is one more benefit, namely that registered religious communities come under the law that protects against breaches of the sanctity of religion.

In 2010 it had been reported that one of Finland's ancient sacrificial cupstones[6] was going to be removed because of the expansion of a car dealership in the city of Hämeenlinna. The Finnish Antiquities Act protects the cupstones so that one cannot break them, but the Act does not protect the original location. This means that cupstones can be removed if they are removed as a whole. This is exactly what happened in Hämeenlinna.

One of the main motivations for founding People of the Bear and applying for the status of registered religious community was this cupstone case. People reasoned that if they formed an association, registered it as a religious community, and stated in their application that cupstones are 'sacred' to their religion in their original locations, the cupstones would be protected. This means that if in the future cupstones are about to be removed, the group could refer to the law concerning breach of the sanctity of religion.

This is a simple example of how an attempt to get the status of religion can be a useful strategic move for certain actors. These privileges reserved for groups classified as religious are key drivers in the move towards 'religionization' of minorities. If you are registered or regarded as a religion, you have better means to get your voice heard in society, rather than simply being a 'non-religious' minority. Evidence of 'religionization' is not limited to the cases I have analysed. There are several ways to collect more evidence of the 'religionization' process. In Finland, the increase in registration of religious communities is a case in point.

In addition to two churches – the Evangelical Lutheran Church of Finland and the Orthodox Church of Finland – whose special status is guaranteed by law, there are currently about 170 registered religious communities in Finland. When local organizations are counted, the total amount rises to more than 500. The increasing tendency to register is obvious: it took twenty-five years, from 1980 to 2005, to double the number of registered religious communities (from 28 to 59), but only ten more years to double that number again (from 59 in 2005 to 116 in 2015). There are two main reasons for this development. First, it is typical that new migrant communities organize themselves according to the new host society. Immigration increased in the 1990s and it took a while until these communities began to develop their organizational structures (Martikainen 2013: 46–60). As a result, some communities, particularly Muslims, have 'religionized' themselves; that is, they have started to present themselves as *religious* communities in public and registered themselves as religious communities.[7] In Finland, 'minority religions are consciously or unconsciously expected to follow this model, and the legislative norms also guide them in that direction' (Martikainen 2013: 53). Second, by registering as a religious community and becoming classified as religious rather than a general association, minorities get benefits, so it is useful to try to get the application through and become labelled as religious.

In this research, the five steps began with identifying the case (step one), then getting to know the context (step two). As a Finn who had been studying similar registration cases previously, my main task here was to understand People of the Bear more generally. Then more specific questions were posed and concepts identified (step three). The key element was that I approached 'religion' as a discursive technique by which the applicants aimed to get their voice heard, especially in the cupstone case. The questions I avoided were whether People of the Bear is really a religion and whether they should be registered as a religious community. Due to the limited amount of material, I was able to study the original documents in detail: two applications and expert committee reports; Finnish law on religious freedom; previous cases; and media discussion relating to People of the Bear (step four). Step five was to contextualize the specific case in terms of larger social processes: the process of 'religionization' of minorities, as well as the possible maintenance of Lutheran hegemony through the selection of expert committee members (discussed in Taira 2022: 69–91).

Culturalization of Christian majorities: Singing of the Summer Hymn in Finnish schools

The religionization of minorities seems to go hand-in-hand with the culturalization of Christian majorities. Culturalization has been theorized by several scholars (Beaman 2020; Beaman, Steele and Pringnitz 2018; Joppke 2015, 2018; Roy 2019). Their views differ slightly from one to the next, but what these scholars share is an idea of 'culturalization' that refers to the process in which practices, symbols or groups which have been previously conceived as religious are now increasingly justified by classifying them as cultural, part of tradition or heritage. This process is most obvious in Europe and North America, and although scholars have not tried to pinpoint its exact date of origin, it can be suggested that such processes became visible in the 2000s and intensified in the 2010s. My interest in 'culturalization' arose out of a case study on debates around the singing of the Summer Hymn (*Suvivirsi*) in Finnish schools (Taira 2019b; see also Taira and Beaman 2022).

In Finland, most public schools finish their spring term in an event where the Summer Hymn is sung. However, there has been a long debate over whether the practice should be allowed because it might count as religious. The lyrics of the song include references to God and creator, and the hymn is part of a Lutheran hymnal. It is sung in Lutheran Sunday worship in midsummer. On this basis, some suggest that its singing counts as religious practice. According to representative Finnish surveys, approximately 4 per cent of the population oppose the singing, but support by a large majority has not prevented the debate from erupting and enduring (Taira 2019b).

The debate itself reflects the diversification of Finland and a discourse in which the fact of diversity is assumed by all discussants. It is widely agreed that there should not be religious practices in school events which are meant to be obligatory for everyone, because schools are diverse (i.e. some pupils have different religions and some have no religion). However, if the song is classified as something other than religious, the 'problem' is solved.

When I studied how the Summer Hymn is classified in public discussion, it was interesting that very few people classified singing of the hymn as a religious practice. Instead, journalists and editors as well as politicians and church people suggested that the singing of this hymn in schools is part of Finnish culture, heritage and tradition, and not a religious practice. It is mainly some outspoken secularists who state that it is a religious practice and, for the sake of inclusivity in schools, argue that it might be wise not to sing it at school events.

This public debate is an example of how a hymn that in most other contexts would be classified as religious is suddenly not religious – or not religious enough to count as 'religious practice' – but part of Finnish culture. This 'culturalization' of (Christian) majority practices is a means by which the singing can be justified, as it is much more difficult to oppose cultural practice than the religious practice of the majority. This is one of the strategies by which the Lutheran church – the Christian majority in Finland – can maintain their hegemonic position in a situation where 'religious practices' would not be allowed. In this example, I concluded, culturalization is beneficial for Christians.

I conducted this case study by implicitly following the five steps described above. I did not keep the five steps in mind when doing the study, but can identify them retrospectively. Step one, choosing a relevant case, was done on the basis that the debate on the nature of the Summer Hymn has been going on for quite a long time and it includes claims about its religious or (relatively) non-religious nature. In addition, the debate has practical implications in schools.

Step two consisted of knowing the context well. As a Finnish scholar of religion, it has been impossible not to know anything about the case, but this step required a more systematic approach. The appropriate occasion for studying the issue in detail arose when I was teaching a course in which twelve students researched the same case with me under my supervision. Although I had already touched upon the issue in a research project focusing on Finnish media discourses on religion, this course made the Summer Hymn a focus we examined together systematically while reflecting on the Finnish context at the same time. We examined what the law and legal experts say about the case and what type of practices different schools actually follow (since the practices are not uniform but follow the principals' decisions).

Step three included choosing the concepts for thinking about the case. Early on I decided that this study would not make claims about what the Summer Hymn really is, or present prescriptive views about whether schools should stop singing the song or not. Instead, I wanted to pay attention to the classification in the material where people suggest that the song is about something. Very soon it became clear that people claim it to be mainly 'religious', 'part of tradition', 'part of heritage' or 'cultural'. This classification correlated very closely with the speakers' normative views: if it was classified 'religious', its singing should be reconsidered or at least the chance to opt out should be emphasized significantly in schools; if it was considered something else, it almost always was conjoined with support for the continuation of the singing practice. This does not yet determine which scholarly concepts should be used but rather excludes some concepts and approaches. However, at this point I already knew that I would focus on the interests involved in public positions concerning the Summer Hymn, in order to think about hegemony through the question 'Who benefits if the hymn is classified as X?'. I decided to approach the Summer Hymn debate as discourse in the construction of social reality, or part of larger discourses entangled with various institutions and actors such as media, education, law, government and lay people.

In practice, steps three and four were not easy to separate, because they are largely co-constitutive and operate in a hermeneutic circle (or spiral): thinking about data begins with an initial idea of what might be the key concepts, tools and questions relevant for the case, while getting to know the possible data generates ideas of which concepts should be maintained and how they should be operationalized. Step four, choosing the data, was done based on an understanding that there has not been a court decision concerning the singing of the hymn, so it was better to choose the media material as the main focus and include legal statements by the Deputy Ombudsman. Given that I was teaching a short research-based course about religion in the media, students were involved in collecting data and providing initial analyses from a wide variety of Finnish media. All major newspapers were included, from morning papers to tabloids, as well as major news websites and professional papers – including the key publications of teachers and Freethinkers, the latter being the biggest and most visible secularist association in Finland. As some scholars have written about the history of the Summer Hymn, including a 1970s debate, there was no reason to go that far back. It was enough to focus on the 1990s onwards, because database searches demonstrate that it is around the mid-1990s when references to the Summer Hymn increase and stay approximately at the same level to the present day. A further question in this step was which actors should be focused on in this study. A variety of views were presented, but it soon turned out relevant to pay special attention to media professionals and (conservative-populist) politicians who seemed to echo what they thought might be the vox populi: that the song is really part of our culture and is not religious at all or is 'not religious enough' to count as practice of religion if sung in school celebrations. It was a very small minority of teachers and Freethinkers who wished to remind people that the song is religious, and its singing should be reconsidered. It was also striking that there was a relative absence of bishops and other high-ranking Lutheran voices, in addition to the absence of voices of 'minority religions'.

In going back and forth between steps three and four, we examined how the discourses on diversity, nationalism and Christianity were connected to the Summer Hymn debate. They were all explicitly addressed in the data and their theorizing made perfect sense: diversity increased in Finland at the same time as the debate on the Summer Hymn intensified in the mid-1990s; the diversity was connected to nationalism and national identity in the sense that people considered what it means to be a Finn in such a situation; Lutheran Christianity had been strongly linked with the national identity, and increasing diversity challenged its taken-for-granted status while church membership figures were simultaneously decreasing. All these issues were condensed in the insistence on the Summer Hymn being part of Finnish tradition or culture. Therefore, we chose 'culturalization' as a key theoretical concept with which to tie several aspects together.

'Culturalization' provided a key to step five, theorizing the case as part of larger social processes. The data, consisting of comments about the Summer

Hymn, offered a way to think about the question of 'Who benefits?' and to argue that it is most beneficial for maintaining the Lutheran hegemony if the Summer Hymn is classified as cultural. Furthermore, it was possible to connect this case to the previously studied (contrasting) examples in which minorities were seen to become more interested in presenting themselves as 'religious', thus providing some evidence for a thesis about the culturalization of the Christianity majority and religionization of minorities.

This already connects the raw material to larger social processes, but it was also possible to think about the Finnish case in relation to other Euro-American examples of 'culturalization' as theorized for instance by Christian Joppke and Lori Beaman. Since Joppke and Beaman have slightly different views about culturalization, I was able to compare their views to the Finnish case. Joppke (2015, 2018) sees culturalization as benefitting secularists, whereas Beaman argues that it is typically 'non-religious' people who oppose it, because they lose some of their ground in the public arena (Beaman 2015, 2020; Beaman, Steele and Pringnitz 2018). On the basis of the Finnish example, I ended up supporting Beaman's view, suggesting that the 'culturalization' in the case of the Summer Hymn maintains Lutheran hegemony against outspoken secularists – an argument I developed later with Beaman in a joint publication (Taira and Beaman 2022).

Conclusion

In this chapter I have offered some views on why 'religion' is a problematic or at least challenging category in scholarly use and a very interesting category for us to study. I have provided some ideas on how we could proceed if we wish to pursue such a research opportunity and argued that such studies should not be limited to exploring the historical emergence of a modern construction of 'religion' in past centuries, but that present-day societies offer plenty of examples for researching the ongoing negotiations concerning the category of religion, showing that it is one of the categories employed in the organization of societies. I also argued that one could condense the current general development in the statement: 'religionization of minorities and culturalization of Christian majorities' – despite the fact that there are individual cases providing exceptions to the pattern. And I have provided some examples of boundary cases which have led me to argue for this general development, while offering some methodological reflections on how such studies can be done in practice.

It should be clear by now that I disagree with those colleagues who argue that scholars who critique the category of 'religion' are ruining the study of religion (see Taira 2020). My strategy has been to demonstrate through case studies – albeit in brief summary form here – what kind of interesting and socially relevant knowledge can be produced with my chosen approach, and how others might apply or adjust and develop that methodological framework. It is up to you to decide whether you find it inspiring for your own thinking and whether you can do something with it.

References

Arnal, William and Russell T. McCutcheon (2013), *The Sacred is the Profane: The Political Nature of 'Religion'*, Oxford: Oxford University Press.
Barthes, Roland (1977), *Image Music Text*, London: Fontana Press.
Batnitzky, Leora (2011), *How Judaism Became a Religion: An Introduction to Modern Jewish Thought*, Princeton: Princeton University Press.
Beaman, Lori G. (2015), 'Freedom of and Freedom from Religion: Atheist Involvement in Legal Cases', in Lori G. Beaman and Steven Tomlins (eds), *Atheist Identities – Spaces and Social Contexts*, 39–52, Cham: Springer.
Beaman, Lori G. (2020), *The Transition of Religion to Culture in Law and Public Discourse*, London: Routledge.
Beaman, Lori G., Cory Steele and Kelin Pringnitz (2018), 'The Inclusion of Nonreligion in Religion and Human Rights', *Social Compass*, 65 (1): 43–61.
Brown, Candy Gunther (2019), *Debating Yoga and Mindfulness in Public Schools: Reforming Secular Education of Reestablishing Religion?*, Chapel Hill: The University of North Carolina Press.
Chidester, David (1996), *Savage Systems: Colonialism and Comparative Religion in Southern Africa*, Charlottesville: University Press of Virginia.
Chidester, David (2014), *Empire of Religion: Imperialism and Comparative Religion*, Chicago: The University of Chicago Press.
Dreßler, Markus (2019), 'Religionization and Secularity', in HCAS 'Multiple Secularities – Beyond the West, Beyond Modernities' (ed.), *Companion of the Study of Secularity*, Leipzig University. Available online: https://www.multiple-secularities.de/media/css_dressler_religionization.pdf (accessed 22 December 2024).
Dubuisson, Daniel (2003), *The Western Construction of Religion: Myths, Knowledge, and Ideology*, Baltimore: The Johns Hopkins University Press.
Fitzgerald, Timothy (2000), *The Ideology of Religious Studies*, Oxford: Oxford University Press.
Fitzgerald, Timothy (2007), *Discourse on Civility and Barbarity: A Critical History of Religion and Related Categories*, Oxford: Oxford University Press.
Foucault, Michel (2002), *The Archaeology of Knowledge*, London: Routledge.
Goldenberg, Naomi (2015), 'The Category of Religion in the Technology of Governance: An Argument for Understanding Religions as Vestigial States', in Trevor Stack, Naomi Goldenberg and Timothy Fitzgerald (eds), *Religion as a Category of Governance and Sovereignty*, 280–92, Leiden: Brill.

Goldenberg, Naomi (2018), 'Forget about Defining "It": Reflections on Thinking Differently in Religious Studies', in Brad Stoddard (ed.), *Method Today: Redescribing Approaches to the Study of Religion*, 79–95, Sheffield: Equinox.
Grossberg, Lawrence (1992), *We Gotta Get Out of This Place: Popular Conservatism and Postmodern Culture*, London: Routledge.
Grossberg, Lawrence (2010), *Cultural Studies in the Future Tense*, Durham: Duke University Press.
Joppke, Christian (2015), *The Secular State Under Siege: Religion and Politics in Europe and America*, Cambridge: Polity.
Joppke, Christian (2018), 'Culturalizing Religion in Western Europe', *Social Compass*, 65 (2): 234–46.
Josephson, Jason Ānanda (2012), *The Invention of Religion in Japan*, Chicago: The University of Chicago Press.
King, Richard (1999), *Orientalism and Religion: Postcolonial Theory, India and 'The Mystic East'*, London: Routledge.
Martikainen, Tuomas (2013), *Religion, Migration, Settlement: Reflections on Post-1990 Immigration to Finland*, Leiden: Brill.
Martin, Craig (2010), *Masking Hegemony: A Genealogy of Liberalism, Religion and the Private Sphere*, London: Equinox.
McCutcheon, Russell T. (2003), *The Discipline of Religion: Structure, Meaning, Rhetoric*, London: Routledge.
McCutcheon, Russell T. (2005), *Religion and the Domestication of Dissent: Or, How to Live in a Less than Perfect Nation*, London: Equinox.
Owen, Suzanne and Teemu Taira (2015), 'The Category of "Religion" in Public Classification: Charity Registration of the Druid Network in England and Wales', in Trevor Stack, Naomi Goldenberg and Timothy Fitzgerald (eds), *Religion as a Category of Governance and Sovereignty*, 90–114, Leiden: Brill.
Rorty, Richard (1991), *Objectivity, Relativism and Truth: Philosophical Papers Volume 1*, Cambridge: Cambridge University Press.
Rorty, Richard (1999), *Philosophy and Social Hope*, London: Penguin.
Rorty, Richard (2007), *Philosophy as Cultural Politics: Philosophical Papers Volume 4*, Cambridge: Cambridge University Press.
Roy, Olivier (2019), *Is Europe Christian?* London: Hurst & Company.
Schilbrack, Kevin (2014), *Philosophy and the Study of Religions: A Manifesto*, Oxford: Blackwell.
Schilbrack, Kevin (2017), 'A Realist Social Ontology of Religion', *Religion*, 47 (2): 161–78.
Slack, Jennifer Daryl (1996), 'The Theory and Method of Articulation in Cultural Studies', in David Morley and Kuan-Hsing Chen (eds), *Stuart Hall: Critical Dialogues in Cultural Studies*, 112–27, London: Routledge.
Smith, Jonathan Z. (1982), *Imagining Religion: From Babylon to Jonestown*, Chicago: The University of Chicago Press.
Taira, Teemu (2010), 'Religion as a Discursive Technique: The Politics of Classifying Wicca', *Journal of Contemporary Religion*, 25 (3): 379–94.
Taira, Teemu (2019a), 'Reading Bond Films through the Lens of "Religion": Discourse of "the West and the Rest"', *Journal of Religion, Film and Media*, 5 (2): 119–39.
Taira, Teemu (2019b), 'Suvivirsi ja kristinuskon "kulttuuristuminen" katsomuksellisen monimuotoisuuden aikana' ['The Summer Hymn and the

"Culturalization" of Christianity in Times of Diversity'], *Uskonnontutkija* 8 (1). Available online: https://journal.fi/uskonnontutkija/article/view/83000 (accessed 22 December 2024).

Taira, Teemu (2020), 'Historicization of "Religion" and the Devastation of Study of Religion Departments: Siamese Twins or Contingent Acquaintances?', *Implicit Religion*, 22 (3–4): 291–308.

Taira, Teemu (2022), *Taking 'Religion' Seriously: Essays on the Discursive Study of Religion*, Leiden: Brill.

Taira, Teemu and Lori Beaman (2022), 'Majoritarian Religion, Cultural Justification and Nonreligion: Finland in International Context', *Temenos: Nordic Journal of Comparative Religion*, 58 (2): 193–216.

8

Researching 'religion' in Indigenous cultures

Suzanne Owen

In this chapter, I aim to offer a constructive approach to studying 'religion' in Indigenous cultures by building on the work of Chidester, Fitzgerald and McCutcheon, while acknowledging concerns expressed by Indigenous scholars Linda Tuhiwai Smith and the late Vine Deloria Jr about researching Indigenous people and religion. Such scholars influenced the way I approach studying religion in cultures that often reject the categorization of their traditions as 'religion'.

During my doctoral studies in the early 2000s, I became aware of this disconnect between scholars' categories and how others understand them in a discussion I had in Edinburgh with a Cofán activist from Ecuador who referred to the Cofán way as 'tradition' and Catholicism as 'religion'. Thus, I became sensitive to the way groups categorize themselves compared to others' descriptions about them. In addition, I began to question definitions of Indigenous religion based on an ethnic criterion when I observed some similarities in the way Mi'kmaq in Canada and contemporary Druids in Scotland were reconnecting with their local environments, histories and traditions.

Regarding Druids, Vine Deloria (1992: 288) wrote 'each land projects a particular religious spirit, which largely determines what types of religious beliefs will arise on it', implying Druidry was an Indigenous religion. From my reading of this, I came to distinguish between Indigenous 'people' and 'religion', and argued that Druidry could be considered an example of the latter while being excluded from the former (see Owen 2013); that is, Druidry could be regarded as an Indigenous religion while the people who practice it would not. An Indigenous person might argue, however, that one cannot separate Indigenous 'religion' from 'people', and this leads us to the politics of defining such terms, which is a core component of a critical study of religion.

First, I will attend to 'indigenous' as an identification practice before examining the problem of 'religion' (leaving aside the concept of 'culture', often conceptually paired with 'nature'[1]). In both there is often a gap between self-representation and scholarly classifications. The second half of this chapter focuses on the politics of refusal where colonial classifications are rejected in favour of culture-specific ones, exploring the rich body of Anishinaabe scholarship on this. I will also consider issues of legitimization, power and privilege when evaluating 'traditional spirituality' as an alternative to 'religion'. At the end, I suggest ways a critical religion approach can offer a way forward that recognizes these differences in representation.

'Indigenous' as identification practice

'There is no such thing as identity, only operational acts of identification', wrote Jean-François Bayart (2005: 92, originally published in French in 1996). The understanding is that an identity does not identify something in the world; rather it is a discursive practice. I came across Bayart's work through the *Culture on the Edge* research group centred at the University of Alabama, 'whose aim is to use social theory to offer more nuanced understandings of how those things that we commonly call identities are produced, managed, and continually reproduced' (Culture on the Edge, n.d.).

It was reading Russell McCutcheon, a member of that research group, that led me to a theoretical framework for writing about cultural appropriation and ways Indigenous people distinguish it from cultural 'sharing' by paying close attention to the discourse (Owen 2008). In their entry on the word 'Identity' in *Religion in 50 Words*, Aaron Hughes and Russell McCutcheon suggested that: 'To study such tactical operational acts, or what Bayart also terms enunciation of an identity, we must therefore study actions in settings where things are being negotiated and thus where something is at stake' (2022: 125). Indigeneity is such an example. Indigenous rights, recognition, land claims and sovereignty are at stake.

Though each cultural group prefers to be identified by their own names for themselves, wary of another type of erasure as distinct peoples, for broader political aims they gain a collective voice under the 'indigenous' label. This way they aid each other in the struggle for recognition and international protections for their culture and sites. In some cases, it gives them more authority to speak for groups that no longer have a voice. Concerning the extinct Beothuk of Newfoundland,[2] in more recent times Mi'kmaq on the island have been consulted over the handling of Beothuk remains and artefacts.

For contemporary Druids in Britain, the battlegrounds have been over site management of places such as Stonehenge and the treatment of ancient burial remains, with rhetoric borrowed from indigeneity discourse from other parts of the world. However, Druid claims are weak compared to what is at stake for colonized peoples who are attempting to redress several centuries of oppression and decimation caused by European colonization when they assert authority over ancient burial or ceremonial grounds and material culture held in museums.

Similarly, a group of Scottish crofters had sought recognition as an 'indigenous culture' as a strategy to protect their way of life, without claiming to be 'indigenous people', at least in the conversations I had with them. However, they have blurred this distinction in the title of their publication *Crofters: indigenous people of the Highlands and Islands*, and 'consider that indigenousness is an inclusive concept, and is primarily to be regarded culturally, rather than racially or genetically' (MacKinnon 2008: 2). This also applies to those born elsewhere who have adopted crofting in the Highlands and Islands. In such cases, including that of Druidry, the boundaries of a term like 'indigenous' are maintained or expanded to exclude or include based on chosen criteria.

However, in the critical study of religion, we should also examine the power relations in making such distinctions. Vine Deloria Jr, in raising this issue in the ongoing legacy of colonialism, criticized 'the unarticulated assumption that social science scholars . . . should always control the definitions that people use to describe and communicate' (1998: 67–8). As scholars, we *do* control the terms and definitions in our publications and therefore we should take responsibility for them and follow-up the rejection of them by those we study.

Going further than Deloria, Audra Simpson writes that: 'To speak of Indigeneity is to speak of colonialism and anthropology, as these are means through which Indigenous people have been known and sometimes are still known' (2014: 95), expanding on the view of Indigenous people as 'colonized people' (Smith 1999: 7). The term Indigenous is inextricably bound to colonization, which is why for some the decolonizing process includes a rejection of this term in favour of Indigenous peoples' own terms for themselves. A Mi'kmaq in Newfoundland had told me that he preferred 'Mi'kmaq' to 'Indigenous' as he didn't want to lose the specificity of their culture and identity.

In these shifting sands, the rejection of an identification is as significant as the practice of claiming one, leading to the question of how we classify people who have historically had little say in how they have been represented. 'Religion', in the study of Indigenous cultures, is particularly problematic.

Putting aside the problems in defining 'Indigenous', as an umbrella term it has been useful for giving voice to small societies that on their own might not be heard, as in the United Nations Permanent Forum of Indigenous Issues. In the study of religion, there is the Indigenous Religious Traditions Group at the American Academy of Religion (and more recently the *Journal of Indigenous Religious Traditions* published by Equinox), providing a space in the programme for researchers of groups and global issues facing them that might otherwise not have a presence. Nevertheless, as a researcher, if we refer to a Mi'kmaq only as Indigenous we help to erase their distinctiveness.

The problem of 'religion'

During my doctoral studies, David Chidester's *Savage Systems* (1996) was key for helping me to see how 'indigenous religion' was created in the context of colonialism. Addressing this directly, he writes: 'More important to the discovery of indigenous religions was the practice of morphological comparison that established analogies between the strange and the familiar. . . . Through comparison, therefore, the beliefs and practices of "savages" could be reconfigured as religion' (Chidester 1996: 18), giving the example of an eighteenth-century Jesuit father, Joseph Lafitau, who reconstituted ancient 'religions' among the Greeks and Israelites to draw analogies to what he observed among the Iroquois. At this time, this was largely done by Christian missionaries (and later by anthropologists) who at first did not discern any 'religion' among indigenous populations. According to Chidester, this definitional shift 'depended upon the establishment of local control' (1996: 20) in order to subjugate indigenous people and to incorporate them into the colonial system.

Not only was a category for 'indigenous religion' created in the Jesuit example, but also 'religion' as a set of characteristics based on a Christian model that could be applied comparatively, underlying Timothy Fitzgerald's assertions that: '"Religion", rather than being a kind of neutral category which can be created by the scholar for his or her own purposes, is laden with cultural and ideological assumptions and interests' (2007: 40).

Applying the Western category 'religion' to Indigenous traditions also implies a 'secular' (see Fitzgerald 2007), separating supposed 'religious' activities from, say, political ones, which would likely distort those traditions. Yet, even a Christian might say he or she could not separate their religion from other aspects of life, and that it informs everything they do. Chris Jocks (Kahnawà:ke Mohawk) acknowledges this, too, saying: 'the most devout practitioners of almost any religion would insist that their practice is also a way of life' (2022: 22). Familiar with the view that 'religion' connotes 'institutions, mandated beliefs, and formalistic rituals' (2022: 22), Jocks proposes that the rejection of the label 'religion' is also about the idea of salvation: 'Since the Enlightenment, many established religions based on individual salvation have also come to accept and accommodate the European scientific tradition of a physical universe devoid of spirit' (2022: 23). As Afe Adogame says in the same volume: 'Most often, defining an Indigenous religion from its belief system is putting it upside down' (2022: 88). In religious studies, scholars studying phenomena falling within the category 'religion' often begin with 'beliefs' while non-Western cultures might rather start with practices or relationships. The idea of religion as referring to something 'out there', or transcendent, makes little sense when applied to most non-Western cultures.

Mitsutoshi Horii recognizes this disconnect between scholars and the people they study in his study of 'religion' and 'secular' categories in the Japanese context, pointing out 'scholars' tendency to try to find what they call "religion" where people say that there is no such thing. Rather, . . . the scholar should examine what people and institutions mean by "religion" in highly ambiguous and often contested ways' (2021: 212). He provides the example of how some scholars have redescribed Japanese 'lifeways' as 'very "religious", even when Japanese people themselves claim that they are "not religious" . . . when their practices fall into the broad scholarly definition of religion' (Horii 2021: 212).

The reluctance on the part of Indigenous people to equate their traditional ways of life with 'religion' stems from its association with colonialism. Chris Jocks asks 'whether it is respect or colonialism even to assign the label religion to people who explicitly deny that it describes what they do' (2004: 124). In the critical study of religion, what we can do is pay close attention to how terms are used. Although it may be useful to employ the terminology used by practitioners, they require explanation as many terms are understood differently in other contexts. In addition, Indigenous people, as well as those in other colonized contexts, might use one set of terms for themselves and another when speaking to outsiders. While conducting fieldwork among the Dene in the Northwest Territories, David Walsh observed a shift in Dene discourse 'from external, public expressions of identity on the macro-indigenous-religious level to internal, private expressions on the micro-familial-environmentally-relational level' (2017: 205). That is to say, 'indigenous' and 'religious' terms such as 'sacred' are employed when speaking to non-Dene, and social-relational terms when speaking among themselves. According to Walsh, an example of the macro-level 'public indigeneity' is the Idle No More movement (2017: 206). He also claims that 'non-Dene have often denied a Dene religiosity, stating that Dene had no traditional religion or that it was supplanted by Christianity' (Walsh 2017: 206). This colonialist view of Indigenous peoples, challenged here by Walsh, is replicated across the world (as recounted in Chidester 1996), both denying Indigenous people had any religion and deeming what they do have as no more than superstition.

Indigenous scholars within religious studies are faced, then, with a choice about whether to reject or redefine 'religion' when applying it to Indigenous cultures. Suzanne Crawford O'Brien with Inés Talamantez, in their book *Religion and Culture in Native America*, 'hope to push the boundaries of what is thought of as "religion"' (2021: 3) (they do not address the concept of 'culture'); in other words, expanding the category beyond the binaries of religion/profane, religion/secular and so on to include not only 'oral traditions and ceremonies' but also 'YouTube videos, political protests, health clinics, creative arts, and community gardens' (2021: 3). This is good advice for all studies of 'religion' where a scholar's assumptions about what constitutes a 'religion' ought to be interrogated, along with what is being excluded when employing such a category and whether they are making assumptions based on particular models of 'religion' derived from Protestant Christianity.

Indigenous politics of refusal

In *Mohawk Interruptus* (2014), Audra Simpson defines Indigenous refusal 'as a political and ethical stance that stands in stark contrast to the desire to have one's distinctiveness as a culture, as a people, recognized. Refusal comes with the requirement of having one's *political* sovereignty acknowledged and upheld and raises the question of legitimacy for those who are usually in the position of recognizing' (2014: 11). David Jefferess sees this postcolonial resistance as 'a "new humanism" that emphasizes new ways of being, knowing and doing' (2008: 220). Elaborating, he says, 'Unlike a *reactive* notion of "resistance" that opposes or subverts colonial rule, transformational resistance is a *proactive* effort to *transform* colonizer / colonized subjectivity, colonial discourses and material structures' (Jefferess 2008: 220, italics in original). We can see examples of this in the works of Nishnaabeg scholars Audra Simpson and Leanne Betasamosake Simpson, among others, in their rejections of colonial systems of knowledge while proactively asserting Indigenous ways of knowing.

In outlining the issue of knowledge, Audra Simpson states: 'In different moments, anthropology has imagined itself to be a voice, and in some disciplinary iterations, *the* voice of the colonized' (2014: 95). Anthropology's 'interlocutionary role' is:

> accorded with the imperatives of Empire and in this, specific technologies of rule that sought to obtain space and resources, to define and know the

difference that it constructed in those spaces, and to then govern those within . . . Knowing and representing people within those places required more than military might; it required the methods and modalities of knowing – in particular, categorization, ethnological comparison, linguistic translation, and ethnography. (Simpson 2014: 95)

This has a direct bearing on the study of religion, which has also categorized and compared using terms and divisions based on European norms.

The Indigenous refusal of the colonial ways of knowing is connected to the struggles for recognition and sovereignty. One stark example is the refusal of United States or Canadian citizenship in favour of an Indigenous one. The Haudenosaunee passport, which the Iroquois Nationals Lacrosse Team used for international travel, was accepted everywhere they went apart from the UK. They are refusing to disappear by holding such a passport (Simpson 2014: 25–6). It has also been a problem for many communities that Indigenous recognition is bestowed on individuals by the state, creating tensions by furthering a settler-Indigenous binary.

Kelsey Freeman, in her honours paper for Bowdoin College, suggests that in lacking 'viable political avenues available to them to address their grievances, [Indigenous people] may aim to transcend the political opportunity structure. In refusing state power, they seek to create a new order with room for collective, Indigenous identities within the state. To build this new order, however, Indigenous groups must construct a legitimate collective identity that speaks to Indigenous peoples' grievances' (2016: 12).

We can see an aspect of this in Leanne Betasamoke Simpson's *As We Have Always Done* (2017). Building on the work of Indigenous authors such as Audra Simpson, she writes: 'Within Nishnaabewin, refusal is an appropriate response to oppression, and within this context it is always generative; that is, it is always the living alternative' (2017: 33). The refusal of colonial categories involves embracing an alternative, for example their own Nishnaabewin knowledge and theories, including notions of what it means to be *kwe* ('female'). Under colonial rule, when women were told they were no longer status Indians if they married someone who was non-status, Simpson says 'many refused and continued to live as Nishnaabeg' (2017: 33; this discriminatory practice in Canada was removed in 1985). Simpson says she is able to 'exist as a kwe' because of generations of refusal, leading her to become interested in 'all the ways the Nishnaabeg refuse colonial authority, domination, and heteropatriarchy throughout time while generating Nishnaabewin' (2017: 34).

Simpson follows the 'grounded normativity' of Dene scholar Glen Coulthard's place-based practice and knowledge towards a radical 'refusal of state recognition as an organizing platform and mechanism for dismantling the systems of colonial domination' (Simpson 2017: 176). She asks, 'What happens, then, when we build movements that refuse colonial recognition as a starting point and turn inwards, building a politics of refusal that is generative? Well, you get things like the Dene Declaration' for self-recognition, after struggling to gain recognition from other governments (Simpson 2017: 177). In addition, this grounded normativity 'does not allow settler colonialism to frame the issues facing Indigenous peoples, and this is critical because settler colonialism will always define the issues with a solution that reentrenches its own power' (Simpson 2017: 178).

Following this deconstructive analysis, it is worth exploring in the next section ways Anishinaabe scholars do define themselves and their culture, especially if it is considered at odds with Western notions of 'religion'.

Indigenous ways of knowing: Anishinaabe examples

Nishnaabeg[3] terms are utilized in Leanne Betasamoke Simpson's *As We Have Always Done* (2017), where she explores what they mean to her within her experience of Nishnaabeg culture, some of them based on stories and guidance from elders and others. For example, she translates terms such as *aki* ('land') not as a commodity but more as a relationship (2017: 28), and *kwe* ('woman') again not as a commodity but more as a method of 'refusing colonial domination' (2017: 33), citing Audra Simpson's work.

The issue of translatability of emic terms does not necessarily lead to isolation from cross-cultural discourse or to untranslatability outside the group. In most cases, translations are imperfect, losing the sense of a term to some degree, but this is true also of 'religion' when applied to cultures outwith the European context in which it was defined. Given enough context, the sense of the words can be conveyed as much as any word can be.

Lawrence Gross (2014), whose PhD is in religious studies, devotes a whole chapter to the Anishinaabe concept of *bimaadiziwin* (the good life) in relation to the Anishinaabe 'religion'. Earlier in his book, Gross first highlights the role of silence, like that of a hunter who is also listening (2014: 60), reminding me of when I was met with silence in some situations during a visit to the Oglala Sioux Lakota on Pine Ridge. In my observation, sometimes it seemed to mean 'carry on as you are' and other times 'I don't agree but your mistakes are yours to make' or 'these are matters not to be discussed'. In an *inipi* (sweat lodge) ceremony, there is a moment of silence after each person speaks, as with the use of a talking stick passed around to each speaker. This silence does not separate individuals but brings them together in listening and receiving. Gross indicates this when he says, 'I have become more and more interested in the ways in which maintaining silence can help individuals make personal connections' (2014: 63). His story of how he and his wife would spend time in silence reminds me of when a friend and I used to go fishing when I was a child. We listened and observed, much like the silence of the hunter, only exchanging a few words of a practical nature.

The significance of silence in Anishinaabe ways of knowing, and its relationship to the concept of *bimaadiziwin*, could easily be missed by scholars from outside the culture. Gross says *bimaadiziwin*, or more properly *mino-bimaadiziwin*, encapsulates the 'moral structure of traditional Anishinaabe religion', a this-world focus rather than an afterlife, similar to Jocks' view above. He goes on to say: 'And since they do not have a religion but a way of life, *bimaadiziwin* also encompasses the spiritual life for the Anishinaabeg' (Gross 2014: 205). Gross stresses that 'the teaching does not exist as a definitive body of law. Instead, it is left up to the individual to develop an understanding of *bimaadiziwin* through careful attention to the teaching wherever it can be found', and it 'flows through just about every facet of traditional Anishinaabe religion' (2014: 207). While it may be left to the individual to figure it out, I have also observed that if one gets it wrong, they are often corrected by those around them.

Part of this lifelong process as described by Gross is listening to Anishinaabe stories, which do not end with a moral but rather allow the listener to develop their own understanding of the lesson – 'As such, the stories are designed to engage the listener, implanting seeds for later reflection and contemplation' (2014: 208). The opposite of this, one can surmise, is that dogmatism requires following pre-determined morals or laws but does not require any understanding of them.

Other Indigenous cultures in North America have equivalents to the concept of *bimaadiziwin*. Natalie Avalos Cisneros, of Mexican Indigenous descent, says:

> Native lifeways consist of living in an appropriate relationship to other persons and phenomena, meaning to honor the reciprocal nature of relations. Although Indigenous communities may not explicitly refer to themselves as 'religious' we see that Western notions of religiosity coincide with Indigenous notions of 'living right' or in a balanced relationship with the cosmos. (2014: 8)

Therefore, one could describe Indigenous North American equivalents to 'religion' as based on right relationship rather than right belief.

Indigenous tradition versus spirituality versus religion

While Indigenous people are rejecting the term 'religion', partly as a reaction to their experience at the hands of missionaries, many are adopting the term 'spirituality', which, to them, refers to a way of life that is non-institutional and pervasive. It is interesting to observe how their understanding of these categories stems from the meaning given to them by non-Indigenous people. Yet, their rejection of 'religion' is not surprising bearing in mind Indigenous peoples were at first told they had *no religion*, in the reports made by early explorers and missionaries (see Chidester 1996: 11). Furthermore, Indigenous people are not merely passive recipients of Western terminology, which they are compelled to accept or reject, but select and adapt terms for their own purposes.

Ronald Grimes, in seeking comments about non-Natives teaching Native American religions, found that some of his respondents took issue with 'religion' while a Mohawk scholar objected to 'spirituality' as an alternative, 'understanding it to connote a New Age mishmash of borrowed ideas and practices' (Grimes 2000: 86). However, Carrette and King, in their book *Selling Spirituality*, state that: '"Spirituality" has no universal meaning and has always reflected political interests' (2005: 30).

The pervasive assumption, though, is that religion refers to churches and doctrines while spirituality is all-encompassing. When I had once asked Deloria about this via email in 2003, he replied saying '"spirituality" is the popular name for religion because Indians refuse to separate religion from everything else' (in Owen 2008: 12). Whereas 'traditions' are thought to have been handed down through many generations, often adapted freely to present situations, and elude any distinction between religious and/or cultural phenomena.

Yet adding the term 'spirituality' to 'tradition', as in 'traditional spirituality', seems to set it apart from other aspects of culture. 'Spiritual', as a term, conveys the non-material. Something conveyed as a spirituality, understood as 'non-institutional', could make it more susceptible to misuse, appropriation and inculturation because an absence of collective authority is assumed in Western notions of spirituality where the 'self' is the authority. In terms of power, something labelled 'religion' has a greater privilege in society due to legal recognition when compared with something labelled a spirituality. In some cases, gaining recognition as a 'religion' could give the latter more validity and protection in society, but this would require it to conform to Protestant Christian expectations, which give primacy to 'beliefs'. It is, in my opinion, far better to challenge the need for 'religion' as a special entity in law in the first place.

The critical study of religion and the ethics of research

As a non-Indigenous scholar, my own research is enriched by reading about the politics of refusal and the ways Indigenous people identify themselves and what they do, while also analysing the rhetorical moves and implications, including an attention to what is being excluded. However, this has been a difficult chapter to write, in part because of this refusal. I am a non-Indigenous person writing about Indigenous knowledge and practices, which can be considered a form of colonialism. It is a question for anthropology, religious studies and other types of study that involve researching other people's lives, but at the same time it is of little worth to write only about ourselves (unless in some senses that is all any of us are doing). I am also non-religious in the popular sense of not having supernatural beliefs. Therefore, I see myself as a conversation partner where I try to understand myself as much as my opposite. Whatever position we occupy can bring advantages as well as create blind spots in our research. I have observed, especially in studies of Indigenous cultures, that when a critical stance is absent in non-Indigenous scholarship, the tone can be patronizing or, in an attempt to redescribe a group, it ends up getting it wrong because of unacknowledged assumptions at play in the terms chosen by the researcher.

Listening is key, which means being aware of language and our tendency to either 'translate' words into more conventional or familiar terms in our research or to ignore something important to the speaker because it is of little importance to us. One example happened during my doctoral research on cultural appropriation. When I visited the Mi'kmaq in Newfoundland, I heard many times the word 'protocol', which referred to proper conduct, especially in ceremonial contexts, but it took me a while to realize its significance for distinguishing cultural *borrowing* – for example, Mi'kmaq conducting a Plains Indian-style sweat lodge according to established protocols – from cultural *appropriations* of Indigenous practices that make little or no mention of them – such as the sweat lodges I had attended in the UK. It was an issue I thought a European ought to investigate. When I mentioned this to a few white, male anthropologists, they dismissed it, with one calling it a 'red herring', making me wonder if there was a gender element to it. However, Graham Harvey (2003) in religious studies had discussed following protocols in his article on 'guesthood' as an ethical decolonizing methodology, and so I persisted in making it central to my thesis.

Chippewa scholar Duane Champagne had offered guidance for ethical research on Indigenous cultures back in 1998 in his chapter for the volume *Natives and Academics: Researching and Writing about American Indians,* edited by Devon A. Mihesuah. 'As guests, scholars must respect community rules and desires to protect certain information from public view. Many communities, for example the Hopi, forbid publication of the location of sacred places or the details of certain sacred ceremonies. Scholars, Indian and non-Indian alike, must respect such wishes' (Champagne 1998: 183). This might at first seem to make studying Indigenous cultures quite tricky from a religious studies perspective, but it is a matter of respecting certain boundaries and limitations, which ought to be the case for all ethnographic research. After my first fieldwork visit to Newfoundland, I had presented a paper at a First Nations conference which included a discussion of a particular sweat lodge ceremony led by Joey Paul (see Owen 2008: 122–3), which led to a debate between Canadian First Nations participants about whether I had revealed aspects of the ceremony that should remain secret. Although they were generally satisfied that I had gained consent to include certain details of this ceremony in my research, for myself it was a learning experience and made me more careful going forward. On my second visit to Newfoundland, I made sure I had a conversation about my research with the traditional chief of the community, who told me about an anthropologist who had betrayed them and was not allowed to return, which I took as a warning. Looking back on what I had written, I think I did include more details than I needed to have about the ceremonies I participated in during my visits.

How do we combine an ethical approach with the critical religion approach? Critical does not mean 'criticism'; gaining consent and including the voices of Indigenous people does not equate to 'caretaking'. Russell McCutcheon, in the Foreword to the second edition of his book *Critics Not Caretakers*, holds that a critical approach does not mean to 'undermine' a group and nor does its opposite mean to 'support' a group (2024: xiii). A critical approach is to be aware that particular terms we use in the study of religion are not neutral:

> After all, designating something as 'militant,' 'political,' or 'extremist,' as opposed to 'lived,' 'authentic,' 'orthodox,' or 'mainstream,' are hardly innocent descriptive claims; rather they are all socially formative claims inasmuch as they effectively normalize, in the authorized voice of the scholar, but one way of doing, one that is obviously in competition with a variety of others that exist across a broad spectrum. (McCutcheon 2024: xiv)

From what I gather from McCutcheon's response to a Religious Studies Project podcast on the topic, a caretaker is one who takes things 'at face value', marginalizing the marginalized and labelling deviant what is labelled deviant by members of a group, the media or other scholars, whereas a 'critic' regards these moves the object of their study (see McCutcheon 2024: xiv).

Conclusion

Critical religion as a reflexive approach takes into account the colonial origins in employing the term 'religion' as a descriptor, particularly when paired with the term 'indigenous', by examining each category's normative assumptions and how they intersect with each other.

What I have learnt by applying a critical religion approach to the study of Indigenous cultures is that there is often a gap between self-representation and scholarly classifications. Imposing one culturally-derived category from Europe, such as 'religion', in place of a local indigenous one could be regarded as a form of cultural imperialism. 'Religion' is associated with missionary activity and the adoption or rejection of the term has generally assumed a European Christian model of 'religion'.

A critical religion approach acknowledges differences in categorization, and determines how terms are understood and employed or rejected. Scholars need not take sides in the debate about whether or not something is a 'religion', or indeed 'indigenous', but rather could research the assumptions, interests and intentions of those who employ or reject a term. Crucially, we must recognize power issues in all classification systems because decisions over what is included create a normativity and arbitrate on what is regarded as anomalous or deviant.

References

Adogame, Afe (2022), 'What Moral Responsibilities do Scholars and Students Have in Studying Indigenous Religions?', in Molly H. Bassett and Natalie Avalos (eds), *Indigenous Religious Traditions in Five Minutes*, 87–90, Sheffield: Equinox.

Avalos Cisneros, Natalie (2014), 'Indigenous Visions of Self-Determination: Healing and Historical Trauma in Native America', *Global Societies Journal*, 2: 1–14.

Bayart, Jean-François ([1996] 2005), *The Illusion of Cultural Identity*, trans. Steven Rendall, Janet Roitman, Cynthia Schoch and Jonathan Derrick, Chicago: University of Chicago Press.

Carrette, Jeremy and Richard King (2005), *Selling Spirituality: The Silent Takeover of Religion*, London: Routledge.

Champagne, Duane (1998), 'American Indian Studies Is for Everyone', in Devon A. Mihesuah (ed.), *Natives and Academic: Researching and Writing about American Indians*, 181–9, Lincoln and London: University of Nebraska Press.

Chidester, David (1996), *Savage Systems: Colonialism and Comparative Religion in Southern Africa*, Charlottesville and London: University of Virginia Press.

Crawford O'Brien, Suzanne with Inés Talamantez (2021), *Religion and Culture in Native America*, Lanham, ML: Rowman & Littlefield.
Culture on the Edge (n.d.), 'Preface', *Culture on the Edge: A Peer Reviewed Blog*. Available online: https://edge.ua.edu/identity/ (accessed 31 March 2023).
Deloria, Vine, Jr (1992), *God Is Red: A Native View of Religion*, Golden, CO: Fulcrum Publishing.
Deloria, Vine, Jr (1998), 'Comfortable Fictions and the Struggle for Turf: An Essay Review of *The Invented Indian: Cultural Fictions and Government Policies*', in Devon A. Mihesuah (ed.), *Natives and Academic: Researching and Writing about American Indians*, 65–83, Lincoln and London: University of Nebraska Press.
Fitzgerald, Timothy (2007), *Discourse on Civility and Barbarity: A Critical History of Religion and Related Categories*, Oxford: Oxford University Press.
Freeman, Kelsey J. (2016), 'The Rising Tide of Indigenous Mobilization: Identity and the Politics of Refusal in Mexico and Ecuador', *Honors Projects*, 55. Available online: https://digitalcommons.bowdoin.edu/honorsprojects/55 (accessed 19 December 2024).
Grimes, Ronald L. (2000), 'This May Be a Feud, but It Is Not a War: An Electronic, Interdisciplinary Dialogue on Teaching Native Religions', in Lee Irwin (ed.), *Native American Spirituality: A Critical Reader*, 78–94, Lincoln, NE: University of Nebraska Press.
Gross, Lawrence W. (2014), *Anishinaabe Ways of Knowing and Being*, Farnham: Ashgate.
Harvey, Graham (2003), 'Guesthood as Ethical Decolonising Research Method', *Numen*, 50 (2): 125–46.
Horii, Mitsutoshi (2021), *'Religion' and 'Secular' Categories in Sociology: Decolonizing the Modern Myth*, Cham: Palgrave Macmillan.
Hughes, Aaron W. and Russell T. McCutcheon (2022), *Religion in 50 Words: A Critical Vocabulary*, London and New York: Routledge.
Jefferess, David (2008), *Postcolonial Resistance: Culture, Liberation and Transformation*, Toronto, ON: University of Toronto Press.
Jocks, Chris (2004), 'Modernity, Resistance, and the Iroquois Longhouse People', in Jacob Olupona (ed.), *Beyond Primitivism: Indigenous Religious Traditions and Modernity*, 139–48, New York and London: Routledge.
Jocks, Chris (2022), 'Why Do Some Indigenous People Insist that What They Practice Is Not Religion?', in Molly H. Bassett and Natalie Avalos (eds), *Indigenous Religious Traditions in Five Minutes*, 22–4, Sheffield: Equinox.
MacKinnon, Iain (2008), *Crofters: Indigenous People of the Highlands and Islands*, Scottish Crofting Foundation. Available online: https://www.crofting.org/wp-content/uploads/2020/03/crofters-indigenous-peoples.pdf (accessed 21 September 2022).
McCutcheon, Russell (2024), *Critics Not Caretakers: Redescribing the Public Study of Religion*, 2nd edn, London and New York: Routledge.
Owen, Suzanne (2008), *The Appropriation of Native American Spirituality*, London and New York: Continuum.
Owen, Suzanne (2013), 'Druidry and the Definition of Indigenous Religion', in James L. Cox (ed.), *Critical Reflections on Indigenous Religions*, 81–92, Farnham: Ashgate.

Simpson, Audra (2014), *Mohawk Interruptus: Political Life Across the Borders of Settler States*, New York: Duke University Press.

Simpson, Leanne Betasamosake (2017), *As We Have Always Done: Indigenous Freedom through Radical Resistance*, Minneapolis: University of Minnesota Press.

Smith, Linda Tuhiwai (1999), *Decolonizing Methodologies: Research and Indigenous Peoples*, London and New York: Zed Books.

Walsh, David S. (2017), 'Spiritual, Not Religious; Dene, Not Indigenous: Tłı̨chǫ Dene Discourses of Religion and Indigeneity', in Greg Johnson and Siv Ellen Kraft (eds), *Handbook of Indigenous Religion(s)*, 204–20, Leiden: Brill.

9

Managing 'faith' in a modern state

'Time for Reflection' in the Scottish Parliament

Steven J. Sutcliffe

Introduction: Time for Reflection as a new faith ritual

In this chapter[1] I analyse the new ritual of 'Time for Reflection' (TFR), which has been held in the Scottish Parliament since October 1999. The ritual opens the weekly plenary session in the main chamber and consists of a four-minute spoken address to Members of the Scottish Parliament (MSPs) and to visitors in the public gallery. First I argue that, although TFR expands the parameters of 'faith' – a proxy for the increasingly problematized term 'religion' – beyond the established state religion of the UK, this dominant model remains in play and is mediated annually to the Church of Scotland General Assembly via the office of the Lord High Commissioner who represents the monarch of the Church of England. Second, I argue that the scope of this expansion is limited by the historical recruitment and performance of TFR. Third, I argue that the ritual form of TFR, in which usually one person speaks from an approved text at a lectern on a raised platform, inscribes a culturally 'Protestant' template into the performance.

TFR is thus of intrinsic interest in terms of its form and content as a new public ritual, and of extrinsic interest in how it normativizes a particular public performance of 'faith' in a devolved UK. My argument is based on the history of the development of TFR in its material, discursive and ritual contexts, supported by ethnographic snapshots of selected TFR performances during the first parliamentary term in 1999–2003, supplemented with observations from 2016–17 and later. My approach draws on 'category formation' (Baird 1971) in the study of religion/s (Sutcliffe 2020), which treats categories as strategic or tactical concepts deployed by interested agents in specific contexts to particular ends.[2] Previously I have used this method to disentangle emic and etic uses of the category 'new age' (Sutcliffe 2003), ambiguities in the academic formation of 'religious studies' (Sutcliffe 2008) and the taxonomic hegemony of 'world religions' over 'new age stuff' when identifying the historical content of 'religion' (Sutcliffe 2016). Diverse as these examples may seem, each serves as datum for a comparative analysis of 'what what we do does', to quote Foucault. 'Time for Reflection' is another case in point in the political impact of category formation.

State context

Before we explore the specifics of TFR, we need to get a sense of the wider political economy. Since 1999 a Scottish Parliament has operated again in Edinburgh, this time as a devolved unicameral (single) chamber within the UK state. Members of the Scottish Parliament (MSPs) are elected via a system of proportional representation and their work is conducted through a combination of plenary sessions and special committees. The Parliament is the material outcome of a long campaign for political devolution in Scotland, which has been shadowed by campaigns in the other nations of the UK, leading to a Northern Irish Assembly in Stormont, Belfast, in 1998, and the Senedd Cymru (Welsh Parliament) in Cardiff in 1999. The Scottish Parliament is the most powerful of these devolved legislatures in terms of holding a remit for education, health and transport. Other functions, notably defence, energy and immigration, are reserved to the UK Parliament in Westminster.[3]

In Scotland, the pageantry of devolution is displayed at the annual opening of the General Assembly of the Church of Scotland in May. Since 1929 it has met in the Assembly Hall in Edinburgh, which is now part of the New College complex that also houses Edinburgh University's School of Divinity (where I was based during most of the research for this chapter). It is noteworthy that the first session of the Scottish Parliament, between 1999 and 2004, was held in the Assembly Hall while new, bespoke premises were built. The General Assembly is opened by a visit from the Lord High Commissioner representing the UK monarch, whose roles also include being 'Supreme Governor' of the Church of England and a de facto member of the Church of Scotland. In this intricate political nexus, the imbrication of Protestantism and the UK state, as backdrop to the formation of TFR, can be traced.

Context and representation of religions in TFR

Both Scottish and UK Parliaments continue to retain a privileged space for the exercise of a 'religious' – historically, Christian – function despite the evidence of recent Censuses showing a steady decline in Christian identification. For example, in England and Wales in 2021, Christians were returned as a minority group: '46.2 per cent of people identified themselves as Christians, compared with 59.3 per cent of the population in the 2011 census, a 13-percentage point drop in a decade' (Duncan, García and Swan 2022). In Scotland the numbers were even less: just 38.8 per cent of the population identified as Christians, with the sharpest fall being in membership of the Church of Scotland, which in 2022 was recorded as 20 per cent of the population in contrast to 32 per cent in the 2011 Census and 42 per cent in the 2001 Census. This loss of half of its membership in just over a generation – from 42 per cent in 2001 to 20 per cent in 2022 – was accompanied by significant rises in 'no religion' in the 2021–22 Census: 37 per cent in England and Wales, 51 per cent in Scotland (Scotland's Census 2022).

Despite this evidence of UK decline in established (Christian) religion, the Westminster Parliament continues to host short worship rituals: daily sittings in both Houses of Parliament ('Commons' and 'Lords') begin with prayers spoken by the Speaker's chaplain (in the House of Commons) or by a senior Bishop (in the House of Lords). Their content should 'follow the Christian faith and there is currently no multi-faith element'.[4] In Stormont, 'prayers' are also held before the day's business but are less prescriptive: 'a period of two minutes silent prayer or contemplation' is indicated, which 'shall take place in private' (Northern Ireland Assembly Standing Orders 2024). However, the evangelical organization 'Transformations Ireland' has organized bi-monthly prayer meetings inside Stormont since 2003 with the aim to 'see God's Kingdom come and His will done and so we have prayed without any political bias or agenda' ('Stormont Prayer' on Transformations Ireland website). The standing orders of Senedd Cymru give no mention of prayers. However, the Senedd hosts an annual St David's Day Prayer Breakfast 'to share in the spirit of prayer and thanksgiving for the nation of Wales and our rich Christian heritage . . . to build relationships between church leaders and Members of the Senedd, and to reflect upon the relevance of the Christian faith in public life' (St David's Parliamentary Prayer Breakfast website).

Against the almost entirely Christian content in the other legislatures, TFR is clearly the most inclusive UK forum for the representation of 'the pluralization of life worlds' characteristic of late modern societies (Berger et al. 1973).[5] TFR has gradually encompassed not only representatives of 'world religions' – Buddhists, Christians, Hindus, Jews, Muslims and Sikhs – but also, more rarely, speakers from 'new religions' such as Baha'i, Brahma Kumari, Christian Scientist and Church of Jesus Christ of the Latter-Day Saints. Pagans, Humanists and Atheists have also appeared, although such 'outliers' are arguably the exceptions which prove the rule.[6]

The selection of TFR presenters would seem to gesture towards a kind of 'proportional representation' of religions with rough affinity to the voting model in Scotland's parliamentary elections. That said, there is no accurate transfer of the percentage of specific religious and indeed 'no religious' affiliation in the population at large into TFR representation, which, as we have seen, draws from a diminishing field of practice. In other words, the TFR profile does not represent an accurate proportionality of 'worldviews' in the Scottish population; otherwise, between one third and one half of all speakers would need to speak with the voice of 'no religion'.

Nevertheless, an early document entitled 'Time for Reflection: Background' states that TFR 'will follow a pattern based on the balance of beliefs in Scotland'.[7] Scottish Parliament Fact Sheet FS4-01 (2009), which lists all TFRs for the first session (1999–2003), unwisely adds '(based on the Census)'. The 'Background' continues: 'Invitations to address the Parliament in leading Time for Reflection will be issued by the Presiding Officer on advice from the Parliamentary Bureau'. Fact Sheet FS4-01 adds: 'In general, *nominations for contributors* are proposed to the Presiding Officer *by MSPs or by the religions or faiths directly*' and also that '[t]here have been occasions when *individuals* have written to the Presiding Officer with nominations' (emphasis added). These statements are confusingly hedged around with qualifications such as 'on advice', 'in general', 'reflects' and 'occasions when'. It also seems to be the case that MSPs, 'individuals' and even 'religions or faiths directly' can make nominations. 'It's not very scientific', I was told early on in my research in a conversation with the officer then responsible for TFR. I was also told that no applicant had (yet) been rejected, although some groups 'ruled themselves out' after reading the guidelines. Managing TFR therefore includes the Presiding Officer triaging nominations with a variety of proposers as well as following the advice of the Parliamentary Bureau and the Scottish Churches

Parliamentary Office, and eliciting agreement from successful applicants to perform TFR in a prescribed manner. How all this activity is coordinated remains opaque.[8]

The ritual content of TFR

TFR presenters are required to follow the Parliamentary Bureau's guidance, which has been revised on several occasions since 1999 in response to controversial renditions of TFR, discussed below. The current guidance requires the presenter to deliver a short text – 400 words maximum – at a stipulated position in the parliamentary chamber, to supply the text in advance, and not to deviate from it in delivery. The guidance advises that the Parliament's 'dignity and respect' policies should be upheld and that 'contributors may be asked to revise text that may be deemed to be sensitive'.

TFR itself is described as 'an opportunity for MSPs and members of the public to join together before a [plenary] meeting of the Parliament commences'. I quote the most recent guidance in full to show the granularity of management of the ritual:

1. Time for Reflection will normally be held in the Chamber of the Scottish Parliament as the first item of business each week (i.e. on Tuesdays at 2.00 pm) and recorded in the Official Report. Time for Reflection will last for a <u>maximum</u> of 4 minutes (up to 400 words at normal speaking speed). The Presiding Officer will invite contributors to deliver Time for Reflection.

2. The content of Time for Reflection should adhere to the following guidelines:

    (a) it will be in public and should be led in the context of both Parliament and the Scottish people as a whole;

    (b) it should consist of **either** a short narrative relating to personal experience or current affairs **and/or** prayers/readings from appropriate texts;

    (c) it should normally reflect the practice of the faith or belief community to which the Time for Reflection contributor belongs (if any);

    (d) it will not make political points;

    (e) it will not denigrate another faith, belief or none;

(f) it will be consistent with the principle of equal opportunities for all and should not include remarks or comments which are discriminatory; and

(g) the text should be submitted in advance to the Clerk and the content of the Time for Reflection should not deviate from the text provided.

3. Time for Reflection will be held in public, but Members and the public can be encouraged to enter the Chamber during the duration of Time for Reflection.

4. The procedure will be as follows:

(i) the person leading Time for Reflection will follow the Presiding Officer into the Chamber (once the gavel has brought the Chamber to attention) and take the seat to the left of the Presiding Officer. Members stand as the Presiding Officer comes into the Chamber and sit once he/she is seated;

(ii) the Presiding Officer will introduce Time for Reflection;

(iii) on completion, a Clerk will escort the Time for Reflection contributor out of the Chamber and the Presiding Officer will move on to the next item of business.[9]

TFR texts have been published in the parliamentary report since the first TFR in October 1999 and the Parliament has produced six online Fact Sheets documenting all dates and contributors with hyperlinks to texts (searchable on the Scottish Parliament website). Since January 2017, TFR has been video recorded on in-house television (see 'TV Archive' on the Scottish Parliament website). This forms an immense body of data with considerable detail and granularity. Here I can do no more than tease out some of the main lines of analysis for the 'category formation' approach I recommend.

Several initial critical points can be made about the guidance document. For example, a text is central to the ritual, and this must be submitted in advance and not deviated from (2g). Furthermore, its content must conform to stipulations including equal opportunities and non-discrimination (2f), and should not make 'political points' (2d); a further safety net is provided in the warning contained in the brief introduction to the guidance that 'contributors may be asked to revise text that may be deemed to be sensitive'. TFR has a national-state dimension – 'the Scottish people as a whole' (2a) – which may explain this caution. Finally, the spatial performance is tightly controlled by parliamentary ushers who steer the entrance and exit (point 4). The sum, I argue, is that TFR, while modestly expanding the representation of the 'plurality of life-worlds', is a closely choreographed ritual whose latent function lies in the reproduction of a culturally Protestant template for 'religion', recast as a matter of interiorized 'faith'. In the remainder of this chapter, I will attempt to substantiate this argument spatially, discursively and ethnographically.

The spatial context of TFR

The performance of TFR has been shaped by material space. As we have seen, the ritual takes place in an enclosed bureaucratic space to and from which entrance and exit are closely superintended, with the performance reduced to reading from a text at a lectern. The architecture of the ritual space plays a wider role here. Since 2004, the Parliament has occupied a new building at the foot of Edinburgh's High Street opposite Holyrood Palace. However, for its first session in 1999, it met in the Assembly Hall of the Church of Scotland on the Mound. This was built in 1858–9 for the Free Church of Scotland, which had split from the Church of Scotland in 1843. In 1900, use of the Assembly Hall passed to the United Free Church of Scotland and, after 1929, to the Church of Scotland following unification with the United Free Church. Since 1929, the Assembly Hall has hosted the annual General Assembly of the Church of Scotland. Thus, when the Parliament moved into the Assembly Hall, it was sharing a key space for Scottish Presbyterianism.

In 1998 a firm of Edinburgh architects was commissioned to convert the Assembly Hall into a parliamentary debating chamber. They described their remit as to produce 'a more politically-correct and non-confrontational horseshoe pattern' to break up the 'existing rectilinear tiering' of seating (Simpson and Brown website). The design for a new build had meanwhile been awarded to Catalan architect Enric Miralles (1955–2000), and his building duly opened in 2004 with an eclectic postmodern style:

> [T]he Parliament is an almost overwhelming sensory experience of complex shapes, materials, and structural devices. Every feature of the building is uniquely detailed. . . . Soaring spaces are juxtaposed with intimate, human-sized niches that create an exciting and unpredictable maze of architectural stimuli . . . which serves to emphatically reject the establishment of spatial hierarchies. (Langdon 2011: n.p.)[10]

Despite the radical differences between the nineteenth-century Scots Baronial style of the Assembly Hall and Enric Miralles' twenty-first-century Holyrood Parliament, a similar functionality shapes the actual performance space of TFR. In both buildings, the ritual must be performed at the secular equivalent of a pulpit. Beneath the surface of macro-scale architectural change from Scots Baronial to Postmodern lies ritual continuity.

Performing TFR: Early iterations

All iterations of TFR since the first on 27 October 1999 have been archived and, with patience, can be located on the Scottish Parliament website in the form of six Fact Sheets listing speaker, date, affiliation and hyperlink to the text. By the end of 2024, a total of 814 TFRs had been given across the twenty-five years of the Parliament, almost entirely solo but with occasional duets after 2011. As already noted, this represents an enormous quantity of data, including content of texts and details of speakers' affiliation, status (professional or lay) and sex, which I cannot analyse in any detail here. As also noted, there is evidence of increasing diversity of content (of text) and representation (of speaker) across the quarter-century since 1999, as we might reasonably expect in a period marked by decreasing church attendance and increasing 'non-religion' (charted by the three Censuses since 2001 which have kept pace with TFR). A full content analysis is required to nuance the present account. Here I focus on delineating the prototypical form and content of TFR, which was created in the first term and is still in service with only superficial changes.

The first TFR was given on 27 October 1999 by a Church of Scotland minister, Reverend Doctor Graham Blount, who spoke in his role as Scottish Churches Parliamentary Officer. Blount's text began with a reading from the Hebrew Book of Psalms, which he said 'express[es] the common ground of Christian and Jewish faith'. This was followed by an extract 'from the new hymn book that celebrates the common ground of faith shared by the Scottish Churches'. He completed his address with a prayer ending with a traditional Christian benediction: 'May the grace of our Lord Jesus Christ, the love of God and the friendship and fellowship of the Holy Spirit go with us now and always. Amen.'[11] The next seven TFRs before the end of 1999 were given by the Catholic Cardinal in Glasgow, the Catholic Archbishop of St Andrews and Edinburgh, the Primus of the Scottish Episcopal Church, the Church of Scotland minister of Greyfriars Tolbooth and Highland Kirk (representing Gaelic speaking Christians), the Principal of the Free Church of Scotland College, a Muslim Lecturer in Arabic and Islamic Studies in Glasgow, and the current Moderator of the General Assembly of the Church of Scotland. Among the Christian texts – which constituted all but one – the Reverend David Beckett departed from the non-political policy in TFR guidance by invoking the political value of the church-state relationship:

> The very existence of this Parliament is the fulfilment of a long-expressed wish of the Kirk's general assembly. Even at this early stage, it is interesting how often the concerns of Church and Parliament converge. . . . Social justice is perennially on the Church's agenda. If it ever disappeared . . . the Church would no longer deserve to exist.[12]

The text that would seem to differ most noticeably from the template was delivered by Dr Mona Siddiqui:

> As a Muslim, I stand here proud to be representing a faith and a community. . . . In giving recognition to the faith, the Scottish Parliament is giving recognition to a whole ethos and to different cultures, a commitment to religious communities and a willingness to show that Scottish society is a multi-faith society. . . . Our sacred books sometimes come with different stories, different social laws and even different routes to salvation, but one thing that they all share is a simple belief in God's love and mercy.[13]

The text then interprets a passage from the Qur'an. However, despite the landmark inclusion of Dr Siddiqui as a female Muslim speaker in a UK political assembly, the ritual prototype remains. That is, the address takes the form of a text, includes a reflexive identification, references a contemporary issue, quotes an authoritative scripture and ends with a homily. The meta-communication would seem to be that (religious) difference is acceptable as long as it is communicated in the approved form.

Although TFR has certainly diversified over the past twenty-five years, its formative content can be gleaned from analysis of the first parliamentary term, October 1999 to March 2003, in which the ritual became embedded into the weekly plenary session and began to develop a tradition of performance. The first term contained 127 addresses, which can be examined according to four main categories: Christian denomination, 'other' religion, sex and status (lay or professional). The first three categories are used in the Parliamentary Fact Sheet, and I have inferred the new category of status from supplementary notes to each TFR.

Male speakers gave 90 (or 71 per cent) iterations, and female speakers 37 (or 29 per cent). The three Christian denominations with the largest representation were the Church of Scotland (39, or 31 per cent), Roman Catholic (25, or 20 per cent) and the Scottish Episcopal Church (11, or 9 per cent); together these accounted for 75 (or 59 per cent) iterations. At least an additional 25 (or 20 per cent) were given by smaller Christian groups, including Methodists, Baptists and the Free Church. Also, on closer inspection, three out of four TFRs categorized as 'inter-denominational' were given by members of Christian organizations.[14] Thus at least 103 (or 81 per cent) of first term

TFRs were given by Christians of various denominations. The next largest group were Jews and Muslims (5 and 4 respectively), followed by Buddhists and Sikhs (2 each). Other groups appeared once, such as Brahma Kumari, Christian Scientist, the Church of Jesus Christ of Latter-Day Saints, Hindu and Humanist. In terms of occupational status, overwhelmingly the speakers were professionals: ministers, priests and convenors, with perhaps six TFRs led by lay or non-professional people including two secondary school students.

On this rough count, the first term of TFR was overwhelmingly led by male (71 per cent), Christian (81 per cent) and professional elites (c. 95 per cent). This sample is out of balance with the 2001 Census data on females (52 per cent) and males (48 per cent) in the Scottish population at large, and with the ratio of female (54 per cent) to male (46 per cent) identifying as Christian. The 81 per cent Christian TFR is somewhat closer to the 65 per cent of the wider population identifying as Christian in the 2001 Census, although that figure has dropped significantly to 39 per cent in the 2022 Census. The question of the gap between TFR representation and wider public practice returns when the status of contributors is considered, for clearly the vast majority of those identifying as 'religious' in the population at large will be lay practitioners rather than ministers, priests or other trained professionals.

Watching TFR: Ethnographic snapshots

To enrich the analysis, between 2001 and 2017 I conducted a peripatetic longitudinal study of TFR based on in-person observations of more than twenty-five separate TFRs, plus scrutiny of related debates and issues in the media. First, I present a few ethnographic snapshots which describe the ritual as I observed it from the public galleries in the two different parliamentary chambers. During my first visits in the Assembly Hall, I noticed that the chamber as a whole – MSPs as well as the public – would become quiet and attentive as TFR began. My fieldnotes describe a '"sermon-like" quality of address'.[15] Nevertheless, many MSPs remained outside the chamber and slipped in after TFR had finished. On one early visit, only around one-fifth of MSPs were present for TFR, although the public gallery was busy with two secondary school parties. On this occasion, the TFR leader was a male Free Church minister who began with the words 'let us hear the word of God' and proceeded to read from Isaiah ch. 6, finishing with the ritual invitation 'let us pray'. Of those in the chamber, I noticed one MSP yawning and another reading.[16]

Public access to the weekly plenary was 'walk in' during the first term. After the move to the new build, I had to book in advance. On one occasion in September 2016, having passed the metal detector, a security officer enquired (pleasantly), 'what's the purpose of your visit to the Parliament this afternoon?' When I said I was attending TFR, he said: 'You're in good time, the prayer group's in [the public gallery] already'. Once inside the building, two security personnel vetted entrance to the public gallery itself. I counted sixteen MSPs in the chamber and sixty people in the public gallery. Eight sat together wearing crimson tops, whom I assumed were the prayer group. This particular TFR was given by a Pastor from the Assemblies of God, Champion Life Church, in Glasgow's East End, and ended with the affirmation 'God bless you', which received a smattering of applause in the gallery. After TFR ended, a few people entered who had been prevented while it was in progress.[17] This interdiction on disturbing TFR was repeated to me by the usher on another visit in October 2017, who added: 'it's not us who make the rules'. This TFR was delivered by Alan Spence (b. 1947), a Scottish writer and a follower of the Indian *guru* Sri Chinmoy (1931–2007).[18] On this occasion I counted around twenty MSPs in the chamber and around eighty people in the public gallery, including twenty from the Prayer Group.

My ethnographic impressions were of an ambiguous event: an avowedly 'new' ritual, performed initially in an ecclesiastical building and subsequently in a postmodern new build, framed by interdictions to 'remain silent' and to 'refrain from opening and closing the doors', enforced by prohibition of entry when in progress, yet recorded in the official business of a European state parliament. The UK Parliament also holds prayers, as noted earlier, but this is done 'by tradition' and their content does not form part of the official Hansard record (see 'Prayers' on UK Parliament website). The Scottish Parliament had broken with Christian exclusivity in TFR's representation of a measure of religious diversity, yet its ritualization of 'faith' had been constructed along culturally Protestant lines and then inscribed in the official 'business' record.

Constructing TFR: Discourse analysis

At this point we need to back-pedal to uncover the discursive process behind the creation of this ambiguous ritual. In May 1999, Conservative MSP Alex Fergusson (1949–2018) lodged the first parliamentary motion (S1M-1), which was 'for prayers to be held on a non-denominational basis, at the start of each plenary session'. In his preamble to the motion, Fergusson addressed the Presiding Officer, Sir David Steel (b. 1938), as follows:

> I, like you, Sir David, am a son of the manse. I was, therefore, brought up in a Christian, God-fearing household, although I admit that for much of

my early upbringing I tended to fear the wrath of my father on earth rather more than my father in heaven. None the less, throughout the years I have found the occasional moment of prayer or simply of quiet and reflective thought to be of great assistance in my daily business.

Note the encoded Presbyterian genealogy: patriarchal ('father on earth / in heaven'), dwelling ('manse', a word with strong Presbyterian association), ontology ('God-fearing'), ritual ('prayer'), piety ('quiet and reflective'). Fergusson argued that Parliament 'should ask for a little daily advice and guidance from the greatest expert of all ['my father in heaven'] . . . particularly as it meets in the assembly building of the Church of Scotland'. In support, Fergusson referred to MSPs' inaugurations: although one third had made secular affirmations, 'two thirds of us chose . . . to swear our allegiance in the name of God'.

In response, Scottish National Party (SNP) MSP Alex Salmond (1954–2024) moved that Fergusson's term 'non-denominational' be replaced by 'interfaith':

in other words, relating not only to Christian denominations, but to the various other faiths in Scotland. It is important that this Parliament affirms that the Muslim, Hindu, Sikh and Jewish communities are important in the wider Scottish community and that, if we have some form of religious or other observance in our proceedings, it should encompass all the faiths of Scotland.

Salmond advocated for 'a two-or-three minute thought for the day' to be based in 'advice from representatives of the faiths of Scotland'.[19] SNP MSP Dorothy-Grace Elder (b. 1942) was supportive of Fergusson's motion, describing herself as 'a poor sinner' and calling for an 'element of spirituality in this Parliament'. Fergusson's fellow Conservative MSP, Annabel Goldie (b. 1950), declared her support as 'a member of the Church of Scotland and an elder of the kirk'.[20] Although rejecting the concept of 'prayers', then Labour First Minister Donald Dewar (1937–2000) supported 'a quiet period of contemplation and reflection'. Supporting Salmond, Green MSP Robin Harper (b. 1940) proposed 'a period of contemplation preceded by a talk from a representative of a religion'. Liberal Democrat MSP Donald Gorrie (1933–2012) called for 'proportional praying': 'We must embrace all religions . . . all the Christian denominations and all the other faiths.' But Labour MSP John McAllion (b. 1948) requested 'assurance that no two faiths would be able to form a coalition to impose their prayers on the rest of the faiths', and argued that 'not only is Scotland multifaith, it contains people who do not have any faith in God'. The debate is rich in detail and deserves detailed discourse analysis. In the end, Salmond's advocacy for an 'interfaith' interpretation of 'prayers' led to a revised recommendation that plans for TFR 'on a non-denominational basis' be drawn up by the

Parliamentary Bureau: A slender majority of MSPs supported this amended version of S1M-1.[21]

TFR: Representing diversity in a particular way

Thus far I have argued that analysis of the history of the debate on the motion for 'non-denominational prayers', supported by ethnographic observation and content analysis of early texts, reveals TFR to constitute a normative ritual performance of 'faith' moulded by culturally 'Protestant' and specifically 'Presbyterian' discursive elements. The historical domination of the ritual by Christian representatives supports this thesis, and not only in the first term. For example, the count for the third parliamentary session (2007–11) included 18 (or 13 per cent) 'no religion' contributions while 105 (or 74 per cent) were given by Christian speakers; of these, 45 (or 32 per cent) Church of Scotland members formed the largest group of all TFRs as well as nearly half of Christian TFRs. In the most recent Fact Sheet for 2021–25, 81 (or 62 per cent) out of 132 TFRs were delivered by Christians from various denominations. Church of Scotland contributors once again formed the largest (if declining) TFR representation overall (38, or 29 per cent), but this time 34 (or 26 per cent) were categorized as 'non-faith'.

Despite the continuing sizeable representation of Christians, there is a modest yet increasing 'post-Presbyterian' diversification in the TFR portfolio that requires comment. Let us briefly examine the seeds of this in the first parliamentary term. A first index concerns contributions by Catholics, who historically have borne the brunt of sectarian discrimination in Scotland. 20 per cent of TFRs in the first session are Catholic, a little more than Catholic identification in the population as a whole (16 per cent) and hence gaining approximate representational parity. Church of Scotland representation in TFR stands at 31 per cent compared with 42 per cent of the population as a whole. In this sense, the initial TFR demographic – whether by design or accident – is weighted against the dominant religion. A similarly contested topic is the status of 'new' religions, which forms a second index of the scope of 'post-Presbyterian' representation. Several are represented in the first term, including the Church of Jesus Christ of Latter-Day Saints and the Brahma Kumaris, both of which have been pejoratively constructed as 'cults' by some commentators.

A third index is the various groups classifiable as 'interfaith', 'inter-denominational' or 'ethical'. For example, one TFR presenter was convenor of the newly established Scottish Interfaith Council (in 1999), now called Interfaith Scotland; however, in the Parliament's own count she was included under the category 'inter-denominational' alongside three other presenters representing Christian umbrella groups.[22] 'Ethical' contributors included a Humanist and charity representatives. The inclusion of the Scottish Interfaith Council in the first term is a particularly noteworthy development and indeed the term was explicitly used by Alex Salmond in the debate on S1M-1 above. Explicitly 'interfaith' initiatives have begun to enter wider displays of civic religion in the twenty-first century: for example, the 'kirking of the Parliament' service in St Giles Cathedral in May 2003 incorporated Qur'anic recitation into an ecumenical Christian programme, while at least one long-standing Edinburgh secondary school, the Royal High School, organizes its 'religious observance' programme around the concept of 'Time for Reflection' following the steer by Education Scotland in 2014.[23]

Pushing back and managing controversy

Thus far I have argued that TFR is a tightly controlled and carefully managed ritual which has as its aim the production of a specific, normative expression of public faith for post-devolution Scotland. Occasionally some contributors have pushed back against this norm, which has in turn led to amendments to the ritual.

An interesting although uncontroversial early variation in performance came from a Brahma Kumari (13 February 2002) who introduced a guided meditation into TFR. This shifted the model away from a Reformed acoustic model of 'hearing the word' into a more participative, psychological mode. Arguably, this only marginally disturbed the template since the meditation itself was designed to be internalized by listeners and required no change in bodily deportment. But could a TFR presenter move their body or arms in some way, and/or require MSPs and the public gallery to do the same? Could incense be lit to accompany the ritual? Could a statue or icon be placed on the lectern? Could a glossolalic or mediumistic performance be accommodated? These examples may seem exaggerated in the context of a parliamentary chamber but in other ritual contexts they are, of course, unremarkable or even mandatory for proper practice.

That the Parliamentary Bureau is alert to the impact of performances that push the boundaries of the protocol is evident in revised guidance for TFR issued in April 2005. This followed a high-profile pre-Christmas TFR on 22 December 2004 by Cardinal Keith O'Brien (1938–2018) which contrasted the concrete experience of prisoners in Edinburgh's HMP Saughton with the metaphorical experience of 'captives' in wider society 'to an addiction to drink, drugs, sexual aberrations or whatever'; to both parties, O'Brien concluded,

Isaiah and Jesus offered a message of liberty. Green MSP Patrick Harvie (b. 1973) issued a press release the next day calling for MSPs 'to condemn [O'Brien's] remarks' on the grounds that 'to compare lesbian and gay people to criminals and to describe them as aberrations . . . was an insult to the Parliament and amounted to promoting intolerance and bigotry'. Harvie duly drafted a motion condemning O'Brien's 'gratuitous insult' to Scotland's LGBT community and called for 'the choice of speakers at Time for Reflection . . . to fully reflect the attitudes, values and beliefs which Scotland, as a modern society, encompasses'.[24] In April 2005 the Parliamentary Bureau issued revised guidelines for TFR, notably stressing that 'contributions will be consistent with the principle of *equal opportunities for all* and should not include remarks or comments that are *discriminatory*' and that 'it will not denigrate another faith *or those without a faith*' (emphasis added). *The Herald*, Glasgow, reported the response of a Catholic church spokesman:

> Discrimination is in the ear of the beholder. . . . If MSPs don't want to be questioned or challenged, it calls into question the whole purpose of [TFR]. Maybe they should consider scrapping it altogether if they are not willing to entertain freedom of expression. (Quoted in *The Herald*, 1 May 2005)

It fits the logic of my argument that the first public challenge to TFR should come from a Cardinal of the Catholic Church, historically Scotland's pre-eminent religious minority, and that this should in turn be met by a robust response from a pre-eminent civil society minority. To use de Certeau's terminology, the strategic positioning of TFR could be pushed back on from a variety of tactical positions.[25]

A very different challenge was mounted in 2014 by Norman Bonney (1944–2015), Professor of Sociology at Edinburgh Napier University and founder of the Edinburgh Secular Society. Bonney presented a petition to the Parliamentary Bureau arguing for greater representation of atheists, humanists and 'non-religious' in TFR to more accurately reflect the socio-demography of the Scottish Census; he also pitched for an 'open public debate' on the scope of TFR (Bonney 2014). His case, made by letter and in public, was considered by the Parliament's petitionary committee. The decision was no action on Bonney's petition for boosted atheist representation, but some acknowledgement of the need for a future review of TFR.

Further insight into the behind-the-scenes negotiations preceding his TFR in 2015 is provided by Gary McLellan of the Humanist Society in Scotland, who writes:

> My words were carefully chosen, and there was a lot of tense negotiation with the Parliamentary authorities – although . . . they never at any stage

sought to change the content of my message, they were very anxious to avoid my words being too critical.[26]

McLellan gamely adds:

I'm going to continue to encourage the Parliament to publish details of all those who have applied or been recommended, we need much more transparency in this area.

From a very different public perspective to Bonney and McLellan, there is at least one religious group which proactively engages TFR. Parliamentary Prayer Scotland describes itself as a 'non-denominational Christian group that exists to pray for the needs of the Members of the Scottish Parliament'. Its website contains a picture of a crown with the title 'Jesus King of Kings' and it describes itself as 'non-party political'. It states its main activity as praying for individual MSPs, justified by a Christian text, 1 Timothy 2.1-3, which urges 'prayers, intercession and thanksgiving' for 'kings and all those in authority, that we may live peaceful and quiet lives in all godliness and holiness'. Members gather in the public gallery during TFR, as I observed above, although I had been unaware of their ritual purpose: 'The core prayer group . . . pray[s] inside the chamber while the time for reflection is being held' (Parliamentary Prayer Scotland website).

TFR and the category of faith

The status of TFR as a public ritual would seem to be attractive for numerous groups with vested interests in acquiring a measure of the symbolic capital of a pluralizing 'religious' field. From a Bourdiesian perspective, TFR could be seen as a point of entry into a new field of competition for the kind of symbolic capital previously called 'religion' but increasingly retooled in the public domain as 'faith'. Although the category 'religion' has received much critical attention in recent years due to its historical entanglement with Protestant theology and European colonialism, the category 'faith' has not (yet) attracted such scrutiny. This category is widely used within traditional UK state discourse, for example to describe the monarch as 'defender of the faith'.[27] Theologically, 'faith' appears in influential liberal Protestant models of religion, especially as developed in 'the long 1960s' (Marwick 1998): for example, in Wilfred Cantwell Smith's seminal separation between (personal, interior) 'faith' and (historical, collective) 'cumulative tradition' in *The Meaning and End of Religion* (Smith [1962] 1995) and in *The Faith of Other Men* (Smith 1962). Another powerful strategy behind the shift to 'faith' may be a rebranding exercise to create blue water: first, from 'religion', as the term has been tainted in the early twenty-first century by association with 'terror' and 'fundamentalism' especially after 9/11; second, from 'spirituality', increasingly preferred in popular discourse to 'religion' for talking about emotional and psychological aspects of experience, but tainted in public discourse by perceptions of superficiality (Sutcliffe 2022). 'Faith' communicates the ethos of belief, tolerance and personal relationships associated with politically liberal understandings of 'religion', while quietly dropping that increasingly problematized term.

However, analysis of the discourse of 'faith' from the perspective of category formation and function remains under-developed. In the UK, James Beckford argues that its increasing public use, especially in such amalgams as 'faith sector' and 'multi-faith', was in part a product of the ideological preference of the UK New Labour government from the mid-1990s to 2010 to foster a 'partnership' between state and church, in which the state took a new lead in working with the third sector of voluntary organizations. Beckford argues that this approach amounted to 'a subtle but significant change' in policy which 'introduced a discourse of "faith", "faith traditions", "faith communities" and "faith-based" activities' which had the effect of 'shift[ing] the focus of public attention away from the differences between religions and, instead, emphasized their common properties as faiths' (Beckford 2010: 126). A discourse emerged on the value of faith as 'a unitary and potentially unifying force that was capable of enhancing public – as well as private – life' (Beckford 2010: 127). This *lingua franca* has since firmed up at numerous sites: for example, in the 'Faith Zone' in London's Millennium Dome (Gilliat-Ray 2004); in the protected category of 'faith schools'; in the consolidation of 'interfaith' dialogue (Sutherland 2025); and in advocacy projects such as the 'Three Faiths Fellowship' of Abrahamic religions. Teemu Taira has also noted 'indicators of discursive change from "religion" to "faith" . . . for example in television programmes (especially documentaries) as well as in political treatments' (2013: 40). Like Beckford, Taira argues that 'one of the reasons for these changes is the idea that *religion separates*, while . . . *faith connects* people by emphasising *something in common*' (2013: 40; emphasis added).

Conclusion: Managing TFR as a 'faith' ritual in a state parliament

I argue that the cumulative evidence presented in this chapter – based on discourse analysis, spatial contextualization and ethnographic snapshots – suggests the existence of a devolved strategy for modelling TFR as a normative public expression of 'faith'. Here, 'faith' represents a set of pluralistic, 'post-Presbyterian' practices that are to be ritually performed in the Parliament as a form of 'proportional praying' (Bonney 2013b). As Lanouette argues from his review of Commonwealth countries, 'to date, no legislature rooted in the British parliamentary system has been so innovative . . . despite the fairly high percentage of people who state they have no religion . . . which may seem paradoxical' (Lanouette 2009: 6). Not only that, but careful analysis of the management of TFR indicates the existence of mechanisms designed to inculcate and monitor a particular representation of 'faith' according to a ritual prototype laid down early on in the development of the Scottish Parliament. In other words, while TFR has undoubtedly broadened representation of the plurality of life-worlds in Scotland, it has done so through the creation of a ritual form indebted to a Protestant and particularly Presbyterian prototype.

Modest as this weekly four-minute ritual might seem, TFR raises questions about the ideological control of the means of production of representations of 'faith/religion' in a public state forum. As we have seen, the very first motion of the Scottish Parliament concerned a perceived need for prayers which immediately established a principle that could be moderated and qualified but not easily unpicked. Since then, some parties have sought to increase the scope and inclusivity of TFR from different – and not necessarily complementary – perspectives. For others, especially secularists such as Bonney, TFR raises pressing questions about the legitimacy of holding a religious address within the premises of, and as part of the official business record of, a modern state parliament. The careful superintendence of the content and conduct of the ritual by the Parliamentary Bureau signals awareness of these political delicacies. At the very least, the evidence reviewed in this chapter provides further empirical support for Beckford's argument that 'religions', as social constructions, remain 'active in the British public sphere [but] the level and manner of this religious activity are strongly conditioned by government policy and state structures' (Beckford 2010: 133).

References

All-Party Parliamentary Humanist Group (2020), *Time for Reflection: A Report of the All-Party Parliamentary Humanist Group on Religion or Belief in the UK Parliament*. Available online: https://humanists.uk/wp-content/uploads/APPG-report_religion-in-parliament_Jan2020_print.pdf (accessed 6 March 2025).

Baird, Robert D. (1971), *Category Formation and the History of Religions*, The Hague: Mouton.

Baldwin, Nicholas D. J. (2013), 'Introduction I: Legislatures', in Nicholas D. J. Baldwin (ed.), *Legislatures of Small States: a Comparative Study*, 1–11, Abingdon: Routledge.

Beckford, James A. (2010), 'The Return of Public Religion? A Critical Assessment of a Popular Claim', *Nordic Journal of Religion and Society*, 23 (2): 121–36.
Berger, Peter L., Brigitte Berger and Hansfried Kellner (1973), *The Homeless Mind: Modernization and Consciousness*, Harmondsworth: Penguin.
Bonney, Norman (2013a), 'Established Religion, Parliamentary Devolution and New State Religion in the UK', *Parliamentary Affairs*, 66 (2): 425–42.
Bonney, Norman (2013b), 'Proportional Prayers: Time for Reflection in the Scottish Parliament', *Parliamentary Affairs*, 66 (4): 816–33.
Bonney, Norman (2013c), 'Scotland's Pagan Parliament: A Token Atheist in Time for Reflection', 4 March 2013. Available online: https://paganparliament.blogspot.com/2013/03/an-atheist-at-holyrood.html (accessed 26 December 2024).
Bonney, Norman (2014), 'PE01514: Making Time for Reflection Representative of All Beliefs', Petition to the Scottish Parliament, 16 April. Available online: https://webarchive.nrscotland.gov.uk/20240327083803/http://archive2021.parliament.scot/GettingInvolved/Petitions/equaltimeforreflection (accessed 11 June 2023).
Church of Scotland website, 'Eldership', https://www.churchofscotland.org.uk/get-involved/serve/office-bearers/eldership (accessed 3 January 2025).
Church of Scotland website, 'Scottish Churches Parliamentary Office', https://www.churchofscotland.org.uk/get-involved/scottish-churches-parliamentary-office (accessed 26 December 2024).
Common Ground Editorial Committee (1998), *Common Ground: A Song Book for All the Churches*, Edinburgh: St Andrew Press.
De Certeau, Michel ([1980] 1984), *The Practice of Everyday Life*, Originally Published as *L'Invention du Quotidien*, Berkeley: University of California Press.
Donovan, Paul (1997), 'The Breakfast Pulpit', in *All Our Todays: Forty Years of Radio 4's Today Programme*, 149–73, London: Jonathan Cape.
Duncan, Pamela, Carmen Aguilar García and Lucy Swan (2022), 'Census 2021 in Charts: Christianity Now Minority Religion in England and Wales', *The Guardian*, 29 November. Available online: https://www.theguardian.com/uk-news/2022/nov/29/census-2021-in-charts-christianity-now-minority-religion-in-england-and-wales (accessed 29 December 2024).
Education Scotland website, 'Religious Observance – Time for Reflection', https://education.gov.scot/resources/religious-observance-time-for-reflection/ (accessed 2 February 2025).
Gilliat-Ray, Sophie (2004), 'The Trouble with "Inclusion": A Case Study of the Faith Zone at the Millenium Dome', *The Sociological Review*, 52 (4): 459–77.
Langdon, David (2011), 'AD Classics: Scottish Parliament Building / Enric Miralles', *ArchDaily*, 14 February. Available online: https://www.archdaily.com/111869/ad-classics-the-scottish-parliament-enric-miralles (accessed 7 February 2025).
Lanouette, Martin (2009), 'Prayer in the Legislature: Tradition Meets Secularization', *Canadian Parliamentary Review*, 32 (4): 2–7.
Learmonth, Andrew (2024), 'Pagan to Deliver Holyrood's Time for Reflection Slot', *The Herald*, 15 January. Available online: https://www.heraldscotland.com/news/24048776.pagan-deliver-holyroods-time-reflection-slot/ (accessed 31 July 2024).
Lloyd-Jones, Naomi and Margaret M. Scull (2018), 'A New Plea for an Old Subject? Four Nations History for the Modern Period', in Naomi Lloyd-Jones

and Margaret M. Scull (eds), *Four Nations Approaches to Modern 'British' History: A (Dis)United Kingdom?*, 3–31, London: Palgrave MacMillan.

Marwick, Arthur (1998), *The Sixties: Cultural Revolution in Britain, France, Italy and the United States c. 1958 to c. 1974*, Oxford: Oxford University Press.

McKean, Charles (1999), 'Theatres of Pusillanimity and Power in Holyrood', *Scottish Affairs*, 27: 1–22.

Northern Ireland Assembly Standing Orders (2024), 'Item 8: Prayers', 26 November. Available online: https://www.niassembly.gov.uk/assembly-business/standing-orders/standing-orders-26-november-2024/#a8 (accessed 26 December 2024).

Parliamentary Prayer Scotland website, https://www.ppscotland.org/ (accessed 3 February 2025).

Prideaux, Mel and Andrew Dawson (2018), 'Interfaith Activity and the Governance of Religious Diversity in the United Kingdom', *Social Compass*, 65 (3): 363–77.

Royal High School website, 'Time for Reflection', https://royalhighschool.co.uk/time-for-reflection/ (accessed 2 February 2025).

Samuel, Raphael (1995), 'British Dimensions: "Four Nations History"', *History Workshop Journal*, 40: iii–xxii.

Scotland's Census 2022 (2024), 'Ethnic Group, National Identity, Language and Religion'. Available online: https://www.scotlandscensus.gov.uk/2022-results/scotland-s-census-2022-ethnic-group-national-identity-language-and-religion/ (accessed 29 December 2024).

Scottish Parliament Official Report (2024), 'Meeting of the Parliament: Tuesday 29 October 2024'. Available online: https://www.parliament.scot/chamber-and-committees/official-report/search-what-was-said-in-parliament/meeting-of-parliament-29-10-2024?meeting=16058&iob=137115 (accessed 1 February 2025).

Scottish Parliament website, 'Parliamentary Bureau', https://www.parliament.scot/about/how-parliament-works/parliament-organisations-groups-and-people/parliamentary-bureau (accessed 29 December 2024).

Scottish Parliament website, 'Presiding Officer and Deputy Presiding Officers', https://www.parliament.scot/about/how-parliament-works/parliament-organisations-groups-and-people/presiding-officer-and-deputy-presiding-officers (accessed 29 December 2024).

Scottish Parliament website, 'TV Archive', https://www.scottishparliament.tv/archive (accessed 2 February 2025).

Shephard, Mark (2013), 'Scotland: Britain Devolved – The Scottish Parliament', in Nicholas D. J. Baldwin (ed.), *Legislatures of Small States: a Comparative Study*, 158–74, Abingdon: Routledge.

Sherwood, Harriet (2017), 'John Humphrys says *Thought for the Day* message "deeply boring"', *The Guardian*, 30 October. Available online: https://www.theguardian.com/media/2017/oct/30/john-humphrys-says-thought-for-the-day-message-deeply-boring (accessed 27 February 2025).

Simpson and Brown website, 'The Interim Scottish Parliament', https://www.simpsonandbrown.co.uk/architecture/leisure-commercial/the-interim-scottish-parliament/ (accessed 1 February 2025).

Smith, Wilfred Cantwell (1962), *The Faith of Other Men*, Toronto: Canadian Broadcasting Company.

Smith, Wilfred Cantwell ([1962] 1995), *The Meaning and End of Religion*, Minneapolis, MN: Fortress Press.

Standing Orders of the Scottish Parliament (2024), 'Chapter 5: The Parliamentary Bureau and Management of Business', 6th edn, 2 July. Available online: https://www.parliament.scot/about/how-parliament-works/parliament-rules-and-guidance/standing-orders/chapter-5-the-parliamentary-bureau-and-management-of-business#topOfNav (accessed 30 December 2024).

St David's Parliamentary Prayer Breakfast website, 'About Us', https://ppb.wales/about-us/ (accessed 26 December 2024).

Sutcliffe, Steven J. (2003), *Children of the New Age: A History of Spiritual Practices*, London: Routledge.

Sutcliffe, Steven J. (2008), 'Historiography and Disciplinary Identity: The Case of "Religious Studies"', in Simon Oliver and Maya Warrier (eds), *Theology and Religious Studies: An Exploration of Disciplinary Boundaries*, 101–18, London: T and T Clark / Continuum.

Sutcliffe, Steven J. (2016), 'The Problem of "Religions": Teaching Against the Grain with "New Age Stuff"', in Christopher R. Cotter and David G. Robertson (eds), *After World Religions: Reconstructing Religious Studies*, 23–36, Abingdon: Routledge.

Sutcliffe, Steven J. (2020), '"What's in a Name?": The Case for "Study of Religions"', *Religion*, 50 (1): 129–36.

Sutcliffe, Steven J. (2022), 'Spirituality', in George Chryssides and Amy Whitehouse (eds), *Contested Concepts in the Study of Religion: A Critical Exploration*, 117–21, London: Bloomsbury.

Sutherland, Liam T. (2025), *One Nation, Many Faiths: Religious Pluralism and National Identity in an Interfaith Organisation*, London: Bloomsbury Academic.

Taira, Teemu (2013), 'Making Space for Discursive Study in Religious Studies', *Religion*, 43 (1): 26–45.

The Herald (2005), 'Crackdown on Preachers' Attacks on Minorities at Holyrood', 1 May. Available online: https://www.heraldscotland.com/news/12494643.exclusive-crackdown-on-preachers-attacks-on-minorities-at-holyrood/ (accessed 7 March 2025).

Transformations Ireland website, 'Stormont Prayer', https://www.transformations-ireland.org/stormont-prayer (accessed 26 December 2024).

UK Parliament website, 'Prayers', https://www.parliament.uk/about/how/business/prayers/ (accessed 12 July 2024).

Younger, Steve (2018), *Time for Reflection: A Guide to School Chaplaincy and Spiritual Development*, Edinburgh: St Andrew Press.

10

Thinking outside of the 'religion and politics' duality

The Jewish-Israeli case*

Yaacov Yadgar

Introduction

Taking the critical epistemological arguments made in the wider fields of 'critical religion' and 'post-secularism' seriously, we are left with a quandary: How can we understand and interpret the complicated relations of the politics, or even theopolitics, of the modern state with what the nation-statist configuration of power itself terms as apolitical, private and non-rational 'religion'? In this essay I suggest that we approach this relation via the ubiquitous yet often misinterpreted concept of tradition. I approach the Israeli and Zionist cases, seeking to reframe and reinterpret what would usually fall under 'religion and politics' or 'religion and nationalism'. Specifically, I offer a reinterpretation of the role of Jewish traditions in the shaping of the Zionist project, the shaping of the Israeli public sphere as a form of dialoguing with these traditions, and the development of Jewish identities in Israel in light of the question of Israeli Jews' relation to tradition.

Prevalent and supposedly self-evident as the discourse on religion and politics in Israel is, I would nevertheless argue in this essay that overcoming

---

*This chapter revises and adapts material from a previously published article: 'Overcoming the "Religion and Politics" Discourse: A New Interpretation of the Israeli Case', *Journal of Religion & Society*, 16 (2014): 1–15.

this discourse is essential for understanding some of the most fundamental issues in Israeli politics. Having been implanted into the Jewish-Israeli, Zionist context by way of adopting and translating some of the most basic dominant Western premises regarding theology, religion, secularism and politics, this discourse not only forces a foreign (Christianity-based) framework on the Zionist/Jewish-Israeli case, but more critically it also carries over to the Israeli case some of the most fundamental misunderstandings and misinterpretations characterizing this discourse in its original context (which are, of course, the focus of the 'critical religion' field).

Given this discourse's dominance, most commentators tend to assume, whether implicitly or explicitly, that Jewish religion and Israeli politics are two separate, essentially distinguishable, realms that, for some historical and political reasons, tend to be entangled and confused. They view Israeli society and politics as essentially dictated by the basic tension between religion and politics and by the socio-cultural cleavage between 'secular' and 'religious' Jews in Israel, generally characterizing the former as committed to liberal democratic (secular) values and the latter as an anti-democratic, theocracy-craving conservative minority.

Needless to say, this premise regarding a categorical distinction between religion and politics reflects a broader worldview that dominates corresponding discussions on similar issues outside of Israel (often constructed as matters of 'church and state'). Moreover, as highlighted by the critical religion field, the assumed dichotomy between religion and politics is attributed to a modern, Protestant notion, with only limited validity (in the best of cases) in Jewish history and thought. In other words, even before we challenge the dichotomy itself, it is rather obvious that it is essentially foreign to Jewish traditions (Batnitzky 2011; cf. Walzer et al. 2003a, b). It is doubly regrettable then that the discourse built around this dichotomy is largely mistaken and misleading.

To understand why this is so, we have to first keep in mind – or rather to make explicit – what this discourse assumes to be an unchallenged 'given'. I am referring here to the taken-for-granted conceptual and epistemological basis of our analysis of politics. This discourse first assumes religion to be a transhistorical and transcultural, rather abstract concept – indeed, one that has been stubbornly avoiding agreed-upon definitions. (This latter fact, it is commonly argued, should not deter us from further using the concept 'religion', as we supposedly all know what it means.) Second, this discourse takes religion to be essentially, fundamentally independent from the almost-just-as-abstract (and surely also transhistorical and transcultural) notion of 'politics'. Indeed, the discourse goes further to advocate the separation between these two realms as a precondition for the viability of modern democracies. Doing so, this discourse assumes the secular(ist) epistemology as obvious, viewing the distinction between religion and not-religion (i.e. the secular) as the foundational basis of (at least) modernity. (This, of course, is a point commonly made by the critical religion field, discussed throughout this volume, and it would be redundant to offer the customary list of representative references here.)

Now, as William Cavanaugh (2009) has convincingly shown, this very common use of 'religion' is fundamentally wrong: it ignores the specific history of the term, its cultural (or rather theological) origins and developments, and, most importantly, the configurations of power that drive these developments, especially that of the currently common use of the term. As he sums up the conclusions of his penetrating critical interpretation:

> The first conclusion is that there is no transhistorical or transcultural concept of religion. Religion has a history, and what counts as religion and what does not in any given context depends on different configurations of power and authority. The second conclusion is that the attempt to say that there is a transhistorical and transcultural concept of religion that is separable from secular phenomena is itself part of a particular configuration of power, that of the modern, liberal nation-state as it developed in the West. In this context, religion is constructed as transhistorical, transcultural, essentially interior, and essentially distinct from public, secular rationality. (Cavanaugh 2009: 59)

It is the modern political – that which is constructed as essentially secular, the not-religion – that gives birth to our common, just-as-modern use of 'religion'. In other words, the order of the modern, sovereign, 'secular' nation-state, with its insistence on a monopoly over its subjects' lethal loyalty, is what drives the invention of 'religion'; 'To construe Christianity as a religion, therefore, helps to separate loyalty to God from one's public loyalty to the nation-state' (Cavanaugh 2009: 59). Another way of putting this is to say that the discourse on church (or synagogue) and state camouflages the many ways in which the latter is playing a major role in the very construction of the former, for its own needs.

Carried over to the Zionist and Israeli case, the 'religion and politics' framework perpetuates the misconception that Zionism has been an essentially secular project. The argument here uses the very terms by which this epistemology constructs the Western, liberal democracy as essentially secular. It also propagates a narrative that assumes Israel to be a secular, liberal and democratic nation-state, which for various reasons is forced or coerced to pass and enforce laws that impose Jewish 'religion' on the (otherwise 'secular') public sphere and on the private lives of the Israeli citizens. This is blamed primarily on the representational and coalitional structure of the Israeli political system, which allegedly endows the 'religious' political parties with the ability to extort compromises and concessions from the 'secular' majority.

This, after all, is the idea encapsulated in one of the basic notions of Israeli politics, namely the (in)famous 'status quo' – or, in a longer form: 'the secular-religious status quo' – a title commonly used to denote the otherwise strange mixture of the two supposedly distinct realms of religion and politics, or even more confusingly, of the two mutually exclusive categories of 'the religious' and 'the secular' in Israel. The 'status quo' is largely understood to be a 'conflict-neutralizing, consociational arrangement' regarding 'the proper place of Judaism in the Jewish state' (Cohen and Susser 2000: 18). It is usually presented as a 'compromise' (Barak-Erez 2008: 2496) or an 'accommodation' (Don-Yehiya 1999: 1) between two sides: the 'secular camp' (which is supposedly committed to the aim of establishing a secular, liberal and democratic regime, in which religion is excluded from public matters) and the 'religious camp' (which is allegedly committed to the enforcement and coercion of Jewish law onto the state and its citizens).

This bipolarity generates severe misunderstandings and prevents us from carefully assessing the unresolved nature of the relationship between Zionism (followed by the nation-state it has established) and what it, Zionism, has viewed (following the cue of contemporaneous Jewish-European thought) as 'Jewish religion', distinguishable from 'Jewish nationality'. This distinction, it should be noted at the outset, is an idea borne out of the coercion of Jewish traditions into the splint of the essentially European Christian historically situated categories of 'religion' and 'nationalism'. As such, this discussion hides several important foundational facts regarding the meaning of Jewish and Israeli identity and encourages a misrepresentation of the diversity of Jewish identities in Israel (to note but two of its regrettable consequences).

A 'traditionist' alternative

I would argue that a fruitful way to transcend this discourse's narrow horizon and to engage in an examination – a construction, even – of its alternatives, is to identify the matters at hand *not* as an issue of religion and politics in Israel, but rather as a (quintessentially political) issue of our relations with our traditions (Yadgar 2013). In other words, I would propose that we engage in a critical reading of the unresolved, problematical, often manipulative nature of the State of Israel's approach to the numerous histories of Jewish communities, histories that are manifested in the Jewish traditions that preceded the Zionist project and its culmination in the State of Israel.

Thus we come to grips with the central issue to be addressed: How does the nation-state's theopolitics – constituted, as it is (symbolically, at least), on an 'invented' (Hobsbawm and Ranger 1992; Liebman and Don-Yehiya 1983;

Zerubavel 1995) national tradition – approach Jewish traditions that preceded it and continue to live alongside it?

A note on terminology is in order here: 'Theopolitics' (borrowed here from Cavanaugh 2003) is meant to highlight that foundational institutions of modern, so-called secular politics, such as the state, are 'ways of imagining [that] organize bodies around stories of human nature and human destiny which have deep theological analogies. In other words, supposedly 'secular' political theory is really theology in disguise' (Cavanaugh 2003: 2). Crucially, theopolitics signals the fact that 'the modern state is built upon a soteriology of rescue from violence', a foundational 'myth of the State as Savior' (Cavanaugh 2003: 2), the basis of the modern concept of sovereignty. In order to establish itself, the sovereign nation-state also 'imagines' collectives (Anderson 1998) and 'invents' traditions (Hobsbawm and Ranger 1992) that narrate theopolitics and sustain the state's existence.

The term theopolitics, then, helps us in overcoming the debilitating predominance of the secular vs religious dualism. Informed by a post-secular critique, theopolitics is a discursive tool that enables us to both see the theological aspects of the supposedly secular nation-state, and to devise a meaningful discourse on how the state uses so-called religious traditions in the process of constructing an imagination of the nation and the sovereign state as secular.

Returning to our case, the 'problem' with those Jewish traditions is that they do not fit easily, if ever, into commonly used categorical frameworks that originate in modern Western discourse such as 'nation', 'ethnicity', 'race' and, maybe most importantly, 'religion'. Let us ignore for a moment, even if only for the sake of argument, the tendency to view these categories – borne as they are from a specific European Christian history (W. C. Smith 1963; J. Z. Smith 1982; cf. Asad 1993; Masuzawa 2005; Dubuisson 2007; Cavanaugh 2011) – as if they were a universal language of human order, which is necessarily also applicable to the histories of Jewish communities. What is critical to note is that in many meaningful senses 'Judaism' fits both and at the same time each and every one of these terms/categories, and none of them (cf. Batnitzky 2011: 1–3; Satlow 2006). This is so because Jewish traditions are comprehensive ways of life that touch upon various dimensions of human experience, which are sometimes labelled under one of the abovementioned categories, while at others they are labelled under another.

Bearing this in mind, I would like to offer below a short discussion of several notions that become further clarified by refocusing the framework of discussion and analysis on matters of tradition. These touch upon three central issues: the role of Jewish traditions in (a) the shaping of the Zionist project, (b) the shaping of the Israeli public sphere and (c) the formation and development of Jewish identities in Israel.

Zionism and Jewish traditions

One of the more fruitful ways to understand Zionism is *not* to identify it as an attempt at secularizing Judaism (or 'Jewish tradition') through the invention of a national tradition. Predominant as such a description is (e.g. Avineri 1981; Shimoni 1995: 269–332), it nevertheless suffers from some obvious deficiencies (cf. Salmon 2002), not least of which is its lack of clarity as to the very meaning of 'secularization'. Instead, I would argue that a fruitful starting point would be to view Zionism as a counter-reaction to another act of invention, which preceded this ideological project: the making of Judaism into a 'religion' (or, in other words, the invention of 'Jewish religion'). I am referring here to the modern reinterpretation and reformation of the very meaning of Judaism and Jewishness that originated in Europe from the eighteenth century onwards, whereby Jewish traditions were reread so as to fit the allegedly universal (but essentially European, Protestant), apolitical category of 'religion', in itself an invention of its times and politics (Batnitzky 2011 offers a compelling narrative of this 'invention' and its consequences).

Viewed from this perspective, it is rather clear that Zionism emerged as a forceful argument against the idea that Judaism is in essence a 'religion', that is, a system of belief, a 'faith' that is mostly a personal, apolitical matter of 'spirituality'. Needless to say, this perspective does not capture Zionist ideology in its entirety. For one thing, it downplays (if only for the sake of focus) other forceful drivers of Zionism, such as a European-Jewish rebellion against what was viewed as Jewish passivism and an attempt at liberation from gentile political authority. Furthermore, my argument here is focused on mainstream Zionist ideology, which tended to view itself as 'secular', postponing my discussion on the minor-yet-influential stream of Religious Zionism (see my discussion below).

Moses Mendelssohn (esp. 1983) is commonly identified as the most representative and influential formulator of the argument that Judaism is a religion – exactly that which is labelled under this title and nothing beyond it. This argument, which was further developed and articulated mostly by other German Jewish philosophers, brought about the formation of Reform Judaism, encouraged the shaping of the Historical Positivist position (better known today, especially in the United States, as Conservative Judaism), and, ultimately, facilitated the shaping of Jewish Orthodoxy and Ultra-Orthodoxy as counter-reactions to the Reform interpretation of the implications of this argument.

By making Judaism a 'religion', modern European Jews had allegedly solved the potential tension in their identification as members of an alien, foreign nation living among host nationalities. This is so because the argument that Judaism is a religion renders Judaism essentially apolitical, and denies that Judaism fits in the category of nationality, at least in the prevalent contemporaneous European nation-state-oriented sense of this term. It thus enabled Jews, as the famous turn of phrase goes, to become 'German (or French, or otherwise) nationals/citizens of the Mosaic faith': loyal citizens and servants of the nation-state who differ from the non-Jewish majority only in the limited realm of religious belief, which lacks any political implications. Against prevalent anti-Jewish arguments which advocated a *political* view of Jews, depicting them as an 'alien nation' living among (Christian) host nations, the insistence that Judaism is a religion (and so: not a nationality) sought to diffuse this hatred by reiterating the non-political nature of Judaism and the Jews' organic belonging to these host nations.

Zionism sought to negate the argument that depoliticized Judaism by rendering it (only) a religion. The driving ideological force of this historical project had revolved, fundamentally, around a competing argument, which also used the European political discourse of the time: The Zionist idea in its various formulations states that Judaism (or – keeping in mind the secular/religion distinction that tends to equate Judaism with 'Jewish Religion' – let us say: *Jewishness*) is a *nationality*, and hence political in its very essence. Jewish religion, this argument poses, has indeed been *part* of the history of the Jewish nation, but Jewish nationality is that which ultimately constitutes and defines the people. As such, it must be expressed and realized in the political framework of a nation-state, in which the true meaning of Jewishness as a nationality will be reincarnated (Avineri 1981; Laqueur 1989; Shimoni 1995).

This nationalism – which many Zionist thinkers preferred to label 'Hebrew', not 'Jewish', betraying some of their unease with the historical 'baggage' of Judaism, in the name of which they made their nationalist claims – was thus presented as a broader frame of meaning, which incorporates in it 'Jewish religion' but is surely not dictated by this religion, nor is it identical or reducible to it.

As in other cases of emerging nationalist movements (Hobsbawm and Ranger 1992), the Zionist enterprise has also involved a wide-ranging project of 'inventing' a national tradition: Zionism was required to instil the notion of a national Jewish identity with a positive meaning, and Zionist thinkers were required to rewrite Jewish history, to reinterpret Jewish meanings and subjects, so as to render these consistent with the national meta-narrative (Liebman and Don-Yehiya 1983; Luz 1988; Zerubavel 1995).

Needless to say, Zionism has found the building blocks for this rewriting in the histories of Jews, that is, in Jewish traditions. But it had arrived at this undertaking as it has been already deeply immersed in the context of the 'secularization' of Judaism (a move that culminated in the movement of Jewish Enlightenment, *Haskala*). That is to say, this project of a national rewriting of traditions was, from the outset, based upon the false distinction between Jewish 'religion' and other, allegedly 'essentially secular', dimensions (e.g. political, national, cultural, linguistic etc.) of Judaism. Moreover, prevalent streams in Zionist ideology tended to view this same 'religion' as oppressing the national vitality, and as the root cause of what they viewed as the historical decline of the Jewish people.

How, then, has Zionism constructed its position vis-à-vis Jewish traditions that had preceded it (and were, so the mainstream argument has claimed, besmirched by the stain of 'religiosity')? Several Zionist leaders and thinkers chose largely to ignore these traditions, focusing instead on the notion of Jewish political power by way of imagining the 'Jews' State' as a sort of European nation-state that is ruled by Europeans of Jewish descent. Others, who were fiercely critical of this indifference to tradition, viewed the Zionist project as primarily obligated to 'secularize' Judaism, that is to reinterpret Jewish traditions so as to make them consistent with a rationalist, modernist, utilitarian worldview, which would be the basis of the (secular) nation-state of the Jews (Shimoni 1995: 269–303).

A similar notion of reinterpretation lay at the root of the self-image of those Socialist-Zionist ideologues who arrived in Palestine with the declared aim of rewriting the meaning of their Jewish (or Hebrew) identity. These ideological founders, most of whom had received a traditional Jewish education and many of them driven by a rebellion against the authority of the traditional way-of-life into which they or their parents were born, had an intimate, unmediated familiarity with certain Jewish traditions (mostly Eastern European ones), and they sought to reinterpret parts of these traditions. They did so from a confrontational, aggressive position, never hesitating to rewrite traditional rituals and instil them with what they viewed as more appropriate and relevant content (Lilker 1982; Don-Yehiya and Liebman 1981).

It should be noted that this aggressive confrontation with tradition nevertheless manifests a certain kind of conversation with it, a fierce dialogue based upon relative fluency in matters of this tradition. A rebellion against authority is also an acknowledgement of it, and it is surely based upon a familiarity with it. But once the ideological enthusiasm had ebbed, and the unmediated familiarity with tradition was lost, the sons and daughters of these ideological pioneers were left with a sour residue of resentment against Jewish tradition and 'religion', while being largely ignorant of the content of these objects of their derision. They have, of course, continued to identify as Jewish. But the positive meaning of this identity, beyond the fact that they have been committed to the establishment of a nation-state for Jews, became increasingly vague. The dialogue between them and their Jewish tradition fell gradually silent (cf. Kurzweil 1953; Yadgar 2012: 66–86).

The State of Israel and the 'secular-religious status quo'

The establishment of the State of Israel did not resolve this dilemma of how to classify – or rather fundamentally to understand – Judaism and Jewishness in the prevalent modern terms of religion and secularity. In the end, the state seems to have chosen to focus primarily on the constitution of a Jewish majority – a matter of 'demography' (cf. Yonah 2004) – as the principal condition for its existence as the state of the Jewish People; it put relatively few resources into answering the questions of how to converse with and reinterpret the Jewish traditions of the communities that constitute this majority. In the famous contest between two possible translations of Theodor Herzl's *Judenstaat*, the state's political elite has chosen to focus on the establishment of a 'State of Jews', not necessarily on the constitution of a 'Jewish State'. Indeed, this seems to be the core understanding of the meaning of Israel's being a Jewish nation-state among liberal, secularist Zionist circles, such as *Haaretz*'s editorial board, which clearly states:

> Zionism dreamed of a state for the Jews, not a Jewish state: a refuge for members of the Jewish people, not a state with an official religion like Muslim Saudi Arabia. The Balfour Declaration promised a national home, not a religious one. On Israeli identity cards, 'Jewish' describes a nationality. (*Haaretz* 2013)

But even such a limited understanding of Jewish politics – this, simply, is politics run by people of Jewish origins – is required to address certain issues of Jewish identity in order to run a nation-state that identifies as the state of the Jews. Primarily, the state is required to decide who counts as a Jew and who does not – to outline, in other words, the borderlines and definitions of that nation in the name of which it claims sovereignty. The solution devised by the allegedly-secular state was to rely on the supposed official representatives of Jewish 'religion' (namely, rabbis and politicians who adhere to a conservative, Orthodox interpretation of Jewish tradition) to function as the nation's gatekeepers – whether by assigning them the responsibility to decide 'who is a Jew?' (cf. Gavison 2010) or by giving them the monopolistic authority to manage the Jewish citizens' personal matters (marriage and divorce), essentially preventing marriages between Jews and non-Jews (Halperin-Kaddari and Yadgar 2010), thus preserving the distinction between these two primary groups.

It is worth noting here that the State of Israel has never attempted to genuinely build an *Israeli* national identity that would be 'liberated', so to speak, from Jewish 'religion' and would naturally include the non-Jewish citizens of the state. Indeed, this point was made by none other than the Israeli High Court of Justice, who ruled that 'the existence of an Israeli nation has not been proven' (Vogelman 2013), denying the appellants their demand to be registered not as Jewish nationals but rather as Israeli ones in the state's official registry. Israel, as the State and its High Court of Justice have reiterated, is sovereign in the name of *Jewish*, not Israeli, nationality.

Instead, the State of Israel has been fostering a de facto identification between Israeliness and Jewishness, as it has focused on the construction of a *Jewish* national identity, which although highly problematical in its Jewishness (indeed, the meaning of this identification is far from being clear) is nevertheless distinct in one critical respect: it is a national identity reserved for Jews only (Peled 1992; Rouhana and Ghanem 1998; Smooha 1997; Yiftachel 2006). In addition, the state has viewed the diversity of Jewish traditions as a threat to what it views as national unity, and devoted its resources and attention to the forceful project of 'the melting pot', which, as its name suggests, viewed these traditions as objects that must be dissolved in order for the state's identity to prevail (cf. Buzaglo 2001, 2002).

Of course, the state still espouses a notion of a distinction between Jewish 'religion' and 'nationality', but – as has been demonstrated by the political and legal debates surrounding the 'paradoxes' this distinction creates, especially those surrounding the 'who is a Jew' conundrum (see Gavison 2010) – in practice the state, as well as the culture it has built, remains loyal to the notion that these two alleged categories are essentially identical. This idea stands at the core of the national school curriculum, and it feeds a series of laws that enforce a certain, notoriously narrow, interpretation of Jewish tradition (mainly, if not solely, in terms of practice, or rather the prohibition of certain practices) on the public sphere.

This, then, is the key to understanding the Israeli 'status quo'. It is not a matter of a compromise and a submission of the secular majority to the whims of the religious minority; rather, it is an expression of the state's reliance – a state, it should be stressed, that is ruled by representatives of that same secular majority – on a narrow, 'religious' (indeed: Orthodox) interpretation of the meaning of Jewish traditions for the purpose of regulating the public sphere and administering national politics.

It is worth stating this explicitly: The secular majority needs this alleged religious coercion more than any other party in this relationship. This coercion is what secures the maintenance and preservation of this majority's Jewish identity in a nation-state that self-identifies as the state of the Jews. Being a Jew in Israel means belonging to the majority, which enjoys a privileged position in every aspect of life; whoever is Jewish enjoys political, symbolic and cultural capital that is reserved for Jews only (Peled 1992; Rouhana and

Ghanem 1998; Smooha 1997; Yiftachel 2006). And were it not for the state's enforcement of its narrow interpretation of Judaism on the public sphere, most members of this majority would have been left lacking a possibility to positively understand the meaning of their Jewish identity. The state, in other words, enforces 'religion' on the public sphere, through the 'status quo' arrangements among other ways, and guarantees by this the distinction between Jews and non-Jews, as well as the privileging of the former over the latter (cf. Levy 2011).

Jewish identities in Israel: Beyond the 'religious-secular' divide

A focus on the issue of tradition also sheds new light on the matter of Israeli Jews' Jewish identity. Primarily, it exposes the negative and distorting influence of the 'cleavage' discourse (cf. Cohen and Susser 2000), which tends to view the binary distinction between 'secular' and 'religious' as the constitutive axis of Jewish identities in Israel. It is the cleavage discourse that gives birth in the first place to such baseless bipolar images of 'the religious' as supposedly purely theological, while 'the secular' is its complete opposite. Instead, we would be better advised to adopt a 'traditionist' (Yadgar 2015) point of view, one that raises the question of Jewish-Israelis' attitudes to their Jewish traditions as the main focus of a nuanced understanding of Jewish identities in Israel.

Take, for example, the secular majority. The positive meaning of its secularity is so enigmatic as to have encouraged the pollsters running the most comprehensive survey on Jewish beliefs and practices among Israeli Jews to replace the label 'secular' in their questionnaires with the negative designation 'not-religious' (Levy, Levinsohn and Katz 2002).

I have already outlined above the background for the formation of Jewish-Israeli secularity – or at least the Jewish identity of most of those who identify as secular as a matter of designating a 'default' option in terms of their Jewishness, not as a matter of identifying with an explicit secularist ideology – as an outcome of the waning of dialogue between the individual and her reference group and their traditions. These secular as a matter of 'default' (Liebman and Yadgar 2009: 156) Israeli Jews have assigned (mostly passively so) the state and its institutions the role of maintaining their Jewish identity: The state's institutions educate their children to know certain aspects of Jewish history as their history; they force on them the Jewish (or Hebrew) calendar; they compel them to recognize Shabbat as their day of rest; and they make it difficult for them to marry non-Jews (to mention but some of the facets of this 'religious coercion', or rather 'the status quo').

The key to understanding Jewish-Israeli secularism, then, is its inability to conduct a meaningful dialogue with the Jewish traditions from which it has emerged. This lack has been acknowledged by an important minority of certain intellectuals and elite circles, and it is the driving force behind what is sometimes dubbed the 'Jewish renaissance', which revolves mainly around a mostly textual (at least for the time being) endeavour to get reacquainted with these traditions (Azulay and Tabory 2008; Katz 2011; Sheleg 2010; Werczberger and Azulay 2011).

A lack of dialogue is not reserved for secular Israeli Jews alone. A negation of such a dialogue has also become the founding ideology of Jewish ultra-Orthodoxy, which prefers to view its relationship with tradition as a dictation or obedience, surely not as a dynamic conversation: Tradition, so the (problematic) ultra-conservative argument goes, is set and sealed, and we are to obey it. As a prevalent Orthodox argument states (in the words of 'Hatam Sofer', Rabbi Moses Schreiber, 1762–1839): 'Anything new is prohibited by the Torah'. This stance is of course riddled with contradictions (Sagi 2008: 5–14). It denies the dynamic nature of tradition, and ignores the fact that even the greatest conservative is forced to continuously and incessantly interpret the meaning of tradition's dictation, consequently updating the meaning of this tradition (Yadgar 2013).

'Religious Zionism', which views itself as committed to a reinterpretation of its Jewish tradition in light of modern politics, conducts this reinterpretation under the heavy shadow of its commitment to a foreign European tradition (i.e. nationalism) and to synthesizing two apparently alien organs. Religious Zionism thus tends to view the nation-state, or its geopolitics, in the colours of 'religious' theology – indeed, as a central element of a messianic project (Batnitzky 2011: 91–100; Schwartz 2008; Hadad 2020).

At times it seems that Jewish-Israeli *masortim* (sg. *masorti*; derived from *masoret*, Hebrew for tradition) – who are mostly Mizrahim (i.e. they or their parents originate from Muslim and Arab lands) and tend not to accept the dichotomous distinction entailed in the cleavage discourse as the constitutive axis of their Jewish identity – are those who find themselves faced with the most challenging dialogue with their Jewish traditions. But they do so without much institutional support, and are constantly, harshly criticized for what both 'religious' and 'secular' Israeli Jews depict as the inconsistent nature of the *masorti* way of life. *Masortim* represent in a rather immediate, ever-developing way the possibilities and challenges of dialoguing with tradition while nevertheless remaining a participating actor in modern life. It is not hard to see how they become threatening to both of those competing opponents, the 'religious' and the 'secular', who build their identity as mutual opposites, assuming as they do that modernity leaves us with only a limited choice: Either we abandon tradition, or we blindly obey its dictates (Yadgar 2011).

Concluding remarks

While this essay is obviously focused on a specific Israeli rendition of the secularist epistemology, I would argue (as I have done in more detail elsewhere: Yadgar 2020) that in a deep sense this is but a socio-historically specific appearance of a prevalent, predominant understanding of the politics of the modern nation-state.

The Israeli case merely exposes some of the foundational tensions in the European, historically-embodied Christian notions of politics, religion, nation, ethnos, race and nation-state. In doing so, it directs our attention to an essential matter regarding the secularist nation-statist (liberal democratic or otherwise) order of the world: The nation-statist rules of the game assume (if they are not outright enabled by this) an infrastructure of collective political preferences that are clearly of an order that may be described (at least in the European case) as ethnic, religious, cultural and even racial. A liberal democratic polity that is built on this nationalist infrastructure does not erase or overcome this infrastructure, but rather assumes it and is ultimately enabled by it.

If anything, the contested politics of immigration, multiculturalism, religion and secularism in Europe during the past few decades have stressed this point to an alarming degree. This contested, bitter politics seems to expose the high degree to which the liberal democratic state (in the context of a global nation-statist division of the world, of course) assumes a pre-existing particularistic infrastructure – of values, preferences, worldview, ways of living in the world and so on – as the foundational bed upon which liberal democracy is enabled. A challenge against these particularistic presumptions (in the form of adherence to a different set of cultural values or the practice of other ways of being in the world, for example) is too often taken to be not only an inconvenience but a direct threat to the very viability of the polity.

The need to transcend the 'religion and politics' discourse is far from being limited to the Jewish-Israeli case. Indeed, it is the critique of the very categories that lie at this binary's foundation in a Western, Christian context that encourages a re-evaluation of some of the more taken-for-granted aspects of Israeli politics. What seems more perplexing in the Jewish-Israeli case is not only the (allegedly modern, secular) nation-state's essential reliance on what it – or rather the Zionist ideology upon which it is based – views as the essentially foreign 'Jewish religion' for the management of the state's ethnopolitics, but rather the insistence on viewing this as '*Jewish* politics'. In terms of a traditionist discourse, one that is concerned with the phenomenological and existential matter of our relations with our traditions, this is indeed a misnomer. As I suggested above, a focus on this traditionist point of view exposes what may be termed the misinterpretation and misappropriation of Jewish traditions in modern Israeli politics, used as they are mainly to delineate the borderlines between the collective, national self and its other(s). Such a focus would also offer, I would argue, alternative venues through which 'Jewish politics' can be properly and more constructively understood. This, surely, is a matter for an interpretation of a different type than the one offered above.

References

Anderson, Benedict (1998), *Imagined Communities: Reflections on the Origin and Spread of Nationalism*, London and New York: Verso.
Asad, Talal (1993), *Genealogies of Religion: Discipline and Reasons of Power in Christianity and Islam*, Baltimore: Johns Hopkins University Press.
Avineri, Shlomo (1981), *The Making of Modern Zionism: Intellectual Origins of the Jewish State*, New York: Basic Books.
Azulay, Naama and Ephraim Tabory (2008), 'A House of Prayer for All Nations: Unorthodox Prayer Houses for Nonreligious Israeli Jews', *Sociological Papers*, 13: 22–41.
Barak-Erez, Daphne (2008), 'Law and Religion Under the Status Quo Model: Between Past Compromises and Constant Change', *Cardozo Law Review*, 30: 2495–508.
Batnitzky, Leora Faye (2011), *How Judaism Became a Religion: An Introduction to Modern Jewish Thought*, Princeton, NJ: Princeton University Press.
Buzaglo, Meir (2001), 'Educational Ideologies: The Mizrahi Point of View', in Y. Iram, Y. Shkolnikov, Y. Cohen and A. Shechter (eds), *Crossroads: Values and Education in Israeli Society*, 480–521, Jerusalem: Ministry of Education.
Buzaglo, Meir (2002), 'Mizrahiness, Masortiyut, Melting Pot: A Philosophical-Political Study', in Zeev Harvey, Galit Hazan-Rokem and Y. Shiloah (eds), *Zion and Zionism*, 623–44, Jerusalem: Misgav Yerushalayim.
Cavanaugh, William T. (2003), *Theopolitical Imagination: Christian Practices of Space and Time*, London and New York: Bloomsbury T&T Clark.
Cavanaugh, William T. (2009), *The Myth of Religious Violence: Secular Ideology and the Roots of Modern Conflict*, New York: Oxford University Press.
Cavanaugh, William T. (2011), *Migrations of the Holy: God, State, and the Political Meaning of the Church*, Grand Rapids: Wm. B. Eerdmans Publishing Company.
Cohen, Asher and Bernard Susser (2000), *Israel and the Politics of Jewish Identity: The Secular-Religious Impasse*, Baltimore: Johns Hopkins University Press.
Don-Yehiya, Eliezer (1999), *Religion and Political Accommodation in Israel*, trans. Deborah Lemmer, Jerusalem: The Floersheimer Institute for Policy Studies.

Don-Yehiya, Eliezer and Charles S. Liebman (1981), 'The Symbol System of Zionist-Socialism: An Aspect of Israeli Civil Religion', *Modern Judaism*, 1 (2): 121–48.

Dubuisson, Daniel (2007), *The Western Construction of Religion: Myths, Knowledge, and Ideology*, Baltimore: Johns Hopkins University Press.

Gavison, Ruth (2010), *The Law of Return at Sixty Years: History, Ideology, Justification*, Jerusalem: The Metzilah Center for Zionist, Jewish, Liberal and Humanist Thought.

Haaretz (2013), 'The Jewish Coercion Administration', editorial, 22 May.

Hadad, Noam (2020), *Religious Zionism: Religion, Nationalism and Politics*, Jerusalem: Carmel.

Halperin-Kaddari, Ruth and Yaacov Yadgar (2010), 'Between Universal Feminism and Particular Nationalism: Politics, Religion and Gender (in)Equality in Israel', *Third World Quarterly*, 31 (6): 905–20.

Hobsbawm, Eric J. and Terence O. Ranger (1992), *The Invention of Tradition*, Cambridge: Cambridge University Press.

Katz, Gideon (2011), *The Pale God: Israeli Secularism and Spinoza's Philosophy of Culture*, Boston: Academic Studies Press.

Kurzweil, Baruch (1953), 'The New Canaanites in Israel', *Judaism*, 2: 3–15.

Laqueur, Walter (1989), *A History of Zionism*, New York: Schocken Books.

Levy, Gal (2011), 'Secularism, Religion and the Status Quo', in Jack Barbalet, Adam Possamai and Bryan S. Turner (eds), *Religion and the State: A Comparative Sociology*, 93–119, London: Anthem Press.

Levy, Shlomit, Hanna Levinsohn and Elihu Katz (2002), *A Portrait of Israeli Jews: Beliefs, Observance, and Values of Israeli Jews, 2000*, Jerusalem: Avi Chai and the Israel Democracy Institute.

Liebman, Charles S. and Eliezer Don-Yehiya (1983), *Civil Religion in Israel: Traditional Judaism and Political Culture in the Jewish State*, Berkeley: University of California Press.

Liebman, Charles S. and Yaacov Yadgar (2009), 'Secular-Jewish Identity and the Condition of Secular Judaism in Israel', in Zvi Gitelman (ed.), *Religion or Ethnicity? Jewish Identities in Evolution*, 149–70, New Brunswick: Rutgers University Press.

Lilker, Shalom (1982), *Kibbutz Judaism: A New Tradition in the Making*, Darby: Norwood Editions.

Luz, Ehud (1988), *Parallels Meet: Religion and Nationalism in the Early Zionist Movement*, Philadelphia: Jewish Publication Society.

Masuzawa, Tomoko (2005), *The Invention of World Religions: Or, How European Universalism Was Preserved in the Language of Pluralism*, Chicago: University of Chicago Press.

Mendelsohn, Moses (1983), *Jerusalem: Or on Religious Power and Judaism*, trans. Allan Arkush, Hanover: Brandeis.

Peled, Yoav (1992), 'Ethnic Democracy and the Legal Construction of Citizenship: Arab Citizens of the Jewish State', *American Political Science Review*, 86 (2): 432–43.

Rouhana, Nadim and Asad Ghanem (1998), 'The Crisis of Minorities in Ethnic States: The Case of Palestinian Citizens in Israel', *International Journal of Middle East Studies*, 30 (3): 321–46.

Sagi, Avi (2008), *Tradition vs. Traditionalism: Contemporary Perspectives in Jewish Thought*, Amsterdam and New York: Rodopi.
Salmon, Yosef (2002), *Religion and Zionism: First Encounters*, Jerusalem: Hebrew University Magnes Press.
Satlow, Michael L. (2006), 'Defining Judaism: Accounting for "Religions" in the Study of Religion', *Journal of the American Academy of Religion*, 74 (4): 837–60.
Schwartz, Dov (2008), *Religious Zionism: History and Ideology*, trans. Batya Stein, Boston: Academic Studies Press.
Sheleg, Yair (2010), *The Jewish Renaissance in Israeli Society: The Emergence of a New Jew*, Jerusalem: Israel Democracy Institute.
Shimoni, Gideon (1995), *The Zionist Ideology*, Hanover and London: University Press of New England.
Smith, Jonathan Z. (1982), *Imagining Religion: From Babylon to Jonestown*, Chicago: University of Chicago Press.
Smith, Wilfred Cantwell (1963), *The Meaning and End of Religion: A New Approach to the Religious Traditions of Mankind*, New York: Macmillan.
Smooha, Sammy (1997), 'Ethnic Democracy: Israel as an Archetype', *Israel Studies*, 2 (2): 198–241.
Vogelman, Uzi (2013), 'Ornan et al. v. Ministry of the Interior', CA 8573/08, Opinions of the Supreme Court of Israel, 2 October. Available online: https://versa.cardozo.yu.edu/opinions/ornan-v-ministry-interior (accessed 3 January 2025).
Walzer, Michael, Menachem Lorberbaum, No'am Zohar and Yair Lorberbaum, eds (2003a), *The Jewish Political Tradition: Volume One: Authority*, New Haven: Yale University Press.
Walzer, Michael, Menachem Lorberbaum, No'am Zohar and Ari Ackerman, eds (2003b), *The Jewish Political Tradition: Volume Two: Membership*, New Haven: Yale University Press.
Werczberger, Rachel and Na'ama Azulay (2011), 'The Jewish Renewal Movement in Israeli Secular Society', *Contemporary Jewry*, 31 (2): 107–28.
Yadgar, Yaacov (2011), *Secularism and Religion in Jewish-Israeli Politics: Traditionists and Modernity*, London: Routledge.
Yadgar, Yaacov (2012), *Beyond Secularization: Traditionists and the Critique of Israeli Secularism*, Jerusalem: The Van-Leer Institute/Hakibutz Hameuchad Publishing House.
Yadgar, Yaacov (2013), 'Tradition', *Human Studies*, 36 (4): 451–70.
Yadgar, Yaacov (2015), 'Traditionism', *Cogent Social Sciences*, 1 (1061734): 1–17.
Yadgar, Yaacov (2020), *Israel's Jewish Identity Crisis: State and Politics in the Middle East*, Cambridge and New York: Cambridge University Press.
Yiftachel, Oren (2006), *Ethnocracy: Land and Identity Politics in Israel/Palestine*, Philadelphia: University of Pennsylvania Press.
Yonah, Yossi (2004), 'Israel's Immigration Policies: The Twofold Face of the "Demographic Threat"', *Social Identities*, 10 (2): 195–218.
Zerubavel, Yael (1995), *Recovered Roots: Collective Memory and the Making of Israeli National Tradition*, Chicago: University of Chicago Press.

11

The category of religion in the technology of governance

An argument for understanding religions as vestigial states*

Naomi Goldenberg

My goal in this essay is to contribute to the body of theory that is currently called 'critical religion'. I understand this label to include a wide range of scholarship and critique that clarifies and interrogates binaries such as religious/secular and religion/politics as well as terms such as post-secular that are fundamentals of scholarship both inside the discipline of religious studies and outside it in such areas as political science and international relations (Arnal and McCutcheon 2013; Balagangadhara 1994; Fitzgerald 2011, 2007a, b, 2000; King 1999; Masuzawa 2005; Nongbri 2013; McCutcheon 2007, 2003, 2001, 1997).

Interest in the topics denoted by these terms and linguistic pairings testifies not only to the attention given to them by think tanks and granting agencies in Europe and North America, but also, I think, to widespread uncertainties about how religion ought to be defined and approached in national and international

---

*This chapter was previously published in Trevor Stack, Naomi Goldenberg and Timothy Fitzgerald (eds), *Religion as a Category of Governance and Sovereignty*, 280–92, Leiden: Brill, 2015. It is reproduced here, with some updates (see especially note 1), with permission of the author and of Brill, conveyed through Copyright Clearance Center, Inc.

policy-making institutions. I hope to suggest a trajectory for thought and theory that might prove useful in debates and discussions pertaining to law and public policy and that will aid in further analysis and critique of the concepts and vocabularies clustering around popular and academic ideas about the contested division between what is and what is not religion.

In order to push theory in what I consider to be salutary directions, I want to focus on how the concept of religion functions as a key component in the technology of contemporary statecraft. As an initial step along this trajectory, I suggest that we begin to think about religions as vestigial states[1] – that is, as the institutional and cultural remainders of former sovereignties surviving within the jurisdictions of contemporary governments. I am aware that if the term vestigial state has any resonance, it will be as a provisional notion that might lead to more precise concepts in critical religion. Scholars who are experts in particular periods of history in varied regions of the globe would have to evaluate the idea to judge its use as a hermeneutic in specific contexts.

I also want to clarify that I consider the terms 'religion' and 'state' as concepts that do not denote a singular or consistent meaning throughout their linguistic and political history. The significance of both words shifts considerably through time and continues to change. Nevertheless, in current usage, religion and state, however they are defined, are generally imagined to refer to separate or separable institutions and/or spheres of human ideation and activity. Entertaining the notion that religions are vestigial states is meant to productively disturb that perception by interrogating the evolution of the putative separateness of religion and state. By calling attention in specific times and places to the nuances, contradictions and consequences of the discursively positioned distinctness of the two concepts in institutional and cultural spheres, a theory of religions as vestigial states could direct thinking along original and fruitful lines. Two promising trajectories are: one, to analyse particular histories in which religions develop or are solidified in distinction to states; and two, to foreground how current governments use these classifications as management techniques.

The work I need each term to do in the phrase 'vestigial state' will, I hope, become clearer as the argument proceeds. I understand the word 'state' to refer broadly to a ruling government. According to James Crawford, in *The Creation of States in International Law* (2007), a text recognized as a benchmark in international law, a state is determined by the following six criteria: (1) Defined territory; (2) Permanent population; (3) Governing structure; (4) Capacity to enter into relations with other states; (5) Independence and (6) Sovereignty (37–95). I suggest that these six attributes of a state cluster around two qualities: (1) Jurisdiction (regarding either space and/or population) and (2) Effective authority over such jurisdiction.

By reducing Crawford's six criteria down to two, I highlight the importance that international law places on the effectiveness of governance and geographical jurisdiction in reference to states. A major thrust of my argument about considering religions to be vestigial states is one of distancing religion from definitions that use the word to imply any special spiritual essence to psychological or social experiences classified as religious, and instead to focus on how institutions and aspects of culture come to be classified under the heading of religion. Issues of jurisdiction are central to the argument I want to build about the position and use of the category of religion in the administration of states and the management of populations within their territories.

While Crawford's work is helpful in outlining the contemporary legal parameters of what is meant by a state, it is Max Weber who pointed to its most salient feature over a hundred years ago. In *Politics as a Vocation*, he writes:

> It is . . . the case that in the final analysis the modern state can be defined . . . by the specific means that are peculiar to it, . . . namely, physical violence. . . . [W]e must say that the state is the form of human community that (successfully) lays claim to the monopoly of legitimate physical violence within a particular territory. . . . [A]ll other organizations or individuals can assert the right to use physical violence only insofar as the state permits them to do so. (Weber 2004: 33)

Weber thus identifies the major power a fully enabled state always reserves for itself in the jurisdiction it claims. His linkage of the state with legalized violence is key to distinguishing a recognized state from what I am naming a vestigial one. Although states vary widely in regard to the functions they cede to the religions they licence in their territories, the right to commit violence by means of military or police actions or to enforce a decision made in a court of law is one power that states insist upon retaining. If a religious group engages in acts of physical violence, it is no longer seen as properly 'religious'. It ceases to be unproblematically referred to as a religion; but instead acquires qualifying adjectives and epithets such as 'terrorist' and 'militant' to mark its renegade status.[2]

Innovative vocabulary pertaining to Islam has blossomed in recent years. Terms such as political Islam and Islamism are invented to cordon off appropriate forms of Islam from those that are considered dangerous to public order as defined by ruling governments. I suggest that Islam is in the process of being turned into a religion – that is, of being made vestigial – within some contemporary states at the same time that it functions non-vestigially in other parts of the world. Debates about Islam illustrate how religion as a discursive category operates as a regulatory description in Western democracies.

The adjective vestigial is only halfway adequate for the theory I am advancing. Although the word serves well to point backward in time through history and thus to deflect attention from the present appearances of institutions, ideally I need a term with a Janus-like quality that would also suggest time to come. Vestigial states tend to behave as states in waiting, or as states in hibernation. A more accurate statement of the theory might describe religions as once and future states. I am reluctant to adopt the phrase because it seems distractingly comic and reminiscent of fairy tale monarchs. Nevertheless, I ask readers to take note of the connotation of time to come that I wish the word vestigial would convey.

Vestigial states that I identify as religions are not static. On the contrary, they tend to be restive, ambitious and keen to take on whatever social, cultural or managerial functions dominant states will cede to them. For example, presently in contemporary states, categories of custom and law pertaining to the 'family' are considered proper spheres of influence for the exercise of religious authority. Because family life is commonly considered a legitimate jurisdiction of religion, vestigial states I am naming religions often contest state jurisdiction about matters pertaining to domestic life. Marriage, divorce and children's education are domains in which states frequently allow religions to set rules and policies. Thus, these are also the social arenas in which states and religions often conflict. I argue elsewhere that thinking of religions as vestigial states can help to clarify what is at stake in debates about family matters (Goldenberg 2013a, b).

By designating religions as vestigial states, I am identifying them as the structures of former sovereignties that continue to operate with differing degrees of autonomy within present-day governmental domains. Vestigial states called religions are composed of discursive and institutional practices similar to those of fully functioning states. However, the particular non-vestigial states that contain their predecessors determine the parameters of the vestigial varieties: religions are accorded limited powers and special privileges by the states in which they operate. They differ from the states that encompass and authorize them mainly in regard to what they are allowed to do and what abstract principles they cite to ground their authority. For example, while some contemporary states allude to 'freedom', 'justice' or 'equality' as their raison d'etre, and others claim to be the proper homeland of a cultural group with a particular, idealized way of life, vestigial states called religions often derive their founding tenets from a charismatic, inspirational figure, often divine and more often male.

I consider Wicca and other pagan movements to be consistent with this account of religions as vestigial states, even though such groups cite female deities as foundational. Wiccans construct their histories around claims about the superior qualities of past modes of governance in which imagery pertaining to goddesses and the female qualities of natural phenomena abounded (Gimbutas 1989). Whether such accounts can be proven historically is tangential to my argument. I am describing a discursive pattern utilized by groups aspiring to be defined as religions. Dislocation of a past sovereignty as a result of circumstances such as war or invasion is essential to the narrative. Each contemporary religious group understands itself as embodying and safeguarding the values, practices and symbolic systems in the only form intelligible within current governments – that is, the form known as religion.

Curiously, governments designated as secular ritually cite elements of the vestigial states they have superseded to justify contemporary authority. President Dwight Eisenhower's move in 1954 to add the words 'under God' to the US Pledge of Allegiance illustrates how a generalized reference to religion as a more exalted form of sovereignty is conjured to bolster and validate government.

Canada provides another example when, in 1982, a constitution was passed into law to replace the British North American Act. The Canadian constitution opens with the following phrase: 'Whereas Canada is founded on principles that recognize the supremacy of God and the rule of law . . .' The importance of linking present legislative authority to a supreme deity was underlined when Member of Parliament Svend Robinson tabled a petition from constituents to have the reference to God removed. In an exceedingly rare show of unanimity, all three major political parties refused to allow Parliament to even consider the request. Although Canada was ready to distance itself further from Britain by enacting an independent foundational document, in order to take that step, language preserving connection with a vague but nevertheless putatively superior power was necessary. The words 'supremacy of God' function in the Canadian constitution as a metaphorical reference both to recent colonial history and to a theistic authorization of government as in the US pledge of allegiance. Allusion to God as a distant yet grander sovereign force bestows gravitas on non-vestigial states as a justification for the violence in their power and serves as a mystified and glorified reference to former governing systems they portray themselves as having rightfully succeeded.

Key to my argument is that vestigial states that are now called religions begin their evolution and development when there is a major shift in governing structures. Frequently, such shake-ups have taken place when a territory controlled by a distinct population is invaded and conquered. If the new government does not banish the remaining local population or commit genocide, the subjugated people might be allowed to maintain a semblance of their customs and institutions in attenuated form. Former governmental structures are granted limited recognition and functionality and particular clusters of practices and ideas associated with the now marginalized group can live on vestigially as what in time comes to be called 'religion'.[3]

The evolution of vestigial states into religions has ancient roots. Two early Greek texts in which I see the process depicted are Hesiod's *Theogony* and Aeschylus' *Eumenides*. In the former, the at one time fearsome Uranos is portrayed as a beneficent and harmlessly remote counsellor after he is conquered by the Titans (*Theogony*: 463, 470). In the latter text, when Athena disempowers the Furies by assigning them a limited jurisdiction below the earth, they are nevertheless acknowledged in the new governmental order and accorded specific honours (*Eumenides*: 1021–31). Although applying the term religion to the narratives of both texts is anachronistic, the succession of sovereignties is still marked by relegating former ruling orders to the status of what I am labelling a vestigial state. Eventually, these remainders of former ruling orders become what is more currently called religion as the term takes on traction through history. It is possible that what are referred to as 'cults' in ancient civilizations are the surviving remnants of previous governmental structures.

The history of the Druids provides additional support for the hypothesis that religions – at least in some times and places – have evolved as institutions used by states to contain displaced sovereignties. In Book VI of his commentary on the war in Gaul, Julius Caesar describes the Druids as the central authorities in their territory. He writes that they concern themselves with 'divine matters', conduct sacrifices and interpret 'matters of religion', but, at the same time, take charge of deciding almost all 'public and private' disputes. His account of the Druids' extensive powers shows that 'religion' in Gaul was synonymous with government rather than separate from it (*Bello Gallico*: 6.13). Caesar's text accords with suggestions by S. N. Balagangadhara and Brent Nongbri that in Greece and Rome religious rites and practices are described as traditions supporting the reigning state and thus appear as coextensive with it (Balagangadhara 1994: 34–8; Nongbri 2013: 50–3).

After the Romans succeeded in their conquest of Gaul, the Druids' jurisdiction was limited to Iona and perhaps a few other islands and outlying districts. They finally lost all sovereign power and were restricted to doing what a succession of rulers either allowed or ignored. They became practitioners of a religion – that is, they maintained as best they could the traditions and ceremonies of a disempowered and limited government. Although pagans in the UK have long considered themselves a religion, it was not until 2010 that the Druid Network was legally awarded the title in England and Wales (Owen and Taira 2015).

The proposition that both fully functioning states and remnants of conquered or colonized states come to make use of the category of religion for their own purposes is applicable to Jewish history. I draw on the work of Daniel Boyarin and Seth Schwartz for material in support of this line of argument. According to Boyarin (2004), Christian theologians play a major role in the creation of what gets to be thought of as Jewish religion. In order to define Christianity as a unique body of thought and practice, theorists who understand themselves to be Christians need an ideology that will fit the category of other so that they can decide what they are not. The producers of texts that set out Christian dogma engage in a centuries-long task of self-creation and identity formation that uses 'Judaism' as a foil to separate orthodoxy from heresy. The ideologies attributed to both camps over time grow out of group affiliations that precede articulated philosophies a.k.a. religions. 'One might say', writes Boyarin, 'that Judaism and Christianity were invented in order to explain the fact that there were Jews and Christians' (2004: 21).

Of course Jews take part in this process of identity formation as well because they are 'empowered by the Christian interpellation of Judaism as a religion' (Boyarin 2004: 225). But, argues Boyarin, unlike Christians, Jews do not insist that group membership be predicated on acceptance of particular beliefs. 'The Rabbis', he maintains, 'reject and refuse the Christian definition of a religion, understood as a system of beliefs and practices to which one adheres voluntarily' (224). In contrast to 'the Church' for which, Boyarin says, 'Judaism is a religion', for Jews it is so 'only occasionally, ambivalently and strategically' (224).

Nevertheless, although Christianity and Judaism evolve as religions with their own fluctuating rules about membership, I suggest that each group comes to use the category of religion in much the same way. Religion for both Christians and Jews is a container for attenuated authority, a state-sanctioned placeholder for states-in-waiting. Being a religion permits a group to survive and cohere within a fully functioning state and perhaps to exert significant influence upon practices of governance and institutions under state control.

Boyarin explains that his work with Christian theology and Jewish scholarship shows how three 'religions' – namely Christianity, Judaism and Paganism – 'came into being . . . as distinctions produced (and resisted) for particular purposes by particular people' (2004: 19). I suggest that the discursive production that Boyarin analyses so ably and carefully might well be secondary to the particular contexts of statecraft in which the texts were composed. Jews existed as a marginalized and conquered group within a succession of empires. I understand the creation of the religion of Judaism as one important way in which Jews dealt with perpetual displacement. As the category of religion becomes available, both Jews and the imperial rulers who dominate them put it to use for both containment and survival. The present state of Israel is evidence that a vestigial state known as a religion can transform through tumults and agonies of history into a fully functioning sovereign state with all the levers of military power.

Seth Schwartz's work in *Imperialism and Jewish Society 200 BCE to 640 CE* (2001) supplements Boyarin's intricate and multifaceted analysis of the ways in which Judaism and Jewish identity form in dialogue with and reaction to the philosophical and theological positions of outsiders. I consider such discursive production secondary to negotiations that took place over centuries between successive dominant groups – that is, Assyrians, Babylonians, Persians, Greeks, Egyptians and Romans – and Jews as an ethnic constituency within imperial jurisdictions. Except for relatively brief periods of autonomy such as in the Hasmonean dynasty, ascendant foreign states empowered local Jewish oligarchies to exercise a mélange of civic, legal and so-called 'religious' powers. Texts, buildings and assorted paraphernalia that are often thought to be artefacts pertaining to distinct Jewish religious practice once served in the mechanisms of day-to-day processes of governing. Often, foreign rulers were both the guarantors and enforcers of Jewish law. For example, in reference to first-century history, Schwartz writes, 'it would not be an exaggeration to say that the Torah was the constitution of the Jews of Palestine. Its authority rested not simply, and initially perhaps not at all, on the consensus of the Jews, but on the might of the imperial and native rulers of Palestine' (56).

I read Schwartz's work as demonstrating that governing roles assigned to Jewish leaders under imperial domination were not functionally separated into religious and non-religious spheres, but rather were inextricably implicated in one another. Over a long and complicated history, powers of Jewish leaders and practices of Jewish communities uneasily coalesce under the heading of Judaism as a religion, the institutional rubric that permits the existence of a quasi-state within a state.

Although Schwartz is uncomfortable with any interpretation of Jewish history that does not somehow recognize an originary 'religious' nature to Jewishness, his objections to understanding religion as embedded in government and administration are largely rhetorical and in opposition to the evidence he recounts and records. For example, Schwartz writes that in late antique Jewish communities 'there was no Jewish ecclesiastical hierarchy . . . It may be worth remembering the Talmudic stories . . . telling of villagers appointing a single functionary to "fulfill all their (religious) [sic] needs"' (2001: 287). When asked about his use of parentheses, a form of punctuation that denotes a word or phrase's presence in the original text instead of brackets that would have indicated an authorial addition or explanation, Schwartz answered by email that he 'takes it for granted that the appointee will NOT [sic] be expected to supervise, say, the water supply or the efficient marketing of their wheat crop' (26 March 2012). However, I find nothing in Schwartz's work to substantiate his opinion that the practical aspects of governance and administration were separated from what he refers to as religion. His emendation of the Talmudic quotation seems to mark unease with a lack of evidence in support of disembedding 'religion' from the Jewish institutional and cultural practices in the history he studies.

In an article that argues more specifically that Jewishness has an intrinsically 'religious' nature, Schwartz writes: 'religion can be salvaged as a heuristic concept if we mean by it: the practices (including cognitive ones) which constitute people's relations with their god(s)' (2011: 230). He adds: 'the great tradition of the Jews was overwhelmingly religious in that it was overwhelmingly concerned with the relations between the Jews and their God. The Jews' laws are all treated as divine in origin, whether or not they are stated explicitly in the Torah' (236). Schwartz's logic consists of calling a group or institution religious if God is cited in laws and central texts. His reasoning brings to the fore the crux of my argument about when and how the term religion has come to be used in statecraft.

Schwartz does not acknowledge that states throughout history have more often than not claimed to be built on theistic foundations. The trope is common practice in the present day. (The aforementioned Canadian constitution serves as an example. I doubt Schwartz would claim that mentioning God in the first line of its constitution establishes Canada as a religion.) Even when states do not hail a divinity as a justification for their existence, other principles and ideals are cited as foundational and thus, I would argue, function as a 'god', that is as a validation of authority.

The assertion that God is the ultimate master of a group and the origin of its rules for living, especially in times when the term religion was not in use, does not constitute the group making such a claim as a religion. Calling on a god as a progenitor or architect of society is not a sufficient condition for a group to be a religion in popular, legal and/or academic discourse. What is required is the dislocation of the group within a dominant population's territory usually because of war and/or colonization. It is then that 'religion' becomes useful strategically both to the weaker and to the more dominant collective as a name to create, sustain and maintain coherence.

Although, as I explained earlier, I see the reference to the authority of a divinity as a metaphor marking a past form of territorial jurisdiction, a group does not adopt either willingly or unwillingly the strategic classification of religion without having endured disruption of its sovereignty. Judaism becomes a religion over the course of centuries not because God is continually referenced by Jewish leaders to justify their *Weltanschauung* and directives but because Jews as an ethnicity endured displacement and colonization. Religion as part of the technology of statecraft evolves as the term designating a weakened state that is permitted a circumscribed existence within a more powerful state.

When in Matthew 22.21 Jesus is quoted as saying 'Render unto Caesar the things which are Caesar's and unto God the things that are God's', he acknowledges more than Caesar's specific entitlement to coins stamped with his image. Jesus is also saying that the displaced and subordinate condition of his own constituency obligates that constituency to give Rome its due as the dominant state. God hailed as deserving of that which is not Caesar's confers an ambivalent autonomy from Rome on the group that recognizes the deity's authority, however limited. God is a leader different in kind from Caesar and thus perhaps not a threat to imperial rule. Yet, the very fact that what is due to God is paralleled with what is due to Caesar could imply sedition. The statement embodies both the submission to dominant authority and the possible challenge to it that Jews, as a loosely organized vestigial state, could pose at a time when Judaism, Christianity and Paganism as terms and concepts destined to refer to separate religions were not yet in use.

The approach of Tibetan leaders to their situation as a government in exile offers a contemporary example of the efficacy of the category of religion in the technology of statecraft. I refer to the canny and highly strategic move by Tenzin Gyatso, the 14th Dalai Lama. On 8 August 2011, Lopsang Sangay was sworn in as the first democratically elected Kalon Tripa, or Prime Minister of the Central Tibetan Administration in Dharamsala. At the swearing-in ceremony, the Dalai Lama expressed his satisfaction at having made good on his intention announced several months previously to separate his religious functions from those of an elected government official. 'This is in keeping with the trend everywhere around the world to move towards democracy', he explained. By divesting himself of what he termed the 'political leadership' that he says he 'inherited' at the age of sixteen, he says he is conferring power on the Tibetan people whom he describes as 'the masters of Tibet and not – [that is, instead of] – the religious heads or their heirs'. 'I always state', he maintained, 'that it is wrong for religious leaders to hold political positions. . . . I will continue to strongly speak about the importance of the separation of religion and politics' (Gyatso 2011).

Thus are the functions of the office of Dalai Lama intentionally restricted by being described as religious. One deliberate result is that the powers of future Dalai Lamas will be limited. Even if the Chinese government realizes its well-known plan to influence the selection of the next Dalai Lama by controlling the Panchen Lama, the authority connected with the unelected and now solely 'religious' leader of Tibet will be appreciably diminished. The Dalai Lama as official head of a religion will, in theory at least, administer and direct a version of Tibetan Buddhism that is no longer institutionally synonymous with Tibet as a state in exile. Contemporary Tibetan Buddhism is in this way being fashioned into what I want to call a vestigial state, a.k.a. a once and future state, a.k.a. a religion, as a way of challenging and restricting the purview of Chinese domination.

The implications of perceiving religions to be vestigial states are many and far-reaching. I envision at least three topics that would be impacted creatively and productively: categories of law, gender arrangements and understandings of identity. To conclude, I'll briefly and broadly indicate possible directions for theory about these themes.

1. Differences between secular and religious law could be clarified. Scholars of jurisprudence are often reluctant to discuss religious law because they think of this form of regulation as qualitatively different from the mundane varieties they are trained to analyse. I suggest that the religious/secular distinction could be helpfully thought of as occurring between the legislative mechanisms of two forms of states. Establishment of law in both instances involves processes of debate and compromise among the contingent interests of constituents. I have argued elsewhere that such an understanding leads to a recognition that religious law in any long and complex tradition is not straightforward and monolithic, but rather is multifaceted and subject to shifts in conventions of interpretation as are all varieties of legislation (Goldenberg 2013a).

2. Discussion about power relations concerning gender could be advanced. Feminist theory has a rich history of interrogating all terms and concepts related to sexual difference and orientation. Queering notions of femininity, masculinity, maleness and femaleness in tandem with concepts such as race, class and ethnicity has evolved as a central practice in feminist analysis. Such bold thinking has helped to further social justice in relation to all levels of so-called secular governments. However, because religion has not yet been queered as energetically, oppression of women within religious organizations continues to be permitted and even at times considered worthy of appreciation (Goldenberg 2015). Indeed, some prominent feminist theorists argue that men and women who express their devotion through endorsing and practicing sexual inequality deserve more respect and should remain off limits to critique (Mahmood 2005). In addition, there has been too little attention paid to how such sanctioned sexism in religions can be contagious by making male hegemony and female reticence as generalized practices seem appropriate and honourable (Dhaliwal 2012). By moving the category of religion into the sphere of statecraft, by understanding that gender arrangements derive from the histories of earlier forms of government rather than from inscrutable structures of mystery, piety might be paralleled more closely with politics and the inferior position of women

within the once and future states named religions might be supported with less conviction.

3. Lastly, discourse reinforcing religious commitments and allegiances might be productively disturbed. Idealizing religious identity as a basic component of a good and proper human life could well be limiting the ways we regard and imagine one another. More generous and inclusive types of interactions and affiliations might become possible if a greater number of us were to understand ourselves as being influenced – but not eternally bounded – by the complex histories of the empires and governments that preceded the present structures in which we live.

References

Arnal, William E. and Russell T. McCutcheon (2013), *The Sacred Is the Profane: The Political Nature of 'Religion'*, New York: Oxford University Press.

Balagangadhara, S. N. (1994), *The Heathen in His Blindness: Asia, the West and the Dynamic of Religion*, Leiden: E. J. Brill.

Boyarin, Daniel (2004), *Border Lines: The Partition of Judaeo-Christianity*, Philadelphia: University of Pennsylvania Press.

Crawford, James (2007), *The Creation of States in International Law*, 2nd edn, Oxford: Clarendon Press.

Dhaliwal, Sukhwant (2012), 'Religion, Moral Hegemony and Local Cartographies of Power: Feminist Reflections on Religion in Local Politics', PhD diss., University of London.

Fitzgerald, Timothy (2000), *The Ideology of Religious Studies*, New York: Oxford University Press.

Fitzgerald, Timothy (2007a), *Discourse on Civility and Barbarity: A Critical History of Religion and Related Categories*, London and New York: Oxford University Press.

Fitzgerald, Timothy (2007b), *Religion and the Secular: Historical and Colonial Formations*, London: Equinox.

Fitzgerald, Timothy (2011), *Religion and Politics in International Relations: The Modern Myth*, London and New York: Continuum.

Gimbutas, Marija (1989), *The Language of the Goddess*, San Francisco: Harper & Row.

Goldenberg, Naomi (2013a), 'Theorizing Religions as Vestigial States in Relation to Gender and Law: Three Cases', *Journal of Feminist Studies in Religion*, 29 (1): 38–50.

Goldenberg, Naomi (2013b), 'Demythologizing Gender and Religion Within Nation-states: Toward A Politics of Disbelief', in Niamh Reilly and Stacey Scriver (eds), *Religion, Gender and the Public Sphere*, 248–56, New York: Routledge.

Goldenberg, Naomi (2015), 'Queer Theory Meets Critical Religion: Are We Starting to Think Yet?', in Richard King (ed.), *Religion, Theory, Critique: Classic and Contemporary Approaches and Methodologies*, 531–43, New York: Columbia University Press.

Goldenberg, Naomi (2018), 'Forget about Defining "It": Reflections on Thinking Differently in Religious Studies', in Brad Stoddard (ed.), *Method Today: Redescribing Approaches to the Study of Religion*, 78–95, Bristol: Equinox.

Goldenberg, Naomi (2019a), 'Religion and Its Limits: Reflections on Discursive Borders and Boundaries', *Journal of the British Association for the Study of Religion*, 21: 1–15.

Goldenberg, Naomi (2019b), 'There is No Religion in the Bible', *Implicit Religion*, 22 (1): 13–29.

Goldenberg, Naomi (2019c), 'Timothy Fitzgerald and the Revival of Religious Studies', *Implicit Religion*, 22 (3–4): 309–18.

Goldenberg, Naomi (2020), 'Toward a Critique of Postsecular Rhetoric', in Leslie Dorrough Smith, Steffen Führding and Adrian Hermann (eds), *Hijacked: A Critical Treatment of Good and Bad Religion*, 37–46, Sheffield: Equinox.

Goldenberg, Naomi (2021), 'The Religious is Political', in Kathleen McPhillips and Naomi Goldenberg (eds), *The End of Religion: Feminist Reappraisals of the State*, 7–25, London and New York: Routledge.

Goldenberg, Naomi (2023), 'Why *'Religion' and 'Secular' Categories in Sociology: Decolonizing the Modern Myth* by Mitsutoshi Horii is a major contribution to critical religion', *Critical Research on Religion*, 11 (1): 109–12.

Goldenberg, Naomi (2024), 'Critical Religion Takes a Punch: Notes on a Scholarly Skirmish', *Method and Theory in the Study of Religion*, 36 (3–4): 287–94.

Gyatso, Tenzin (2011), 'His Holiness the Dalai Lama's Speech at the Swearing-in Ceremony of the Kalon Tripa Lobsang Sangay', 12 August. Available online: https://tibet.net/his-holiness-the-dalai-lamas-speech-at-the-swearing-in-ceremony-of-the-kalon-tripa-lobsang-sangay/ (accessed 22 December 2024).

King, Richard (1999), *Orientalism and Religion: Postcolonial Theory, India and the 'Mystic East'*, London and New York: Routledge.

Mahmood, Saba (2005), *Politics of Piety: The Islamic Revival and the Feminist Subject*, Princeton and Oxford: Princeton University Press.

Masuzawa, Tomoko (2005). *The Invention of World Religions*, Chicago and London: University of Chicago Press.

McCutcheon, Russell T. (1997), *Manufacturing Religion: The Discourse on Sui Generis Religion and the Politics of Nostalgia*, New York and Oxford: Oxford University Press.

McCutcheon, Russell T. (2001), *Critics Not Caretakers: Redescribing the Public Study of Religion*, Albany: State University of New York Press.

McCutcheon, Russell T. (2003), *The Discipline of Religion: Structure, Meaning, Rhetoric*, London and New York: Routledge.

McCutcheon, Russell T. (2007), *Studying Religion: An Introduction*, London: Equinox.

McPhillips, Kathleen and Naomi Goldenberg, eds (2021), *The End of Religion: Feminist Reappraisals of the State*, London and New York: Routledge.

Nongbri, Brent (2013), *Before Religion: A History of a Modern Concept*, New Haven and London: Yale University Press.

Owen, Suzanne and Teemu Taira (2015), 'The Category of "Religion" in Public Classification: Charity Registration of The Druid Network in England and Wales', in Trevor Stack, Naomi Goldenberg and Timothy Fitzgerald (eds), *Religion as a Category of Governance and Sovereignty*, 90–114, Leiden: Brill.

Pump, Andrew (2016), 'The Church in Globalization: A World-Systems Analysis on the Influence of Liberalism in Modern Catholic Social Thought', PhD diss., University of Ottawa.

Schwartz, Seth (2001), *Imperialism and Jewish Society 200 BCE to 640 CE*, Princeton: Princeton University Press.

Schwartz, Seth (2011), 'How Many Judaisms Were There? A Critique of Neusner and Smith on Definition and Mason and Boyarin on Categorization', *Journal of Ancient Judaism*, 2: 208–38.

Weber, Max (2004), 'Politics as a Vocation', in David Owen and Tracy B. Strong (eds), *The Vocation Lectures*, trans. Rodney Livingstone, 32–94, Indianapolis: Hackett Publishing Company.

12

The implications of critical religion for (gendered) Religious Education

Alison Jasper and John I'Anson

Introduction

Rather like marmite, Religious Education (or, more commonly, 'RE'), tends to generate sharply polarizing responses: for some, the subject connotes forms of colonial practice and memories of undergoing activities whose educational value was, at best, questionable. For others, an altogether more positive response is generated: a site that potentially opens to difference, raising significant ethical, political and even existential issues in the process. Either way, an emotive force tends to be associated with RE, which eclipses, perhaps, a more measured and considered response. Indeed, *so* familiar have the words 'Religious Education' become, that it is easy to overlook the sheer oddity of their juxtaposition.

Combining 'Religion' and 'Education' to form 'Religious Education' (RE) might be thought surprising, or even, perhaps, undesirable; and yet, such a conjunction is routinely performed; the connection appears, simply, as a given. Were the two terms to be linked with a preposition, as in 'religion *with* education', or a conjunctive, such as 'religion *and* education', this might offer an invitation to explore *how* the two are in fact related, or, perhaps more to the point, how they *might* be related. Nevertheless, even though 'religious' and 'education' appear to run alongside one another – as precarious runners in a three-legged race, we might say – there is, nevertheless, a space between the terms. François Jullien (2014) suggests that acknowledging a gap provides a means with which to think about how a relationship – here, that between 'religion' and 'education' – has been, and might, in future, be imagined. And so, taking this as an initial point of departure, we raise a simple question in relation to 'RE': what is related with what?

An etymology of 'religion' and 'education'

According to Michel Serres, religion is typically linked to its Latin root *religare*, meaning to 'attach', and this derivation leads to the popular and well-known association of religion with binding or constraint (Serres 1995: 47). However, there is another quite different derivation, via Seneca, where religion translates as 're-reading'. Thus, a lexical reading or definition – such as Thomas Tweed (2006: 33) observes to be concerned with 'the setting of bounds or limits' or rendering 'an object or image distinct to the eye' – suggests an impossible concept: the stability associated with an etymology of attachment/binding is challenged by the association of 'religion' with an open-endedness that characterizes re-reading. If we now turn to an etymology of 'education', we find a parallel tension. According to Maurice Craft, 'education' also has two distinct linguistic roots. On the one hand, *educare* is concerned with alignment to an existing and fixed ordering of things (Craft 1984: 9). On the other hand, *educere* literally means 'to lead out' (Masschelein 2006, 2010a, b).[1] So 'education' – not unlike 'religion' – appears grounded in an impossibility between the already achieved and a radical openness to the new and yet to come.

Writing in 1950s New York, Hannah Arendt (1968) identified a 'crisis' in education between, on the one hand, a focus upon the already known versus, on the other, an openness to the new and unforeseen. While such a crisis can be useful in raising the question of education – as 'the moment in which one asks what something is' (Norberg 2011: 134) – it can also be overwhelming in so far as this challenges our existing capabilities to cope: 'we lose certainty about our navigational ability' (2011: 136). And so, on this reading, the alignment of religion and education together might appear to be doubly problematic.

However, while an etymological approach to definition might suggest that the project of Religious Education is, from the outset, untenable, 'RE' empirically exists, apparently unproblematically, in day-to-day speech and discourse. One reason may be that people identify themselves primarily with one or other of these words, or even with just one of its associated etymologies. This is the case, perhaps, when an uncritical understanding of 'learning and teaching' discourse within educational contexts directs practitioners or policy-makers simply to focus on alignment with pre-given orderings: standards, targets, examination results, etc. In this case, what receives less attention – sometimes much less – is the sense in which education can *also* be defined as having to do with the interruption of our present horizons of expectation through encounter with the radically new, that which is still to emerge, sometimes through an experience of being 'led out' from familiar orientations (Biesta 2005; l'Anson and Jasper 2011). Having pointed to some of the challenges associated with an etymology of 'religion' and 'education', how in practice are these mobilized?

An empirical approach to 'RE'

An empirical approach is concerned with how a concept is mobilized within specific contexts, and with identifying the particular material arrangements and practices to which this gives rise. If we consider how 'RE' is mobilized in practice, it becomes relevant, for example, to look at how these terms have been put together through and across time.

An empirical approach is interested in ways in which knowledge practices also imply different kinds of relation to the matters in hand: for example, notions of objectivity imply some kind of *distance* from a given concept, which implies a spatial image, conceiving relationships in terms of relative nearness and farness. Conversely, being 'too *close* to' – or actually being aligned with – a given concept or issue can be seen as questionable on academic grounds, as some kind of 'critical distance' is usually regarded as a precondition for impartial analysis. Such spatial considerations were crucial in the construction of RE as a subject area from the 1970s. Ninian Smart (1972), in particular, put forward an orientation to Religious Education that positioned this *between*, on the one hand, theological/confessional approaches that were seen as involving too close a relationship to the subject matter of religion, and, on the other, 'extra-religious' or what were characterized as 'reductionistic' approaches, such as sociology or psychology, which tended to translate religious terms within their own characteristic grammars. The new approach to studying religion – through being positioned in a new space between these alternatives – could thereby claim to be neutral and impartial, and therefore preferable, at least on ethical grounds, as a way forward (see Table 12.1).

Consequently, from the early 1970s, there was a significant development in the ways in which the terms 'religion' and 'religious' were mobilized particularly in secondary and primary school contexts, reflecting attitudinal changes towards confessional Christianity that had occurred in the population

Table 12.1 The Spatial Positioning of Religious Education from the 1970s

Theological / Confessional Approaches	Religious Education from the 1970s Onwards	'Extra-religious' Approaches
Assumes the truth and standpoint of a given religion – and so involves an exploration within these terms. Educational purpose is to induct young people into this tradition, so that they become familiar with its concepts, values and practices. In a pluralistic society it becomes difficult to justify the assumption of a singular standpoint.	Methodological neutrality: is rhetorically situated between competing perspectives. Aims to enable an analysis of 'world religions' on their own terms. A basis for comparison and understanding of religions is also provided, such as Ninian Smart's categorization of different 'dimensions' (1969).	Such as sociology, psychology, politics, etc. Aims to analyse and explain 'the religious' through relevant concepts and methodologies within these respective disciplines. Consequently, religious terms may be translated and interpreted differently.

at large since the end of the Second World War (Brown 2001; Brown and Woodhead 2017).

Additionally, some new 'Religious Studies' undergraduate programmes – beginning at Lancaster University – began to be offered in universities that had traditionally taught forms of exclusively Christian theology. Under Smart's direction, *Religious Education in Secondary Schools* – more commonly referred to as 'Working Paper 36' (Schools Council 1971) – represented an important liberalization. Smart and his collaborators proposed 'world religions' as a procedurally neutral domain, which was ordered via a series of empirically verifiable 'religious' dimensions (Smart 1969). Significantly, at the start, the 'New Religious Education' (Smart 1972), set apart from (contentious, Christian) theology or biblical studies, still tried to avoid translating – or 'reducing' – 'religion' into terms derived from explicitly 'non-religious' disciplinary frameworks such as sociology, psychology or anthropology. Instead, it sought to encourage young people to engage with radically different ideas and cultures, taken seriously on their own terms.[2]

It could also be said that the Smartian settlement we have outlined changed RE in Britain in respect to the spatiality of relations. Arguably, it moved from an assumed alignment and identification with core concepts and knowledge practices to one premised upon detachment and distance from these things, as well as upon objectivity as short-hand for the *non-affectingness* of educational matters of concern (l'Anson and Jasper 2017; Latour 2005). Analysis, within these revised terms, has tended to become focused upon understanding and acts of comparison, rather than critical inquiry into the concepts, practices and assemblages that were constitutive of the subject per se or the expectation that young people or students will be, in a significant way, changed through or affected by their encounters.

After the 1970s, the energetic dialogue instigated between universities and secondary or primary school levels lost momentum. Though its conclusions were widely implemented, the exchange and conversation that had led to the publication of texts like the *Schools Council Working Paper 36* (1971) – and equivalents such as the *Millar Report* in Scotland (Scottish Education Department 1972) – slowed or ceased altogether. Subsequently, while subject to many of the same trends or changes, such as an increasing policy emphasis on standards, examination and forms of measurability, differing orientations began to develop in respect of 'RE' without any further collective effort to review progress or come to an agreed position. In universities, under the impact of post-structuralism, the centre of gravity within the humanities shifted towards relational ontologies and contextual approaches (l'Anson and Jasper 2017: 16, 23). These approaches – which also inform critical religion – are set in opposition to abstract uniformities, hierarchical masculinist structures of knowledge and, crucially, objectivity viewed as an achievable goal. In other contexts, however, many scholars and perhaps particularly practitioners in primary and secondary education remained more closely identified with the earlier version of the 'world religions' brand, especially in respect of its notion of neutrality – or, at least, of neutrality understood as an approximation to a putative objectivity. Smart's (1973) own commitment to the complex methodological implications of neutrality as a phenomenological practice of bracketing truth claims – that tried to take different ideas and cultures seriously on their own terms – has not survived very well in these contexts, possibly because it is such a difficult exercise in practice. Instead, neutrality has been increasingly replaced by notions of 'religious literacy' (Wright 2007, 2016), which undercut a number of the procedures and practices that informed the 'New' Religious Education from the 1970s.

Smart's earlier approach aimed at an appreciation of the phenomenon of 'religious experience', in its multiple varieties, through the removal of barriers that might get in the way of such hospitality. The bracketing of truth claims, in particular, was seen as a key ingredient in creating the kinds of spaces in which difference might be entertained, rather than becoming a point of contention that might impede further exploration. The focus of critical religious literacy, however, was specifically upon these 'truth claims' and how these might be rationally evaluated. This was to set aside many of the characteristic concerns and practices that had been foregrounded by a 'dimensional' analysis of religion (ritual, story, experience, etc.) and to privilege instead religious texts that were to be read in a particular way and with a particular focus. It could be said that the move towards 'religious literacy' has encouraged the development of a less ethically nuanced, more representationalist approach to the language of 'religion' – one which assumes that a clear and widely shareable word–world correspondence can be established to read across cultures. While this struggles to account for the challenges of profound difference – such as that between literate and non-literate cultures – it nevertheless fits well with the increased focus on forms of accountability that have 'cast [their] shadow' across school – and increasingly, higher education – approaches to RE more generally (Conroy et al. 2013).[3] While a critical religious literacy approach aligned well with an increasing focus on examinations (since its tokens were clear and unambiguous), such a direction of travel can be seen as creating a further divide between RE in schools and developments within universities, where the complex issues of translation and the iterability of language have become key matters of concern.

In sum, the existence of these different orientations towards the study of 'religion' has tended to create significant divisions between the different sectors of education that would-be students of 'religion' have to navigate. This becomes all the more complex when, for example, having studied what might be called 'critical religion' in university spaces, students in professional education then have to translate their new understandings into primary or secondary school contexts where a 'world religions' approach may represent something potentially very different and difficult to reconcile (l'Anson 2004; l'Anson and Jasper 2011). So on closer inspection, an empirical approach to the definition of 'RE', similarly to an etymological approach, suggests real difficulties, belied by much if not most day-to-day use of the term.

Towards an educational approach to RE: A three-elements heuristic

What is perhaps surprising is that the accounts of Religious Education that we have considered so far each address different ways of thinking about religions, foregrounding ways in which a student might relate to the aspects identified as significant. In all this, what is conspicuous by its absence, however, is a more explicit consideration of the second word in the juxtaposition 'Religious Education': education. It might, with some justification, be said that 'education' haunts proposals for Religious Education from the early 1970s – in so far as appeals are made to education as ruling out certain options, while permitting others. A clear illustration of this was the way in which the 'New' Religious Education inaugurated by Smart pointed to extant forms of RE as *not* being sufficiently educational, on account of their presumption of a single confessional standpoint and their not providing opportunities for young people to consider broader cultural perspectives. This, of course, also implied that the approach advocated *was in fact* educational, and was, moreover, legitimated on these grounds. But what this education, with which religion is associated, positively consists in is left largely implicit and unarticulated. In order to think critically about how the relations between Religion and Education might be imagined, it is therefore desirable also to focus upon education, and to ask the question: In what might this education consist? With this in mind, we first set out a brief account of one possible approach to thinking about what an educational account consists in. Our three-elements heuristic, which we first proposed in our book *Schooling Indifference* (l'Anson and Jasper 2017; also 2021), sees education as consisting in the negotiation of pathways that are simultaneously *critical*, *ethical* and *experimental*. With such an approach, it is the mutual interplay of these three elements, within particular scenes, that defines claims to 'education' as such. This will, we hope, provide the basis for imagining how 'critical religion' (Fitzgerald 2001, 2007a, c; McCutcheon 1997, 2003) might connect with 'education' to form a 'critical religious education'.

The critical element

The critical element involves critical reflexivity concerning the various concepts, tropes and practices engaged in making particular kinds of sense in respect of what is called 'education' or 'the educational'. This implies a willingness to interrupt familiar ways of going on – conventions, traditions, unexamined ideas of 'common sense' – and to become aware of the limits of particular framings and approaches: the acknowledgement of *not*-knowing is, therefore, vitally important, especially if we are to avoid projecting limitations onto others (Smith 2016; Latour 2004).[4] In relation to the critical element, we could say that the RE settlement outlined above, while it promotes a critical distance – and a level of abstraction – from its matters of concern, nevertheless offers only a limited understanding of criticality. There is, for example, no attempt to include a critical reflexivity *apropos* the assemblage of concepts, tropes and practices that are mobilized under the sign of 'RE'. In this regard, critical religion, because it problematizes terms, positionings and the consequences of theoretical stances, potentially offers a new way forward that *does* address this element of education.

The ethical element

Since education is a fundamentally relational activity, an ethical element will always be in play the moment one begins to question what these relations imply, and what responsibilities these entail. The ethical element becomes all the more complex and interesting once it is accepted that its many 'different acts, criteria, and accounts' from different cultural contexts are distinct, and cannot be collapsed into a single plane of sense-making (Lambek 2015: 228). The acknowledgement of ethical difference, in other words, requires approaches that are able to register such difference while also giving insight into how this might impact upon us. This may, for example, imply working upon ourselves so as to become more attentive or receptive to the matters before us. As regards the ethical element, it has been noted already that a primary concern of the settlement in RE from the early 1970s onwards was an approach that promoted sympathetic analysis and comparison between so-called world religions. However, the trope of neutrality limits the extent to which the implications of this can be followed through. If educational inquiry is framed as 'non-affecting', then ethical work on the self, which may be necessary if a subject is to change in response to an ethical or ontological demand, becomes suspect (Foucault 2005; McGushin 2007). Critical religion, however, offers an account in which such ethical work is acknowledged as necessary: the invitation to see otherwise is intrinsic to its project.

The experimental element

The experimental element is concerned with imagining otherwise and with the work of translating a given stance within empirical contexts. This is to acknowledge that some insights can only be arrived at through direct empirical engagement, as when a doctor carefully examines (palpates) a patient's wound via a variety of tactile moves that enable them to sense what may be at issue (May 2005: 20). The experimental element constitutes part of an ontology that rejects the idea that education is primarily concerned with the already known. Following Spinoza (1985), we argue that we do not know in advance what a particular being is capable of doing or becoming.[5] A key purpose of education thus becomes the fashioning of events and encounters that lead students out from their point of departure through open engagement and exploration. This involves, in Isabelle Stengers' (1997) terms, a preparedness for 'being at risk'. In this regard, critical religion is acutely attuned to the political and social consequences of mobilizing categories and concepts of this kind.

Critical religion and/with education: Three scenes

Having outlined a possible way of thinking about how the educational might be conceived in practice, what are the implications of linking such a characterization of education (as involving the mutual interplay of all three elements) to critical religion? Moving forward, we consider how far and in what ways critical religion can intersect with education, understood as the task of negotiating pathways within a complex relational milieu. We consider three distinct scenes – that is, three complex, specifically located contexts – that might exemplify how a critical Religious Education might be performed.

After neutrality: Some tools for thinking otherwise

If originally neutrality emerged to safeguard and promote an acknowledgement of different 'religions' on their own terms, in practice procedural neutrality has often come to seem little more than a disguised demand for closer *identification* with dominant preconceptions. What on many occasions has quickly been forgotten is that neither the discourse of religion and religions, nor the discourse of neutrality itself, are simple givens. Assuming that the category of 'religion' exists in the world and that – either explicitly or implicitly – there is an assemblage of practices, beliefs, objects, social placements or whatever else that conform to it does not denote a neutral position. In other words, neutrality is only one particular 'ontocategorical way' of making sense (I'Anson and Jasper 2017: 60; I'Anson 2016). Were this assemblage of 'neutrality' to be substituted, for example, by Karen Barad's (2007: 135) trope of 'diffraction' – a concept concerned with the complexities of relations that exist in any given field and the difference that being implicated within that field makes (I'Anson and Jasper 2017: 69) – this would have very different affordances and consequences. As scholars in the field of critical religion (among others) suggest, the use of terms like 'religion' or 'secular' is *always* contextualized and thus very much dependent on the relations of those who use them within a whole range of socio-material practices. As one recent commentator on critical religion in relation to the history of Indian nationalism warns us (Nadadur Kannan 2016):

> The nationalists indeed used these terms religion, secular, science, and materialism in some instances that pointed to a colonial understanding of these categories. However, there were other complex ways in which these terms were used . . .

Seen through this lens, it is difficult to imagine how the discourse of 'religion' could be promoted as part of the RE curriculum if the goal is to present forms of difference in a disinterested way. As Nadadur Kannan's comments suggest, 'we' have no monopoly on how this discourse of religion is used. Yet currently, encounters with difference under the heading of 'world religions' in the context of a British education system continue to be substantively uncritical in their use of this term. Arguably, the current scene of RE still fails to recognize that education -- as *educere* – implies the possibility of change, of being affected and coming into new ideas and ways of being (Latour 2005). Additionally, as we have previously suggested (l'Anson and Jasper 2017), another difficulty with the settlement of RE proposed by Smart and later collaborators is that insufficient attention is paid to relational aspects of what is happening in spaces we might choose to call the 'educational'. In light of this range of problematic features, we go on to ask, what tools could be helpful in approaching things differently from the current settlement of RE?

We respond to this question, first, by looking at and promoting the work of those philosophers and theorists who offer new ways of articulating differences, challenging or enlivening sense-making practices that (might) also take place in educational spaces. For example, we have found Baruch Spinoza's non-dualistic approach particularly suggestive in giving fuller value to the relational nature of human subjectivity. The contemporary feminist philosopher Luce Irigaray is similarly important for her work that challenges a symbolic masculine singularity at the heart of Western philosophy and culture, proposing instead the fruitfulness of exploring in-between spaces represented by notions of twoness and reciprocity in sexuate relationships. We would also highlight William James' 'relational universe' because, for him, 'it is precisely *relations* that are given in experience, and this provides a valuable point of departure for approaches [such as ours] that are oriented to the empirical' (l'Anson and Jasper 2017: 139). In the simplest terms, these are texts we would recommend while recognizing that in the interplay of the critical, ethical and experimental we can – and should – go beyond the emphasis on the textual that is such a strong characteristic of dominant Western cultural paradigms.

RE and the myth of religious violence

A common view that 'religion' is inherently violent, or that it invariably channels violence, presents us with a second context for thinking about the juxtaposition of 'religion' and 'education' in 'RE'. An article on the 'religion wars debate' (Estrada and Costa 2019) describes this as the kind of mainstream view that is often expressed in news media, as when the huge complexities of the Iraqi civil war or the rise of ISIS were translated into 'a religious war between Sunnis and Shiites regionally, and . . . an Islamic jihad against the secular West globally' (Freedland 2014, cited in Estrada and Costa 2019: 179). The view finds expression in more scholarly circles as well (Schmitt 2014; Kaldor 2001; Münkler 2005, cited in Estrada and Costa 2019: 166), where it sets 'inclusive, universalist multicultural values' in opposition 'to the politics of particularistic identities' (Kaldor 2001: 6, cited in Estrada and Costa 2019: 166) associating the latter with 'religion' and posing it as a danger to the former.

Opposing this coupling of religion with violence as a *myth* (Cavanaugh 2009), a range of critical approaches are cited to support the critique. Sinisa Malešević suggests that violence in religious conflicts differs little from violence in secular or ideological conflicts. What leads to violence, whether state or so-called terrorist sponsored, are crises of material circumstances and inequitable patterns of governance (Malešević 2010, cited in Estrada and Costa 2019: 171). It is a matter of 'power' and not 'religion'; and 'religion' should not be used as a scapegoat for the failure to negotiate just and sustainable relations. Other critics of the mainstream view go still further, taking issue with the terms 'religion' and the 'religious' themselves. Timothy Fitzgerald argues that the very language of 'religion' holds problematic networks of assumptions and social relations in place (Fitzgerald 2015: 304). He maintains that the emergence of the discourse of 'religion' in European and colonial languages was a response to the European Enlightenment (Fitzgerald 2007a; Stack, Goldenberg and Fitzgerald 2015) and to new kinds of relations opening up at this time, forcing a previously all-encompassing Christianity (Fitzgerald 2007b) to negotiate a more limited role in the face of new understandings of science and knowledge, technologies, global exploration and commercial possibility. In consequence, a new religion/secular binary or dichotomy emerged (Fitzgerald 2007b: 214–18). This created a privatized 'sub-national domain of "religions" based on belief in the "supernatural", or in another unseen "spiritual" dimension' but subordinated this firmly to the real public world of natural reason (Fitzgerald 2011: 13, cited in Estrada and Costa 2019: 177–8).

In other words, this critique proposes that the discourse of 'religion' and so-called 'secular neutrality' represents a normative Western or Eurocentric approach. Under the banner of secular neutrality seen as a good achieved and the result of liberal consciousness (Fitzgerald 2015: 305), dominant Western powers have sought to civilize and control, or demonize and destroy, unacceptable forms of difference identified with 'religion'. According to William Cavanaugh (2009: 4, cited in Estrada and Costa 2019: 180–1):

> The myth of religious violence helps to construct and marginalize a religious Other, prone to fanaticism, to contrast with the rational, peace-making, secular subject. . . . In foreign policy, the myth of religious violence serves

to cast non-secular social orders, especially Muslim societies, in the role of villain. *They* have not yet learned to remove the dangerous influences of religion from political life. *Their* violence is therefore irrational and fanatical. *Our* violence being secular, is rational, peace making and sometimes regrettably necessary to contain *their* violence.

If, then, RE is to meet the aims of education as we have described it above – defined by the interplay of the critical, ethical and experimental – it would, we might suggest, be much better aligned with critical religion (the approach taken overall within the article cited above) than with either the post-Smartian settlement or with more recent approaches to 'religious literacy'. According to the approach we have outlined, the interplay of critical, ethical and experimental elements requires us to recognize that 'different acts, criteria, and accounts' are distinct and cannot be collapsed into a single plane of sense-making (Lambek 2015: 228). Adopting a normative view of 'religion' – as inherently linked to violence – is another clear example of this form of collapse. It makes it difficult to register genuine difference (critical work), and it affords little space to the work of self-formation (ethical and experimental) that is necessary once this difference is recognized. Critical religion, because it does problematize the consequences of theoretical stances, potentially offers a fresh approach to RE.

RE and its gendered contexts

A third scene within which the problematic term 'RE' can be explored, and put to work, concerns its relationship with current feminist and gender theory. A feature of this scene is revealed by comparing feminist and gender analysis of a hegemonic male/female binary with the key religion/secular binary identified by some scholars of critical religion such as Fitzgerald (cited in the previous section). These similarities could be said to reflect normative modalities of the European philosophical imaginary as a whole. They highlight a systematic problem within the so-called neutral liberal (and also neutral male/masculinist) domain, in respect of its difficulties with registering difference. In so far as woman and the feminine have any place within this domain or imaginary, it is still today a devalued term. Rosi Braidotti describes it as a 'system of pejoration that is implicit in the binary logic of oppositions that characterizes the phallogocentric discursive order' (1997: 64). And something very similar might be said about the term 'religion'.

Putting a little more flesh on these bones, Simone de Beauvoir – a key voice at the start of a twentieth-century movement towards much greater awareness of gender – suggested that a woman fails to signify within a male normative perspective, except under the sign of 'the Other' ([1949] 2011: 6). In this way, critical feminist analysis calls out the liberal domain's attempts to sell itself as neutral. It is hardly neutral if it is unable to register forms of difference within a scene of dominance and simply obliterates them. And, just as, according to Beauvoir, 'woman' or 'the feminine' can indicate they are not male or not masculine but cannot offer a positive definition of the difference, so a category such as 'religion' or 'the religious' similarly represents obliteration within a scene of non-religious, so-called secular and neutral dominance. The male perspective being absolute (6), that which is outwith the male can only be seen as 'Other' without content. Beauvoir translates 'Other' as 'inessential' in relation to the 'essential' male (6). Other translations of the same idea describe how this normative order *discounts* (Waring 1988) or *makes invisible* (Criado-Perez 2019) differences of gender when they arise within the scene of its dominance. Of course, difference may have the capacity to trouble or challenge the normative order of things, and this idea has inspired much feminist theory (Kristeva [1977] 1986; Irigaray 1985; Cixous [1986] 1991; Gilligan 1982). However, attempts to disturb tend to provoke coercive and sometimes violent responses from the dominant powers. We see what can still happen to women who attempt to enter the public domain perceived as normatively masculine. Like the female commentator Jacqui Oatley when she started as a commentator on the BBC's *Match of the Day* in 2007 (Beard 2017: 31–2), or Caroline Criado-Perez when she campaigned to get at least one female face – apart from the Queen's! – onto the new English banknotes in 2013, such behaviour is still producing 'inappropriately hostile' responses (Beard 2017: 35). Having threatened the masculine/neutral order of things, the underlying lack of neutrality or 'natural reason' in these Western contexts is demonstrated by those who feel they are justified in publicly insulting and threatening women with rape or death (31).

Thus the binary discourses of religion/secular and male/female appear to provide two very similar illustrations of how the normative modalities of a post-Enlightenment domain of so-called 'neutral' liberal values struggle with registering difference. This maps quite neatly onto Fitzgerald's description of the ways in which 'religion' is manifested as a construct (2015: 306). One aspect of this construct faces away from the public domain of power relations and appears as private and, in this way, unthreatening to dominant interests. 'Religion' in this sense can even become a hegemonic marker for what Fitzgerald calls 'civility' (2007a: 110–1), meaning 'properly human', but it is also something that can be discounted with impunity if dominant interests sense a challenge. The feminist historian Barbara Welter detected this process at work in post-revolutionary America when, in line with the Church's diminished role in public life, the discourse of 'religion' began to be seen as something 'for the ladies' and thus, at the same time, 'not very important' (1974: 138). It was thus present but constrained within a scene of dominance. We see here how the two discourses come together, such that we can perhaps claim – within Braidotti's 'discursively phallogocentric' order (1997: 65) that is coterminous with a so-called neutral, liberal domain – that the construct of 'religion' has become gendered or indeed feminized.

The second aspect of the construct 'religion' depicted by Fitzgerald (2015: 306) supports this suggestion more strongly still. It references what is dark, barbarous and irrational or unresponsive to reason. And this identification of 'religion' as dark and barbarous clearly parallels the cultural construction of woman or the feminine, resonating strongly with misogynistic and gynophobic sentiments. Deriving in part from age-old myths of woman's anomalousness (Braidotti 1997: 63), wickedness, unnatural power or hypersexuality, these kinds of casual and exploitative violence against women are all the more intensely evident in the case of women marked by additional differences of colour, ethnicity or culture (hooks 1982: 55; 1997: 113–28). Rosi Braidotti sums up this association of femininity with the abject Other by describing woman as a sign of monstrous difference (1997: 64). The discourse or invocation of 'religion' as a sign of difference can arguably thus be cast similarly as monstrous and barbarously 'Other' (Fitzgerald 2007a: 118), while the neutral domain after the European Enlightenment is definitively secular and also male/masculine.

Thus, if RE is to meet the terms of education as defined by the interplay of the critical, ethical and experimental, it would seem, on the grounds suggested above, that it will certainly need to acknowledge how feminist or gender critique impacts on normative, mainstream approaches to religion and to definitions of the term, and that the RE classroom could not cut itself off from considerations of gendered power in either policy or pedagogical contexts. Once again, distinct 'different acts, criteria, and accounts' need to be acknowledged, and their implications worked through, rather than collapsed into a single plane of sense-making. A 'masculinist' approach would have to be identified as a genuine difference rather than as a neutral position or as the kind of 'language' in which one could simply choose (not) to speak. There would also need to be space provided for acknowledging and working through – ethically and experimentally – the resulting inequities in a process of self-formation and thinking otherwise, which would also involve a wider context than that of individual choice. In this respect, critical religion – again because it problematizes the consequences of theoretical stances – offers fresh options for RE going forward.

Conclusion

In this chapter we have given some consideration to the uneasy juxtaposition of 'religion' and 'education' that forms the subject 'Religious Education'. We have approached this conjunction from both etymological and empirical angles and, through this analysis, have problematized the UK settlement that set the terms for a default approach to the study of religion since the 1970s. In particular, the trope of neutrality, although appearing to resolve cultural challenges at the time, led to pedagogies that, in eschewing the potential affectingness of its matters of concern, ultimately created an approach that was only in a limited sense educational.

Having outlined our three-elements heuristic from *Schooling Indifference* (I'Anson and Jasper 2017), in which education is the outcome of a dynamic interplay between the *critical*, *ethical* and *experimental*, this was then put to work in relation to a possible dialogue with critical religion. With its practice of critique that includes the very terms of its own enunciation, and in turn intersects with its ethical orientation and acknowledgement of ethical work on the self, coupled with an orientation both to ways in which they become enacted and might be thought otherwise, it becomes clear that critical religion potentially offers a more fully *educational* Religious Education going forward. While we have considered how some significant topics such as violence and gender might be engaged within higher education contexts, the possibility of this translating into wider educational contexts remains part of a future agenda.[6]

The development of a discursive tradition of enquiry that brings different players and contexts within education and the academy together more closely will undoubtedly also have to include participation in what Michèle Le Doeuff calls 'the collectivity' to describe a means of prioritizing the unthought, best mediated through a generous range of voices – female as well as male; Western and non-Western – rather than deferring to any one single authoritative voice, tradition, idea or institution (Le Doeuff 1989: 128). Equally, we are looking at the further cultivation of what Pamela Sue Anderson (2020) – reflecting a turn to Spinoza – termed our vulnerability to both risk and affection, indicating that without a capacity to risk being affected in some way, we learn nothing. Hopefully, these are the kinds of tools that will enable student enquirers actively to process the limitations of the normative frameworks into which we enter in the current education system – including the problematic 'discourse of religion' or world religions paradigm. Ultimately our hope is to enable each other in our collectivity to perceive, acknowledge and benefit from a much fuller engagement with what is different.

References

Anderson, Pamela Sue and Nicholas Bunnin (2020), 'Silencing and Speaker Vulnerability: Undoing an Oppressive Form of (Wilful) Ignorance', *Angelaki: Journal of the Theoretical Humanities*, 25 (1–2): 36–45.

Arendt, Hannah (1968), *Between Past and Future: Eight Exercises in Political Thought*, New York: Viking Press.

Barad, Karen (2007), *Meeting the Universe Halfway: Quantum Physics and the Entanglement of Matter and Meaning*, Durham, NC, and London: Duke University Press.

Beard, Mary (2017), *Women and Power: A Manifesto*, London: Profile Books.

Biesta, Gert (2005), 'Against Learning: Reclaiming a Language for Education in an Age of Learning', *Nordisk Pedagogik*, 25: 54–66.

Braidotti, Rosi (1997), 'Mothers, Monsters and Machines', in Katie Conboy, Nadia Medina and Sarah Stanbury (eds), *Writing on the Body: Female Embodiment and Feminist Theory*, 59–79, New York: Columbia University Press.

Brown, Andrew and Linda Woodhead (2017), *That was the Church That Was: How the Church of England Lost the English People*, London, Oxford, New York, New Delhi and Sydney: Bloomsbury.

Brown, Callum G. (2001), *The Death of Christian Britain: Understanding Secularisation 1800–2000*, Abingdon and New York: Routledge.

Cavanaugh, William T. (2009), *The Myth of Religious Violence: Secular Ideology and the Roots of Modern Conflict*, New York: Oxford University Press.

Cixous, Helene ([1986] 1991), 'Coming to Writing', in Deborah Jenson (ed.), *'Coming to Writing' and Other Essays*, 1–58, London and Cambridge, MA: Harvard University Press.

Conroy, James C., David Lundie, Robert A. Davis, Vivienne Baumfield, L. Philip Barnes, Tony Gallagher, Kevin Lowden, Nicole Bourque and Karen Wenell (2013), *Does Religious Education Work? A Multi-dimensional Investigation*, London: Bloomsbury.

Craft, Maurice (1984), 'Education for Diversity', in Maurice Craft (ed.), *Education and Cultural Pluralism*, 5–26, London and Philadelphia: Falmer.

Criado-Perez, Caroline (2019), *Invisible Women: Exposing Data Bias in a World Designed for Men*, London: Chatto and Windus.

De Beauvoir, Simone ([1949] 2011), *The Second Sex*, trans. Constance Borde and Sheila Malovany-Chevalier, London: Vintage Books.

Estrada, Rodrigo Duque and Renatho Costa (2019), 'Religion and the New Wars Debate', *Contexto Internacional*, 41 (1): 163–86. Available online: http://dx.doi.org/10.1590/S0102-8529.2019410100009 (accessed 24 February 2020).

Fitzgerald, Timothy (2001), *The Ideology of Religious Studies*, Oxford: Oxford University Press.

Fitzgerald, Timothy (2007a), *Discourse on Civility and Barbarity: A Critical History of Religion and Related Categories*, Oxford: Oxford University Press.

Fitzgerald, Timothy (2007b), 'Encompassing Religion, Privatized Religions and the Invention of Modern Politics', in Timothy Fitzgerald (ed.), *Religion and the Secular: Historical and Colonial Formations*, 211–40, London and Oakville: Equinox.

Fitzgerald, Timothy, ed. (2007c), *Religion and the Secular: Historical and Colonial Formations*, London and Oakville: Equinox.
Fitzgerald, Timothy (2011), *Religion and Politics in International Relations: The Modern Myth*, London: Continuum.
Fitzgerald, Timothy (2015), 'Critical Religion and Critical Research on Religion: Religion and Politics as Modern Fictions', *Critical Research on Religion*, 3 (3): 303–19.
Foucault, Michel (2005), *The Hermeneutics of the Subject: Lectures at the College de France, 1981–1982*, New York: Palgrave Macmillan.
Freedland, Jonathan (2014), 'The Islamic State Nightmare is Not a Holy War but an Unholy Mess', *The Guardian*, 8 August. Available online: https://www.theguardian.com/commentisfree/2014/aug/08/islamic-state-nightmare-not-holy-unholy-mess-iraq (accessed 24 February 2020).
Freire, Paulo (1972), *The Pedagogy of the Oppressed*, Harmondsworth: Penguin.
Gilligan, Carol (1982), *In a Different Voice: Psychological Theory and Women's Development*, Cambridge, MA: Harvard University Press.
hooks, bell (1982), *Ain't I a Woman: Black Women and Feminism*, London: Pluto Press.
hooks, bell (1997), 'Selling Hot Pussy: Representations of Black Female Sexuality in the Cultural Marketplace', in Katie Conboy, Nadia Medina and Sarah Stanbury (eds), *Writing on the Body: Female Embodiment and Feminist Theory*, 113–28, New York: Columbia University Press.
I'Anson, John (2004), 'Mapping the Subject: Student Teachers, Location and the Understanding of Religion', *British Journal of Religious Education*, 26 (1): 45–60.
I'Anson, John (2010), 'After a Rhetorics of Neutrality: Complexity Reduction and Cultural Difference', in Deborah Osberg and Gert Biesta (eds), *Complexity Theory and the Politics of Education*, 121–34, Rotterdam: Sense Publishers.
I'Anson, John (2016), 'RE: Pedagogy – After Neutrality', in James Arthur and L. Philip Barnes (eds), *Education and Religion: Major Themes in Education*, London: Routledge.
I'Anson, John and Alison Jasper (2011), '"Religion" in Educational Spaces: Knowing, Knowing Well, and Knowing Differently', *Arts and Humanities in Higher Education*, 10 (3): 295–313.
I'Anson, John and Alison Jasper (2017), *Schooling Indifference: Re-Imagining RE in Multi-Cultural and Gendered Spaces*, London and New York: Routledge.
I'Anson, John and Alison Jasper (2021), 'What Is It to Think and Practice Educationally? The Three Elements Heuristic', *SERA Theory and Philosophy of Education Network Bulletin*, 11.
I'Anson, John and Alison Jasper (2025), *A Poetics of Education: Edupoetics and Pathways Towards New Educational Collectives*, London and New York: Routledge.
Irigaray, Luce (1985), *This Sex which Is Not One*, Ithaca, NY: Cornell University Press.
Jackson, Robert (1997), *Religious Education: An Interpretive Approach*, London: Hodder Education.
Jullien, François (2014), *On the Universal, the Uniform, the Common and the Dialogue Between Cultures*, Cambridge and Malden, MA: Polity.

Kaldor, Mary (2001), *New and Old Wars: Organized Violence in a Global Era*, Stanford: Stanford University Press.

Keller, Catherine (2015), *Cloud of the Impossible: Negative Theology and Planetary Entanglement*, New York: Columbia University Press.

Kristeva, Julia ([1977] 1986), 'Stabat Mater' and 'Women's Time', in Toril Moi (ed.), *The Kristeva Reader*, 160–213, Oxford: Basil Blackwell.

Lambek, Michael (2015), 'The Hermeneutics of Ethical Encounters: Between Traditions and Practice', *HAU: Journal of Ethnographic Theory*, 5 (2): 227–50.

Latour, Bruno (2004), 'Why has Critique Run out of Steam? From Matters of Fact to Matters of Concern', *Critical Inquiry*, 30 (2): 225–48.

Latour, Bruno (2005), 'From Realpolitik to Dingpolitik or How to Make Things Public', in Bruno Latour and Peter Wiebel (eds), *Making Things Public: Atmospheres of Democracy*, 14–41, Karlsruhe and Cambridge, MA: ZKM and MIT Press.

Le Doeuff, Michèle (1989), *The Philosophical Imaginary*, trans. Colin Gordon, London: The Athlone Press.

Malešević, Sinisa (2010), *The Sociology of War and Violence*, Cambridge: Cambridge University Press.

Masschelein, Jan (2006), 'Experience and the Limits of Governmentality', *Educational Philosophy and Theory*, 38 (4): 561–76.

Masschelein, Jan (2010a), 'E-ducating the Gaze: The Idea of a Poor Pedagogy', *Ethics and Education*, 5 (1): 43–53.

Masschelein, Jan (2010b), 'The Idea of Critical E-ducational Research: E-ducating the Gaze and Inviting to Go Walking', in Ilan Gur-Ze'ev (ed.), *The Possibility/Impossibility of a New Critical Language in Education*, 275–91, Rotterdam: Sense.

May, Todd (2005), *Gilles Deleuze: An Introduction*, Cambridge: Cambridge University Press.

McCutcheon, Russell T. (1997), *Manufacturing Religion: The Discourse on Sui Generis Religion and the Politics of Nostalgia*, Oxford: Oxford University Press.

McCutcheon, Russell T. (2003), *The Discipline of Religion: Structure, Meaning, Rhetoric*, London and New York: Routledge.

McGushin, Edward F. (2007), *Foucault's Askesis: An Introduction to the Philosophical Life*, Evanston, IL: Northwestern University Press.

Munday, Ian (2013), 'The Classroom Space: A Problem or a Mystery?', in Paul Smeyers, Marc Depaepe and Edwin Keiner (eds), *Educational Research: The Importance and Effects of Institutional Spaces*, 153–66, Dordrecht: Springer.

Münkler, Herfried (2005), *The News Wars*, Cambridge: The Polity Press.

Nadadur Kannan, Rajalakshmi (2016), 'Postcolonial and Subaltern Rethinking of Religion', *The Critical Religion Association: Critical Approaches to the Study of Religion*, 17 September. Available online: https://criticalreligion.org/2016/09/17/postcolonial-and-subaltern-rethinking-of-critical-religion/ (accessed 23 February 2020).

Norberg, Jakob (2011), 'Arendt in Crisis: Political Thought in Between Past and Future', *College Literature*, 38 (1): 131–49.

Peters, R. S. (1966), *Ethics and Education*, London: Allen and Unwin.

Schmitt, Carl (2014), *O nomos da terra no direito das gentes do jus publicum europaeum*, Rio de Janeiro: Contraponto/PUC-Rio.

Schools Council (1971), *Religious Education in Secondary Schools (Schools Council Working Paper 36)*, London: Methuen Education and Evans Bros.
Scottish Education Department (1972), *Moral and Religious Education in Scottish Schools (The Millar Report)*, Edinburgh: HMSO.
Serres, Michel (1995), *The Natural Contract (Studies in Literature and Science)*, trans. Elizabeth MacArthur and William Paulson, Ann Arbor: University of Michigan Press.
Smart, Ninian (1969), *The Religious Experience of Mankind*, New York: Charles Scribner's Sons.
Smart, Ninian (1972), 'Comparative Religion Cliches', *Learning for Living*, 12 (2): 4–7.
Smart, Ninian (1973), *The Phenomenon of Religion*, London and Basingstoke: MacMillan.
Smith, Richard (2016), 'The Virtues of Unknowing', *Journal of Philosophy of Education*, 50 (2): 272–84.
Spinoza, Baruch (1985), *Complete Works*, Princeton, NJ: Princeton University Press.
Stack, Trevor, Naomi Goldenberg and Timothy Fitzgerald, eds (2015), *Religion as a Category of Governance and Sovereignty*, Leiden and Boston: Brill.
Stengers, Isabelle (1997), *Power and Invention: Situating Science*, Minneapolis, MN: University of Minnesota Press.
Strathern, Marilyn (2014), 'Reading Relations Backwards', *Journal of the Royal Anthropological Institute*, 20 (1): 3–19.
Strhan, Anna (2010), 'A Religious Education Otherwise? An Examination and Proposed Interruption of Current British Practice', *Journal of Philosophy of Education*, 44 (1): 23–44.
Tweed, Thomas A. (2006), *Crossing and Dwelling: A Theory of Religion*, Cambridge, MA, and London: Harvard University Press.
Waring, Marilyn (1988), *If Women Counted: A New Feminist Economics*, London: Macmillan.
Welter, Barbara (1974), 'The Feminization of American Religion: 1800–1860', in Mary S. Hartman and Lois W. Banner (eds), *Clio's Consciousness Raised: New Perspectives on the History of Women*, 137–57, New York: Harper Colophon Books.
Wright, Andrew (2007), *Critical Religious Education, Multiculturalism and the Pursuit of Truth*, Cardiff: University of Wales Press.
Wright, Andrew (2016), *Religious Education and Critical Realism: Knowledge, Reality and Religious Literacy*, Abingdon and New York: Routledge.

Notes

Chapter 1

1 Caveat: this chapter and the next present my attempt to sum up, briefly and simply, what seem to me the most important critiques and prevalent directions in the scholarly revolution some call critical religion. While I credit Timothy Fitzgerald's early work above all for its foundational impact on my thinking and many others', Fitzgerald's views have moved on since then as he explains in Chapter 5. Others who broadly agree with the thrust of critical religion, including the scholars represented in this volume, each present and nuance their standpoints in different ways with differing implications (see Chapters 3 and 4, by Aaron Hughes and Russell McCutcheon, for their own perspectives on what it means to be critical about 'religion'). For a review of these strands of scholarship and debates around them, read on to Chapter 2.

2 See 'The Square Hole' entry in the online encyclopaedia *Know Your Meme*, https://knowyourmeme.com/memes/the-square-hole (accessed 1 February 2025).

3 The normative loading of religious-secular classifications has historically favoured the secular to the extent that Fitzgerald and others can refer to it as part of a hegemonic Western ideology. But at a more granular level, the question of who benefits is complex and varied. Teemu Taira explains in Chapter 7 that this 'is an empirical question of what really happens in particular contexts'. See Taira's chapter for a helpful section on *mapping studies of 'religion'* that draw different conclusions in different contexts.

4 Fitzgerald explains: 'I must stress that this argument is not antitheological. It is an argument against theology masquerading as something else' (2000: 20). See Chapter 2 for a discussion of the relationship between critical religion and theology.

Chapter 2

1 The Critical Religion Association currently exists primarily in the form of a website (https://criticalreligion.org/), which hosts a blog and other resources including profiles of scholars in the field, managed by Bashir Saade at the University of Stirling.

2   The Center for Critical Research on Religion (https://criticaltheoryofreligion.org/) organizes conferences and publishes a journal and book series, established and edited by Warren Goldstein. While its mission is not specifically aligned with critical religion, it has provided productive forums for critical religion scholarship and debates around what it means to be critical.

3   *Method and Theory in the Study of Religion (MTSR)* is the journal of the North American Association for the Study of Religion, established in 1989 and currently edited by Mitsutoshi Horii and Tisa Wenger. For recent discussions around the nature of critical religion, see the special issue 'On Critique' edited by Horii, in *MTSR* 36, no. 3–4 (2024); Horii's editorial gives a particularly helpful overview.

4   *Critical Research on Religion* is the journal of the Center for Critical Research on Religion, established in 2013 and edited by Warren Goldstein.

5   *Implicit Religion* was established in 1998 and is currently edited by Carmen Becker and David Robertson. Since 2016 it has been published in collaboration with the Religious Studies Project (https://www.religiousstudiesproject.com/), founded by Christopher Cotter and David Robertson, whose podcast and blog are also an excellent resource for learning about critical religion. For a collection of reflections on the state of critical religion, see the special issue 'Twenty Years of *The Ideology of Religious Studies*' edited by Teemu Taira and Suzanne Owen, in *Implicit Religion* 22, no. 3–4 (2020).

6   I like Matt Sheedy's characterization of critical religion, and what he helpfully expands to 'CR-adjacent scholarship', as: 'orientations toward scholarship that share a few generalized axioms, with a fair bit of methodological variation and disagreement in between' (2022a: n.p.).

7   Russell McCutcheon is highly active in advocating for critical reform of religious studies programmes as a means to their revival and promotion in today's competitive market. He has produced numerous resources for professionals in religious studies and beyond: see e.g. McCutcheon 2024b, d and the REL Toolbox website (https://reltoolbox.ua.edu/).

8   In this retrospective account of critical religion's emergence, it seems an intuitive extension of the critical turn already made in other fields, i.e. denaturalizing boundaries of nation, race and gender. But it is worth noting that the similarity appears less intuitive in practice, so critiques of 'religion' remain obscure to many people across disciplines. Hence a review of recent sociology textbooks still finds a stark difference between their treatments of race versus religion: 'When sociologists come to "race," they usually examine the consequences of the idea of race and racial categories in people's lives . . . they critically study norms and imperatives which drive the practice of making such distinctions. When they come to the idea of "religion," in contrast, sociologists tend not to study "religion" as a constructed idea, but as an independent phenomenon that exists in all forms of life throughout history' (Horii 2021: 141). Horii's book represents an important effort to address this blind spot in sociology. In a response to that book I offered some reflections on why it seems more difficult to get critical

religion into the mainstream of the social sciences and humanities (Henley 2023), but there remains much work to be done in addressing the obstacles to wider implementation of a critical turn in the way we all think and teach about 'religion'.

9 On inventions of 'religion(s)' in Japan, see e.g. Horii 2018; Josephson 2012. On India, see e.g. Bloch, Keppens and Hegde 2010; Mandair 2009. On Middle Eastern and other Muslim contexts, see e.g. Asad 1993, 2003; Mahmood 2016; Tayob 2009. On South Africa, see e.g. Chidester 1996, 2014.

10 In many responses to this article by Watts and Mosurinjohn (2022), it was heavily criticized for treating critical religion as a unified 'methodological school' – an issue I explained in the first section of this chapter. As Matt Sheedy rightly points out, 'this isn't merely a semantic quibble over terminology since the looseness with which "CR" is being applied by Watts and Mosurinjohn risks tarring numerous critical approaches to the category "religion" as driven by a narrow agenda' (2022a: n.p.). That does not mean we cannot generalize at all, but we must take care in what we do with such generalizations. The mistake in this article was to set up 'critical religion' as a singular target for attack, a straw man to be knocked down in one go, rather than engaging with scholars' diverse and developing perspectives in a more nuanced and charitable way. (Its authors are certainly not alone in falling into this trap; it is an occupational hazard of critical scholarship.) Nevertheless, Watts and Mosurinjohn's article proved helpful in drawing attention to concerns that many still harbour about critical religion, and in pushing its advocates to clarify and refine their thinking.

Chapter 3

1 On this trope see the essays in Smith, Führding and Hermann 2020.
2 And, of course, many would indeed say that this is the case. See, for example, Wiebe 1999; McCutcheon 2003; Martin 2012; Arnal and McCutcheon 2013; Nongbri 2013; Chidester 1996 and 2014.
3 I refer here to the Protestant bias in the study of religion that, while dissipated in recent years, still remains. On this bias, see for example, Smith 1990 and Nongbri 2013.
4 Though some have tried to put the origins of the 'objective' study of religion earlier. Most notable are Barton and Boyarin (2016), who put it in late antiquity. Wasserstrom (1988) locates it in the heresiographical literature associated with medieval Islam. And Stroumsa (2010) puts it later in early modern Europe and the Age of Empires.
5 See, for example, the comments found in Tannous 2011.
6 To this end, see Hughes and McCutcheon 2022a and 2022b, two jointly authored monographs along the lines of Williams 1976.

Chapter 4

1 My thanks go also to Andie Alexander and Brent Nongbri for comments on an earlier draft of this chapter and to Martin Lund for some helpful illustrations.

Chapter 5

1 This does not mean that I am a 'socialist' or a 'revolutionary' either. Liberalism and socialism are two mutually parasitic constructions within the same overall paradigmatic set of categories that keep each other perpetually in play. It is these pairs of opposites, which operate as binary signalling, that keep us enthralled and unable to have any new ideas. There is no space to pursue this argument here.
2 For an excellent and fairly recent critical genealogy of the categories 'science' and 'religion', see Harrison (2015).
3 For example, see chapter 12, 'The Critique of "Culture" in Cultural Anthropology' (Fitzgerald 2000: 235–51), where I review some of the critiques of reified 'cultures' and 'societies' made by anthropologists such as Fredrik Barth and Adam Kuper, and then try to save them. Yet the logic of critique has many parallels with the critique of 'religion'.
4 I had been generously given some initial contacts by Richard Gombrich, who taught Pali and Sanskrit at the Oriental Institute in Oxford.
5 The influence of Louis Dumont on *IRS* is evident and palpable.
6 It ought to be mentioned that some of the Dalits and Buddhists I met were pro-British, because they feel they got a better deal under British colonial rule than under the Brahminical hierarchy.
7 Not as a conscious strategy. The originating rhetoric was of course conscious; there were definite goals to be obtained for members of a particular class, but nobody was in control of its unfolding and normalization. The propertied classes are as unconsciously operated on (mystified) as the rest of us.

Chapter 7

1 I define 'religionization' as a process in which it becomes common or even advantageous to classify something (typically a group, practice or symbol) as religious. Similarly, in 'culturalization' it becomes typical or even beneficial to be classified as culture, tradition or heritage. There are other ways to conceptualize 'religionization', such as Dreßler's (2019: 2): 'practices through which religion is homogenized and reified'. I see 'religionization' as a process which may tend towards homogenization and reification of some groups and

practices, but I do not define anything as religion and, therefore, would find it odd to write about religionization of religion.

2   Yoga in legal and educational settings in the United States is a good example. Yoga has been claimed to be 'religious' in order to avoid paying sales tax, and as a 'non-religious' bodily exercise in order to be allowed in public schools (Brown 2019). In the latter case it would have been devastating to perform yoga as religious, because activities classified as 'religious' are not usually allowed. Neither case is a matter of different interpretations of yoga or different traditions or communities, as the claims were linked to the very same person involved in yoga, Eddie Stern.

3   For Rorty, this is not simply a question of our scholarly vocabulary, but it applies to thinking about the value of e.g. God-talk in our society in a different manner. He suggests that 'we should substitute the question of the cultural desirability of God-talk for the ontological question about the existence of God' (Rorty 2007: 24–5), and then it would be possible to negotiate whether it is good for us to articulate our values and deepest wishes in a vocabulary that includes God and puts the term in a central position. This is perfectly applicable to 'religion', although Rorty himself did not pay much attention to the term.

4   For instance, most theories of secularization operate with a (narrow) definition of religion, but precisely because of this they can detect social patterns and correlations between the popularity of certain institutions and/or beliefs (defined heuristically as religious) and, say, wealth, fertility, urbanity, generations, gender, education and so on. A different type of example is my study of Bond films: focusing on occasions in which the word 'religion' is mentioned would not have provided much material to analyse, but operating with a broad definition combining family resemblance with a prototype approach allowed me to study how Christian and Western norms were highlighted and contrasted with less-valued non-Christian traditions outside 'the West' (Taira 2019a).

5   The reference to ethno-nationalist groups seems not to refer implicitly to People of the Bear, but rather to right-wing groups which have gained more popularity in Finland (and elsewhere) during the past ten years or so. This is one of the reasons why People of the Bear has also become reluctant to use the term 'Finnish faith', as one of the community's spokespersons told me in late 2020, others being the fact that 'Finnish' is too restrictive (they see their tradition more Balto-Finnic than Finnish) and misleading in some contexts (in Orthodox Karelia the term 'Finnish faith' has traditionally meant 'Lutheran').

6   Cupstones are ancient rocks with rounded furrows or holes. The Finnish ones are mainly from the Iron Age, and they have most likely been places where food has been sacrificed to spirits and ancestors.

7   Probably a great deal of Muslims and Muslim communities regarded themselves as religious prior to what I call 'religionization', but many of them did not consider it important enough to make sure that the government does it too.

Chapter 8

1 On the discursive aspects of conceptual pairings, see Fitzgerald 2007.
2 There are a few people who may claim descent from the Beothuk, but their culture and language have been lost (barring some material remains and a few hundred words).
3 I have tried to retain the way each scholar spells the term for themselves and their knowledge.

Chapter 9

1 This chapter has been almost as long in the making as TFR itself. I am grateful to the late Norman Bonney and to Liam Sutherland for helpful discussions along the way. Thanks to Christopher Cotter, Suzanne Owen and Teemu Taira on the category 'faith'. Earlier drafts were presented at the Universities of Durham, Edinburgh and Oxford Brookes and at the EASR conference in Helsinki in 2016. Thanks to Lauren Morry and Alex Henley for inviting me to speak at Mansfield College, Oxford, in 2020 and to Alex Henley for his patience in receiving this final version. Last but not least, thanks to Dr Jo Miller for her support.
2 De Certeau ([1980] 1984: 35–7) distinguishes between strategy as 'the calculation (or manipulation) of power relationships' from a position of domination, and tactic as 'a calculated action determined by an absence of a proper locus . . . The space of the tactic is the space of the other'.
3 Devolution in Scotland stems from the creation of the Scottish Office in Edinburgh under the Secretary of State for Scotland in 1885. After devolution in 1999, the Scottish Office remained in place to manage, in Scotland, matters 'reserved' to the Westminster Parliament. For a comparative political discussion, see Shephard (2013) and Baldwin (2013). A Parliament of Northern Ireland operated at Stormont, Belfast, from 1921 to 1973 following a partition of Ireland into two self-governing polities: 'Southern Ireland' (becoming the 'Irish Free State' in 1922 and the 'Republic of Ireland' in 1949) and 'Northern Ireland' remaining within the 'United Kingdom of Great Britain and Ireland'. In Wales, the 1967 Welsh Language Act triggered a campaign for devolution culminating in the creation of the National Assembly for Wales in Cardiff in 1999, which was renamed Senedd Cymru/Welsh Parliament in 2020. On the value of a 'four nations' historiography of the UK, see Samuel (1995) and Lloyd-Jones and Scull (2018).
4 'Sittings in both Houses begin with prayers. These follow the Christian faith and there is currently no multi-faith element. Attendance is voluntary.' For a comparative introduction to the treatment of religion in UK legislatures, see Bonney (2013a: 428–35) and on 'prayers' in Commonwealth legislatures, see Lanouette (2009).

NOTES

5 In a special report on the role played by religion – particularly the Church of England – in the UK Parliament, the All-Party Parliamentary Humanist Group recommended that daily prayers be replaced by 'an inclusive time for reflection' along the lines of the Scottish Parliament (All-Party Parliamentary Humanist Group 2020: 19).

6 Although Nigel Bruce, convenor of the Humanist Society in Scotland, appeared on 8 March 1999 as part of the first tranche of speakers, and the 'celebrity atheist' A. C. Grayling spoke in April 2013 (Bonney 2013c), there has been scant representation of those identifying as 'non-religious' which, according to the 2022 Census in Scotland, forms the majority of the Scottish population at 51 per cent, up from 37 per cent in 2011 (Scotland's Census 2022). It was twenty-five years before a Pagan contributed: the Scottish Pagan Federation's Interfaith Officer, Rev Linda Haggerstone, a Druid and self-described 'Christo-Pagan', led TFR on 16 January 2024 (see Learmonth 2024). According to Scotland's Census 2022, Pagans form the fourth largest grouping at 0.35 per cent (19,113) of the population.

7 'Time for Reflection: Background': text accompanying revised guidance for TFR issued in May 2005.

8 The Scottish Churches Parliamentary Office 'exists to create space for ecumenical fellowship and encounter for Parliamentary and Political affairs in Scotland' ('Scottish Churches Parliamentary Office' on Church of Scotland website). The Presiding Officer chairs meetings in the chamber and represents the Parliament externally (see 'Presiding Officer and Deputy Presiding Officers' on Scottish Parliament website). The Parliamentary Bureau consists of members from parties with five or more MSPs and is chaired by the Presiding Officer; it 'discusses and agrees what the weekly business programme should be for the chamber' ('Parliamentary Bureau' on Scottish Parliament website). There is no information on how the Parliamentary Bureau issues invitations to lead TFR in the otherwise extensive entry describing its functions (Standing Orders of the Scottish Parliament 2024: 'Chapter 5: The Parliamentary Bureau and Management of Business').

9 This guidance was issued in May 2021 and sent to me in January 2025 by the Parliament's information office.

10 For an interesting critical account of the procurement process and architectural design for the new build, see McKean (1999).

11 TFR text 27 October 1999 (Rev. Dr Graham Blount, Scottish Churches Parliamentary Officer). The hymn book is *Common Ground: A Song Book for All the Churches* (Common Ground Editorial Committee 1998). Compare the remarkably similar content of the 25th anniversary TFR given by Lord Wallace of Tankerness (Scottish Parliament Official Report, 29 October 2024).

12 TFR text 24 November 1999 (Rev. David Beckett, Minister of Greyfriars Tolbooth and Highland Kirk, Edinburgh).

13 TFR text 8 December 1999 (Dr Mona Siddiqui, Lecturer in Arabic and Islamic Studies, University of Glasgow).

14 There are also four iterations classed as 'non-denominational' of which at least two were Christian (Prayer for Parliament Scotland, Vision 21).

15 TFR fieldnotes 6 February 2002 (Rev. John Miller, Moderator of the General Assembly of the Church of Scotland). This followed the inaugural instruction of the Presiding Officer that 'those present in the chamber . . . refrain from opening and closing the doors during this time and to remain silent. I ask members and those seated in the galleries to respect the time for reflection' (TFR 27 October 1999).

16 TFR fieldnotes 12 June 2002.

17 TFR fieldnotes 13 September 2016. The latest update in 2021 has changed the April 2005 directive that 'Members and the public will not be encouraged to enter the Chamber during the duration of Time for Reflection' to 'Members and the public can be encouraged to enter the Chamber during the duration'. The Parliament's information office declined to offer the reason for this change.

18 TFR fieldnotes 25 October 2017.

19 The term 'thought for the day' likely refers to *Thought for the Day*, a pre-scripted address (lasting two minutes and forty-five seconds) broadcast on BBC Radio 4 on Monday to Saturday mornings since 1970. Described by one commentator as the 'breakfast pulpit', it can be traced back to the BBC Home Service's *Lift up Your Hearts* in 1939, renamed *Ten to Eight* in the mid-1960s, then *Thought for the Day* in 1970 (Donovan 1997: 149–50). *Thought for the Day* has attracted criticism for denying access to atheists, humanists and secularists: for example, the journalist John Humphrys (b. 1943), who for many years anchored the *Today* programme which hosted the slot, said: 'It seems to me inappropriate that *Today* should broadcast nearly three minutes of uninterrupted religion, given that rather more than half our population have no religion at all . . . [W]e have Hindus of course, and we have the occasional Muslim, the occasional Jew, but by and large it's Christian. Why? . . . Why can't you have an atheist? Or an agnostic?' (Sherwood 2017).

20 See 'Eldership' on the Church of Scotland website. Kirk elders formed around 10 per cent ($n = 12$) of MSPs in the first term of the Scottish Parliament.

21 The official report of the vote on S1M-1 states that 69 (or 54 per cent) of MSPs voted for the motion and only 15 (or (12 per cent) against, with 37 (or 29 per cent) abstaining. But as Bonney (2013b: 820) points out, this count is in error: in fact, thirty-seven (or 29 per cent) voted *against* with only fifteen *abstentions*. The 'for' count is clear, at just over half of MSPs, but close to one third of MSPs opposed the motion.

22 Interfaith Scotland, https://interfaithscotland.org/. The Interfaith Network for the UK was dissolved in January 2025 as a result of losing government funding due to membership on its board of a representative from the Muslim Council of Britain with which the then UK Conservative government held a policy of non-engagement: https://www.interfaith.org.uk/. For critical discussion of the interfaith movement, see Sutherland (2025: 15–24, 42–51) on Interfaith Scotland in the context of contemporary religious diversification; and Prideaux and Dawson (2018) on the UK as a whole.

23 See 'Time for Reflection' on the Royal High School website; and 'Religious Observance – Time for Reflection' on the Education Scotland website. See also Younger (2018).
24 'A Christmas insult', Green MSP Media Release, 23 December 2004, http://www.patrickharviewmsp.com/index.php?page=news.php&story (no longer available online).
25 Bonney (2013b: 824–5) gives three further examples of 'push back' from diverse religious perspectives: a Catholic Apostolic Nuncio who began by saying, 'I am aware of the parameters of the talk, which were clearly indicated by the instructions that were given. . . . [T]he task is particularly challenging, since I am aware that, as a diplomat, I must refrain from any interference in the internal affairs of a country and, as archbishop, I must avoid any remarks that may seem to take sides in a political debate' (Archbishop Faustino Sainz Muñoz, 12 March 2008); a Catholic Sister who began with a blessing, explaining that 'it is not only ordained clergy who have the power or ability to bless; we, too, can offer blessings' (14 January 2009); and a Methodist minister who described music as 'one of the distinctive features of Methodism' but explained that 'in sharing this short time, I was told I could not sing' (Rev. Allan Loudon, Wishaw, 28 September 2011).
26 'Esoteric Ramblings' blog, posted 2 June 2014 (accessed 21 August 2015). At the time of writing Mr McLellan is CEO of Humanists International. See website https://humanists.international/ (accessed 8 February 2025).
27 'The faith' is de facto Protestant in this context, since Catholics are proscribed from holding the position of UK monarch following the Act of Settlement of 1701, which stipulates that only a Protestant in communion with the Church of England can serve as head of state. In February 2025, the Church of Scotland (Lord High Commissioner) Act introduced legislation for Roman Catholics to be eligible to hold the office of Lord High Commissioner to the General Assembly of the Church of Scotland.

Chapter 11

1 I have developed vestigial state theory further in a series of publications since this chapter was first published ten years ago (Goldenberg 2024, 2023, 2021, 2020, 2019a, b, c, 2018). It is also the focus of a collection of essays by various authors under the title *The End of Religion: Feminist Reappraisals of the State* (McPhillips and Goldenberg 2021).
2 Fully functioning states sometimes place forms of 'family' violence under the purview of groups they recognize as religions. Circumcisions of male and female infants might be allowed in some jurisdictions for religious reasons. And, domestic violence is on occasion left to those deemed to be religious authorities to address. For an excellent discussion of how multiculturalism in Britain evolves into multifaithism to the disadvantage of women, see the work of Sukhwant Dhaliwal (2012).

3 Trevor Stack has suggested that religion is probably not the only concept that evolves to create and designate a vestigial state. Andrew Pump (2016), for example, argues that corporations are in the process of making contemporary nation-states vestigial.

Chapter 12

1 Hence different educational theorists tend to focus on one side or other of this divide. Thus R.S. Peters' (1966: 25) definition of education as implying 'that something worthwhile is being or has been intentionally transmitted in a morally acceptable manner', tends towards *educare*, while Paulo Freire, for example, in his *The Pedagogy of the Oppressed* (1972), critiqued what he saw as the deficit framing implied in a transmission account, which he likened to a 'banking' model. Thus, in its orientation to new potentiality, via *concientization*, Freire's work might be seen as tending more towards *educere*.
2 The claim that the 'New' Religious Education enabled a consideration of different religions on their own terms was part of the rhetoric justifying this approach. Critical questions may be posed regarding the extent to which this was achieved, given that the terms for comparison (such as the various 'dimensions' of religion) clearly derived from the West, and many distinctively Western concepts, such as 'belief', continued to inform the analysis offered (see l'Anson 2010).
3 It is noteworthy that, notwithstanding its title, in 'critical religious literacy' one searches in vain for any critical understanding of 'critical', 'literacy' or indeed 'religion'. All three concepts are simply assumed (Strhan 2010; l'Anson 2016). Other approaches, such as those associated with Robert Jackson (1997), promoted ethnographic and interpretive methodologies that fit more easily within the existing Smartian framing. However, ethnographic approaches, in offering more differentiated and contextually nuanced accounts, were arguably less easily examinable.
4 Hence educational sites in such a reading are less problems to be solved than mysteries to be encountered (Munday 2013). Acknowledging the limits of knowing is associated with apophatic traditions (see Keller 2015).
5 Marilyn Strathern amplifies this when she writes, 'relations open up the capacities of properties in unexpected ways and capacities come into existence through new relations' (2014: 4). (See the discussion of this in relation to Deleuze's ontology of the virtual in l'Anson and Jasper 2017: 142ff.)
6 Here, the project of a poetics of education – or what we have termed an 'edupoetics' – has potential resonance (see l'Anson and Jasper 2025).

Index

Note: Page numbers with "n" refer to note numbers

American Academy of Religion (AAR) 52, 62
ancient religions 15–16, 67, 200–4
Anderson, Benedict 28, 183
anthropology 29–30, 80–96, 151–2
anti-realism 37, 95, 123–4, *see also* representation, problems of
anti-theory 52–3, *see also* theory
area studies 56
Asad, Talal 8, 30
Austin, J.L. 14

Barthes, Roland 67, 127
binary oppositions 8–10, 27, 33–4, 63–4, 78–83, 89, 95–7, 124–5, 217–22, *see also* 'religion'
   faith/knowledge 39, 82, 94 (*see also* 'faith')
   private/public 63, 102–4, 126
   religious/cultural (*see* 'culture')
   religious/political 17–18, 102–5, 108–17, 126, 179–92
   religious/secular (*see* 'secular')
   religious/spiritual (*see* 'spirituality')
   religious/superstitious (*see* 'superstition')
   sacred/profane 25, 63, 146 (*see also* 'sacred')
Buddhism 6, 85–8, 107–14, 204

Canada 73, 141–52, 199
capitalism 8–9, 11, 30, 77–9, 81–2, 93–4, 103
categories, *see* binary oppositions; deconstruction; discourse; reification; 'religion'
Cavanaugh, William T. 13, 181–3, 219–20

Center for Critical Research on Religion 23, 230 n.2, 230 n.4
Chidester, David 30, 144–6, 150
China 6, 108–9, 204
Christianity 4–5, 8, 10, 27, 53, 55, 58, 122, 133–7, 200–4
   Protestant Reformation 30, 102
   Protestantism 27, 102–3, 105–8, 150, 157–74
classification, *see* binary oppositions; discourse; 'religion'
colonialism 6–7, 9, 27–30, 65, 77–96, 102–5, 126–7, *see also* Indigenous religion
Confucianism 6, 87–8, 107–9
'critical' 13, 32–8, 47–8, 56–9, 80–3, 152, 215–23, *see also* critical religion; critical theory
critical race theory 22–3, 26, 28, 230 n.8
critical religion 21–40, 61–3, 66–7, 74, 101–2, 195–206, 213–23, *see also* 'religion'
   extended *vs* limited critique 16–18, 23, 33–4, 39, 80–3, 89–97
   methods in 11–18, 30–40, 47–59, 123–30, 141–6, 151–3, 158, 191–2, 205–6
Critical Religion Association 22, 229 n.1
Critical Research on Religion (journal) 24, 230 n.4
critical study of religion and related categories, *see* critical religion
critical theory 27–9, 213–14, *see also* critical religion
critique, *see* 'critical'; critical theory

INDEX

'culture' 10, 80–3, 88–96, 150, *see also* anthropology
culturalization 72–3, 122, 133–7

decolonial theory 18, 28, 39, 84–7, 89–97, 145–8, *see also* postcolonial theory
deconstruction 27, 50, 96–7
discourse 9–10, 13–18, 27–8, 30, 37, 64, 94–7, 101–5, 125–7, 179–81
Dressler, Markus 28, 232 n.1 (ch.7)

education 26, 83–6, 135–6, 209–23, 230 n.8
Enlightenment, European 30, 90, 102, 145
ethics of scholarship, *see* scholarship, good
ethnography, *see* anthropology; representation, problems of

'faith' 17, 29, 64–6, 157–74, *see also* binary oppositions: faith/knowledge
feminist theory, *see* gender studies
Finland 131–7
Fitzgerald, Timothy 4–11, 17–18, 21–4, 29–31, 33–4, 38–9, 77–97, 102–4, 144, 219–22
folk categories 12–14, 64, 68, 104, 117–18
Foucault, Michel 16, 27, 127, 158, 216, *see also* critical theory
freedom of religion, *see* religious freedom

gender studies 16, 18, 26, 28, 205, 220–2
genealogy 15–16, 27, 29–30, 32–4, 47–59, *see also* 'religion', genealogy of
Goldenberg, Naomi 11, 16–18, 25, 28, 34, 126, 195–206
governance, *see* 'religion' as category of governance

Hinduism 6, 83–6
Horii, Mitsutoshi 18, 25, 33–4, 39, 101–18, 145, 230 nn.3, 8

Hughes, Aaron W. 23, 33, 47–59, 142
humanities 26–7, 39, 51, *see also* social sciences

identity 28, 39, 142–8, 183–6
ideology 8, 22, 27–30, 77–82, 89–96, 184–6
Implicit Religion (journal) 24, 230 n.5
India 5–6, 83–7, 231 n.9
Indigenous religion 141–53
intersectionality 28–9, 153, 205, 220–2
invention of religion, *see* 'religion', genealogy of; world religions paradigm
Islam 6, 49–50, 55, 69–71, 197–8, 231 n.9
Israel 179–92, 201

Japan 5–6, 87–9, 105–18, 231 n.9, *see also* Buddhism; Confucianism; Shinto
Josephson-Storm, Jason Ananda 30, 37, 108–9, 127
Judaism 6, 55, 179–92, 200–4

Lincoln, Bruce 57–8
Locke, John 103

Mahmood, Saba 42, 105
Martin, Craig 24, 33–5, 37, 126
Marx, Karl 27, 93, 130
Masuzawa, Tomoko 6, 66–7, 108
McCutcheon, Russell T. 10–11, 17, 22–3, 25–6, 30, 33–4, 36, 38–40, 61–74, 126, 142, 152, 230 n.7
media studies 26, 128–30, 136
metaphor 50–2
Method and Theory in the Study of Religion (journal) 24, 230 n.3
methodology, *see* critical religion, methods in
minorities 73, 121–2, 131–3, 159–60, 171
modernity 27–8, 30, 65, 77–8, 81–2, 125–8, 180–1, *see also* 'religion', genealogy of

monotheism 5, 55
Mosurinjohn, Sharday 24, 31–7, 231 n.10

nation-state 8, 30, 111–17, 126, 157–74, 179–92, 196–9
nationalism 5, 28–9
Native Americans, see Indigenous religion
Nietzsche, Friedrich 27, 50–2
9/11 (attacks of 11 September 2001) 9, 49–52, 173
Nongbri, Brent 15–17, 200
non-religious, see binary oppositions; 'secular'
normativity 34–40, 50, 59, 62, 78–80, 93–4, 152–3, 211–23, see also 'religion' as normative category

objectivity, see normativity
Orientalism 27–8, 82–5, see also Said, Edward

phenomenology of religion 21–2, 211–14, see also 'religion' as sui generis or unique
political science 26, 195–7, see also social sciences
'political', see binary oppositions: religious/political
positionality 22, 29–40, 77–97, 151–3, 211–14, see also reflexivity
post-colonial theory 27–8, 82, see also colonialism; decolonial theory; Said, Edward
Protestant Reformation, see Christianity
Protestantism, see Christianity

'race', see critical race theory
realism, see anti-realism
reflexivity 15–18, 29–32, 36, 47–59, 89, 124, 153, 215–23, see also positionality
reification 7, 11, 28–9, 39, 93
'religion'
    as category of governance 9–11, 14–15, 68–74, 103, 111–18, 150, 172–4, 187–92, 195–206

definitional issues 3–6, 62–4, 195–8
genealogy of 6–9, 29–30, 101–5, 125–7, 180–6
as normative category 8–11, 29–30, 78, 81–2, 89–97, 172–3, 217–23
religionization 28, 121–2, 131–3, 232 n.1 (ch.7)
'religions' (see world religions paradigm)
religion/secular (see under binary oppositions)
as sui generis or unique 5–12, 17, 21–2, 25–6, 53, 58, 62–9, 82
as theological category 10, 17, 29, 38–40, 65–6, 181–3
religious education, see education
religious freedom 9, 70–3, 103, 126
religious studies 21–6, 29–30, 33, 36–40, 47–59, 61–7, 74, 80–3, 94–7
Religious Studies Project (podcast) 67, 230 n.5
religious violence 12–13, 69–70, 197, 218–20
representation, problems of 4–8, 59, 63–4, 80–96, 141–53, 169–74, 187–9, 211–14
ritualization 28, 86–8, 157–74

'sacred' 5, 50, 52, 57, 62–3, 68, 74, 131–2, 145
Said, Edward 27, 69, 82
Schilbrack, Kevin 37
scholarship, good 18, 32–40, 47–59, 78–83, 89–97, 151–3
sciences 8, 26, 78–82, see also binary oppositions: faith/knowledge; social sciences
Scotland, see United Kingdom
'secular' 8–11, 17–18, 25–6, 30, 33–4, 39, 54, 69–73, 78–83, 93–7, 103–5, 181–92, see also binary oppositions
Sheedy, Matt 32–3, 36, 230 n.6, 231 n.10
Shinto 6, 87–8, 107–17
Smart, Ninian 61, 211–15

Smith, Jonathan Z. 6, 29–30, 52–3, 58, 63, 102, 104, 130
Smith, Wilfred Cantwell 6–7, 29–30, 66–7, 172
social sciences 18, 26, 27, 39, 78–83, 88–9, 211–12, *see also* humanities
sociology 26, 39, 82–3, 89, 230 n.8, *see also* social sciences
speech acts 14, 57
'spirituality' 17, 124–6, 150, 173
state, *see* nation-state
study of religion, *see* religious studies
'superstition' 108, 113–15, 124–5, 146

Taira, Teemu 12, 17, 25, 37, 121–38, 173, 229 n.3
Taoism 6
teaching, *see* education
terminology, *see* binary oppositions; deconstruction; discourse; 'religion'

textual study 56–9, 83–5
theology 38–40, 50, 53, 57, 59, 61–3, 189–91, 211–13, *see also* 'religion' as theological category
theory and method, *see* critical religion
tradition 182–92
translation, problems of 6–8, 15–16, 30, 89–91, 108–18, 148–9

United Kingdom 158–60, 172–3, 211–13
 Scotland 157–74
United States 69–73, 102–4
 US–Japan relations 101–18

vestigial states, religions as 195–206

Watts, Galen 24, 31–7, 231 n.10
world religions paradigm 6, 10, 17, 27–8, 39, 52, 65–8, 83–7, 160, 212–14

Zionism, *see* Israel